On 2/11/65, Source advised that on the previous date, 2/10/65, he, in company with [an unidentified individual] had . . . exhibited a motion picture which depicted deceased actress MARILYN MONROE committing a perverted act on an unknown male. According to Source, he claimed that former baseball star JOE DIMAGGIO in the past had offered him $25,000 for this film, it being the only one in existence, but that Source had refused the offer. The above is being furnished to the FBI Lab and the NYO [New York Office] for information purposes in the event reports are received from other divisions describing an obscene film which might be identical to above.

Other Books by Nick Redfern

Body Snatchers in the Desert
Three Men Seeking Monsters
Strange Secrets
The FBI Files
A Covert Agenda
Cosmic Crashes
On the Trail of the Saucer Spies

CELEBRITY
SECRETS

Government Files on the
Rich and Famous

NICK REDFERN

PARAVIEW POCKET BOOKS

NEW YORK LONDON TORONTO SYDNEY

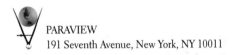

PARAVIEW
191 Seventh Avenue, New York, NY 10011

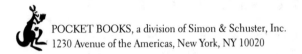

POCKET BOOKS, a division of Simon & Schuster, Inc.
1230 Avenue of the Americas, New York, NY 10020

ISBN-13: 978-1-4165-2866-1
ISBN-10:   1-4165-2866-0

This Paraview Pocket Books trade paperback edition February 2007

10 9 8 7 6 5 4 3 2 1

POCKET and colophon are registered trademarks of
Simon & Schuster, Inc.

Designed by Jan Pisciotta

Manufactured in the United States of America

For information regarding special discounts for bulk purchases,
please contact Simon & Schuster Special Sales at
1-800-456-6798 or business@simonandschuster.com.

To Stephen and Brad:
Brothers-in-law and the finest of friends

Contents

Introduction

Whether we like to admit it or not, we all secretly enjoy reading the latest, salacious gossip about Britney and Kevin, Brad and Angelina, and Paris and, well, whoever this week's star attraction happens to be. But in addition to perusing the pages of the glossy magazines, or tuning into television's nightly exposure fest of Hollywood's finest, there is another avenue that allows us to learn all about the entertaining secrets of our heroes of TV, the big screen, and the stage. That avenue is called the Freedom of Information Act (FOIA).

A very useful piece of government-created legislation, the FOIA allows members of the public access to official files from agencies such as the Federal Bureau of Investigation (FBI), the Central Intelligence Agency (CIA), the military, and a host of others, if the government decides that those files can be released, of course. As will shortly become apparent, in those cases where agencies *have* declassified their surveillance records on the rich and the famous, the FOIA has provided us with a unique, insightful, intriguing, outrageous, sometimes hilarious, but always controversial look at the secret world of the celebrity.

For the most part, a person has to be in the unfortunate position of being dead before the government will reveal its once-secret files to the public. Therefore, it is likely to be several decades before we will get to learn which current pop princess secretly enjoys hot, lesbian action; which rocker is hanging out smoking pot with members of the Communist party; or which actor is having sex with the girlfriend of a Mafia bigwig. From the files of numerous government agencies that were compiled from the 1940s to the present day, however, we learn precisely these types of things, and much more besides, about some very big celebrities of the recent past.

The government's motivation for their surveillance and interest in celebrities has been both wide and varied. In some cases, the celebrity spying was undertaken to find dirt on Hollywood's finest; on other occasions it was to protect famous people who were friends with government officials. Racism and homophobia were unfortunate motivating factors at times, as was the suspicion that some stars were supporters of communism, or were even spying for Russia.

Celebrity Secrets answers some intriguing and notable questions, including: Why did the United States Navy have a file on acclaimed writer Jack Kerouac? Was Frank Sinatra really in league with the Mob? Was the FBI keeping former Beatle John Lennon under surveillance for years because it feared he was donating money to Irish terrorists? And what secrets lay behind the government's interest in, among many others, Abbott and Costello, Marilyn Monroe, Rock Hudson, Mickey Mantle, Jimi Hendrix, Elvis Presley, and Andy Warhol? The revelations are startling, to say the least.

Note from the author

Unless otherwise stated, all the material in this book comes from officially declassified government files.

CELEBRITY
SECRETS

Office Memorandum · UNITED STATES GOVERNMENT

TO : Mr. Wick

DATE: 1-10-48

FROM :

SUBJECT: LOU COSTELLO; LOU COSTELLO, JR. FOUNDATION
Information Concerning

    In accordance with your request there is set forth a summary of available information on Lou Costello, the movie comedian.

I. BIOGRAPHICAL DATA

    Lou Costello was born March 6, 1908, and was christened Louis Francis Cristello. His place of birth is not given. While in his teens, he quit high school and began to work in a haberdashery, which job he soon quit to become an actor. His first attempts were unsuccessful and he then decided to become a prize fighter. Fourteen fights later he ended up on the West Coast where he became a Hollywood stunt man.

    He met Bud Abbott in 1929 at the Empire Theatre in Brooklyn, when his regular straight man was taken ill. Bud agreed to substitute and they have been together ever since. They played most of the burlesque and many of the vaudeville circuits together. Their first break came in 1938 when they were given a 10-minute spot on Kate Smith's program. Their real success came when they began making movies in Hollywood. Since then they have made numerous pictures and their success is well-known. (Current Biography, October, 1941)

II. COSTELLO AN ADMIRER OF CHARLIE CHAPLIN

    In June of 1943 the Bureau received information that Harry Crocker of the Los Angeles Examiner and a close contact of Charlie Chaplin's, intended to launch a publicity program for the purpose of bettering Chaplin's public reputation. Chaplin's reputation, of course, has suffered due to his numerous escapades. Crocker said that Costello, who was a fond admirer of Chaplin, was going to help in regard to this program. (31-68496-x1)

III. COSTELLO REPORTED HAVING LARGE LIBRARY OF OBSCENE FILM

    In October of 1944 during the course of an investigation of a purported ring of obscene motion picture operators in Hollywood, information was received that the best known customers for obscene film in Hollywood were Red Skelton, Lou Costello, George Raft and others. One informant, who, it has been shown, tends to exaggerate the facts, said that Lou Costello had the largest library of obscene film in Hollywood. The informant remarked that Costello "had it running out of his ears." (71-1843-5)

IV. COSTELLO TIE-IN WITH UNDERWORLD

    On October 22, 1946, the Los Angeles Office advised that Lou Costello had requested assistance from one ████████████ of New Jersey to "take care of"

F B I

31 FEB 11 1948

52 FEB 17 1948

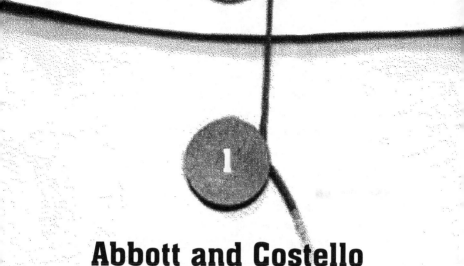

Abbott and Costello

"Costello 'had it running out of his ears.'"

Next to Laurel and Hardy, the most well loved comedic duo of the Golden Age of Hollywood was, for many people, Abbott and Costello. A brief FBI document of January 10, 1948, titled *"Lou Costello, Information Concerning,"* provides background on Costello and reveals how the two met and developed their career:

Lou Costello was born March 6, 1908, and was christened Louis Francis Costillo. While in his teens, he quit high school and began to work in a haberdashery, which job he soon quit to become an actor. His first attempts were unsuccessful and he then decided to become a prizefighter. Fourteen fights later he ended up on the West Coast where he became a Hollywood stunt man. He met Bud Abbott in 1929 at the Empire Theater in Brooklyn, when his regular straight man was taken ill. Bud agreed to substitute and they have been together ever since. They have played most of the burlesque and many of the vaudeville circuits together. Their first break came in 1938 when they were given a 10-minute spot on Kate Smith's program. Their real success came when they began making movies in Hollywood. Since then they have made numerous pictures and their success is well known.

Indeed, their success *was* well known: having signed to Universal in 1939, Abbott and Costello went on to make a wealth of hit movies, including *Buck Privates, In the Navy,* and *Hold That Ghost.* At the height of their phenomenal career, however, Abbott and Costello had more than just faithful fans following their exploits and antics. None other than the all-powerful Federal Bureau of Investigation was secretly doing likewise. Indeed, declassified FBI memoranda on the pair are almost as entertaining as their cinematic output, albeit for *very* different reasons. Stories of covert wartime espionage, "lewd" girl-on-girl action, deep-running Mob ties, impressively huge porno collections, prostitution, and more all made their way to the desk of bureau head honcho J. Edgar Hoover after the duo caught the attention of government intelligence agents.

The first real inkling of FBI interest in Abbott and Costello surfaced in 1943, when, on February 23 of that year, Arthur H. Crowl, the special agent in charge of the bureau's office at Springfield, Illinois, forwarded a highly unusual report to his boss Hoover and to the FBI Technical Laboratory titled: *"BUD ABBOTT and LOU COSTELLO,* Radio Program on February 4 And February 18, 1943. ESPIONAGE."

According to Crowl, he had been recently contacted by a woman from Illinois who was described in the documentation "as writer of radio script and an author," and who had come to the distinctly strange conclusion that Abbott and Costello were carefully and secretly inserting "key words" and phrases into their radio shows that, when correctly interpreted, could potentially be utilized for espionage purposes by unfriendly nations. Given that this was at the height of the Second World War, this could really only mean the Axis powers of Germany, Italy, and Japan. Declassified FBI files demonstrate that the woman had gone to truly extraordinary lengths to carefully record for the bureau's Springfield office no less than eighty-five words and phrases that she believed were directly relevant to her distinctly odd theory. As Special Agent Crowl noted, those same words and phrases included:

"Fog," "Boats," "Rocky coastline," "Kick in the France," "Fire," "South," "Turn north quickly," "Two weeks," "High-powered boats," "Dive bombers hit a rock," "Hole in Boat," "Army and Navy," "Camel caravan," "Telegram," "Important," "Platoon," "Parachute," "Cartographer," "Rand McNally," "T-Zone—Test," "Dead of night," "Twenty miles of desert," "Egypt," "Rommel," "Sphinx," "Battle," "Moonlight," "Guard" [and] "Eleven camps."

Crowl further advised Hoover that the woman was "very nervous and upset over the long illness and loss of her husband," that she was acquainted with "several government officials in Washington," and more intriguing, that she was "distantly related to Mrs. Roosevelt, and assisted in preparing material for the President's recent campaign." Top secret messages and codes, international espionage, and even allegations of presidential links to the story inevitably led Hoover to take a keen and personal interest in the matter. However, after having done so, the crime-fighter-in-chief came away hardly impressed by the woman's so-called incriminating evidence, and he made this clear to Crowl two weeks later.

Stressing that the bureau could "draw no conclusion from the information furnished concerning her reliability," Hoover explained to the Springfield office that "although she has furnished eighty-five key words, she has furnished definitions of only twelve of these words. From the information furnished the Bureau does not understand how or why [she] chose the words contained in the list, labeling them key words, and was only able to give definitions of a small fraction of these." Hoover also rightly noted that selecting such "key words" in such a haphazard fashion "could be similarly applied to practically any radio program." Hoover's final word on the affair was: "No further action is being taken by the Bureau in this matter."

One and a half years after this particularly bizarre episode, the FBI was still carefully watching both Abbott and Costello, but by this time allegations of wartime espionage had been replaced by a plethora of other issues. This is made abundantly clear in a bureau report of 1944 that focused its attention on Costello's private life:

In October of 1944 during the course of an investigation of a purported ring of obscene motion picture operators in Holly- wood, information was received that the best-known cus- tomers for obscene film in Hollywood were Red Skelton, Lou Costello, George Raft and others. One informant, who, it has been shown, tends to exaggerate the facts, said that Lou Costello had the largest library of obscene film in Hollywood. The informant remarked that Costello "had it running out of his ears."

Somewhat amusingly, while J. Edgar Hoover was privately looking at Lou Costello with distinctly disapproving eyes, at a pub- lic level he pretended to be a big fan of the man and his partner, Bud Abbott. "On February 28, 1946," according to an FBI internal memorandum, "the Director wrote a letter to Abbott and Costello in Beverly Hills, stating that he had the pleasure of listening to their radio program the preceding night and enjoyed their play on words on the meaning of the FBI. Costello answered this letter on March 8, 1946, and invited the Director to be his guest at lunch should he come to California." Hoover declined the invitation.

Of greater concern to the FBI, however, was the fact that bu- reau agents had learned that Lou Costello had disturbing links with some distinctly dangerous characters within the dark and feared world of organized crime. On October 22, 1946, the Los

Angeles FBI office had informed Hoover that Costello had then recently "requested assistance" from a New Jersey-based crime lord who was going to secretly arrange for a "hoodlum" in Los Angeles to "take care of" a man who was apparently "making a play for Mrs. Costello."

In monitoring the situation, the FBI learned that Costello had been given a guarantee that the matter would be "handled" to Costello's satisfaction, and that the unnamed Casanova would "cause no further trouble." Given the fact that Costello was later told that the man hadn't been "touched," it seems reasonable to assume that, at the very least, the fear of God was placed in him by the criminal underworld. Ominously, however, Costello's criminal contact elaborated that if stern words were ultimately not enough to convince the man to leave Costello's wife alone, and "additional trouble" loomed on the horizon, he would "hurt him."

"What a tie-up to the underworld," Hoover noted, in a handwritten response to the story. The available FBI files contain no further data on this episode, which strongly suggests that whoever the man "making a play for Mrs. Costello" was, he wisely decided to back off.

Although Lou Costello was fully determined to ensure that his wife did not play away from home, those rules seemingly did not apply to the Hollywood funnyman himself. The FBI knew that the comedian was more than partial to a bit of girl-on-girl action when he was out of town on business. In December 1946, and "during the course of the investigation of a White Slave Traffic Act case in the Portland Division," the FBI learned that "two prostitutes put on a lewd performance for Lou Costello, the movie actor, while he was in Portland in connection with the premiere of a motion picture. The girls were paid $50 apiece for their part in the show." Four months later, on April 17, 1947, the FBI uncovered information to the effect that Lou Costello was a member of a "local Italian-American Citizens Committee" that "planned a banquet for Ferruccio Parri, the non-Communist former premier of Italy."

Interestingly, the FBI noted that Parri was touring the United States under the sponsorship of the American Society for Cultural Relationships with Italy, an organization that, according to the FBI, was "under investigation at the present time as a Communist front."

The following year, 1948, the pair really hit it big with their movie, *Abbott and Costello Meet Frankenstein*—a movie that remains a true favorite among aficionados. That movie also led to a series of highly successful spin-offs, including *Abbott and Costello Meet the Mummy*, and *Abbott and Costello Meet the Wolf Man*. Their television series, *The Abbott and Costello Show*, aired in 1952, and the pair continued to work together through 1957, when they amicably went their separate ways.

The FBI's surveillance continued, however. Like his partner Lou Costello, Bud Abbott also had a great fondness for porno flicks and also possessed a truly huge collection of such movies, something that is borne out by the FBI memorandum of March 5, 1958, titled "Bud Abbott, Interstate Transport of Obscene Matter:"

On 3/3/58 Los Angeles PD [Police Department], advised that a police informant furnished information to the effect that Bud ABBOTT, the well known motion picture and TV star, is a collector of pornography and allegedly has 1,500 reels of obscene motion pictures which he shows in his home where he has a projector of his own. The police informant was approached by ABBOTT to furnish some girls for a private party he is having at an early date.

On 3/4/58 [the police informant] advised he had received no further specific date as to when the party is to be held but stated that Vice intends raiding the party when and if it is held and will confiscate all films they are able to find in their search incidental to their arrests.

Although Abbott is an alleged collector and there is not an allegation of interstate transportation of this matter, a case is being opened in this office as a control file to follow and report to the Bureau information coming to the attention of this office through police liaison with Vice, LAPD. [The police informant] is well aware of the Bureau's interest in this category and any films obtained will be submitted to the FBI Lab for examination and comparison purposes.

This affair ultimately fizzled out, however, and while fans always hoped that the duo of Abbott and Costello would reunite, it was not to be. Lou Costello died from heart failure in 1959 at the tragically young age of fifty-one, and Bud Abbott passed away from cancer in 1974. But hot sex, porn, Mob links, and international espionage would become all-too-familiar themes to the FBI as it delved into the lives of Hollywood's glitterati.

MEDICAL HISTORY

(10) KEROUAC
(Surname)

John   Louis
(Christian name(s))

Born: Place Lowell, Mass.   Date 3-12-22

STATE NAME OF PLACE   DATE EACH NEW ENTRY

C 5-11-43: DIAGNOSIS CHANGED THIS DATE TO
39 DEMENTIA PRAECOX #1509. Reason established, not duty, not misconduct and E.P.T.E.
RA Recommend that he be brought before a
Board of Medical Survey for disposition
as he is unsuitable for Naval Service.
B.L.ALLEN LT.COMDR. (MC) USNR

5-14-43: Board of Medical Survey this
date found Dementia Praecox #1509.
Reason established, not duty, not misconduct and E.P.T.E. Recommends that he
be transferred to the National Naval
Medical Center, Bethesda, Maryland,
for disposition and treatment accompanied
by an officer and two hospital corpsmen.
B.L.ALLEN LT.COMDR. (MC) USNR

T 5-18-43: Transferred this date to the
7 National Naval Medical Center, Bethesda,
Maryland for disposition and treatment
in accordance with approved recommendation and COM One Dispatch #151449 dated
5/15/43.

B. Allen.
B.L.ALLEN
LT.COMDR. (MC) USNR

APPROVED:

C. C. FULLER

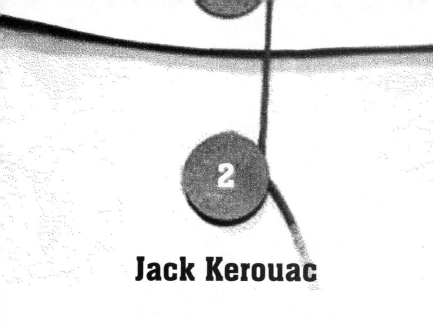

Jack Kerouac

"He imagines in his mind whole symphonies."

Born in Lowell, Massachusetts, in 1922, Jean-Louis "Jack" de Kerouac was the youngest of three children in a Franco-American family and became arguably the finest of those writers that defined the so-called Beat Generation of the postwar era. Kerouac had attended both Catholic and public schools and earned himself a football scholarship to Columbia University, New York City, where he mixed with such luminaries as Neal Cassady, Allen Ginsberg, and William S. Burroughs. After a year, however, Kerouac quit school and joined the merchant marine, ultimately embarking upon the numerous and varied wanderings and road trips that not only defined his life, but also his career as a writer—a career that ultimately inspired and captured the imaginations of millions of like-minded souls across the planet.

While Kerouac's legacy will continue to live on for as long as people devour the written word, the United States Navy has also left us something that is destined to ensure that the legend of this unique wordsmith will always be with us: military medical records from Kerouac's brief time with the navy's reserve in the early 1940s before he joined the merchant marine. Like Kerouac's books, the once-secret documents in question chronicle the life of a man with an infinitely complex mind, a mountain of inner struggles, a wealth of emotional turmoil, and a tortured soul that could never, ever rest.

A 1943 document prepared by staff at the National Naval Medical Center, Bethesda, Maryland, and titled "John Louis Kerouac Admitted from U.S. Naval Hospital, Newport, R.I., '*Constitutional Psychopathic State*' " reveals some notable facts about the twenty-one-year-old Kerouac's personality and state of mind:

A review of this patient's health record reveals that at recruit examination he was recognized as sufficiently abnormal to warrant trial duty status, and that during this period, neuropsychiatric examination disclosed auditory hallucinations, ideas and reference of suicide, and a rambling, grandiose, philosophical manner. At the Naval Hospital this patient appeared to be restless, apathetic, seclusive [*sic*] and described experiences which were interpreted to be visual and auditory hallucinations. The diagnosis Dementia Praecox was established and upon the approved recommendation of a Board of Medical Survey, the patient was transferred to this hospital, arriving here on May 20, 1943.

As a result of the "visual and auditory hallucinations," a careful study of Kerouac's character was conducted while he was in the care of the navy's medical experts. Interestingly, Kerouac was quick to deny assertions that he was suffering from such hallucinations, asserting that they were merely "echo effects in his mind of conversations he had had previously." However, the navy's records continued to paint a notable portrait of Kerouac:

According to the patient, he had made a very poor adjustment in school and in work. He impulsively left school because he felt too stilted [*sic*] and held back in there. Without any particular training or background, this patient, just prior to his enlistment, enthusiastically embarked upon the writing of novels. He sees nothing unusual in this activity. Physical and neurological examinations are negative and mental examination reveals no gross evidence of psychosis. At a Staff Conference on June 2, 1943, the diagnosis was changed to Constitutional Psychopathic State, Schizoid Personality, it being unanimously agreed that this patient has shown strong schizoid trends which have bordered upon but which have not yet reached the level of psychosis, but which render him unfit for service. His discharge from service is recommended. This patient is considered fully competent to be discharged into his own custody. He is not considered to be a menace to himself or to others and is not likely to become a public charge.

We may never know to what extent Kerouac was really plagued by inner voices in his early twenties, but perhaps wisely Kerouac was keen to play down this aspect of his character and was very reluctant to discuss such matters. A *"Medical History"* document of April 2, 1943, prepared by Lieutenant J. J. O'Connell, adds to our understanding and appreciation of the man himself. "He complained of headaches and asked for aspirin," said O'Connell, adding that Kerouac had informed him, "They diagnosed me Dementia Pracecox and sent me here. I was frank with them. I was in a series of ventures and I knew they'd look them up; like getting fired from jobs and getting out of college."

And it did not help Kerouac's position when he advised O'Connell that he was not suited to the military lifestyle and regime: "I just cannot stand it; I like to be by myself." Indeed, a note-to-file from O'Connell added: "He was in the Merchant Marine and was fired because he was bucking everybody." From his conversations with Kerouac, O'Connell was able to determine that the writer's mother was "nervous," his father "emotional," and that at the age of fourteen Kerouac "had a sex contact with a 32 year old woman which upset him somewhat." O'Connell also added that while Kerouac's appearance was "neat," and he was always "cooperative," he was "inclined to exaggerate." O'Connell closed his report on Kerouac in a highly descriptive fashion: "He imagines in his mind whole symphonies; he can hear every note; he sees printed pages of words."

In an interview with medical personnel on April 23, 1943, Kerouac grudgingly conceded that, "I get nervous in an emotional way but I'm not nervous enough to get a discharge. I don't hear voices talking to me from nowhere but I have a photographic picture before my eyes; when I go to sleep and I hear music playing I know I shouldn't have told the psychiatrist that, but I wanted to be frank."

No one who has ever read any of Kerouac's work could accuse him of being anything other than devastatingly open and honest when it came to describing his life, his loves, his adventures, and his experiences on the road. And a series of notes attached to the file provides yet further insights into the unique world and mind of Jack Keroauc:

Patient's father, Leo A. Kerouac, states that his son has been "boiling" for a long time. Has always been seclusive [sic], stubborn, head strong, resentful of authority and advice, being unreliable, unstable and undependable . . . Feels that he has improved. His nervousness had decreased. The first impression that the doctors got of him was incorrect, he states, for he did not take them seriously. Likes the sea and will join the Merchant Marine if he can get out of the Navy . . . Interested in world affairs and political theory. Is gregarious. Has many boy friends. Mother believes him heterosexual but interest in girls shallow. Broods when unhappy or lonely.

In a section of the document titled "Family History," a wealth of further fascinating data on Kerouac and his family was revealed:

Father, French-Canadian birth, living and well, works as a printer, and has always been a pal of the patient's—"more like a big brother." He has worked as a printer most of his life. During the depression years, was on WPA for a time. In 1941, lost his job because his employers wanted him to send his boy to Boston College whereas the boy had already registered at Columbia University. Since then has obtained other satisfactory employment but according to the patient the father feels that the whole town is "against" the family.

Mother, 48, living and well, closely attached to patient. Also French-Canadian by birth. Sister, 24, divorced just recently joined the WAAC's. At 18 she married a man of 30 but divorced him after one year. Because of this she was considered the "black sheep" of the family. Patient remarks that in years past he was the favored child but that recently his role has been reversed so that he is now looked upon as the "black sheep."

Developmental: Denies enuresis, somnambulism, temper-tantrums, nail-biting, etc.

Pre illness personality: Patient enjoyed company of others, but also had periods when he would want to be by himself. Patient believes a change in his personality occurred when he left Columbia.

Sexual and Marital: Has masturbated up until one year ago. Enjoys rather promiscuous relationships with girl friends and is boastful of this. No apparent conflicts over sexual activity noted.

Habits: Enjoys reading and writing. He did enjoy athletics very much and practiced regularly. More recently however is chiefly interested in writing. No drug habits. Has drunken sprees once or twice a year lasting about one week.

On May 20, 1943, an updated summary of the navy's medical assessment of Kerouac was prepared, after it had become abundantly clear that Kerouac and the navy were destined to part ways in the very near future:

The patient was readmitted 4-2-43 to the sick list at the U.S. Naval Training Station, Newport, RI, because at recruitment he exhibited vague, disconnected thoughts. He has been fired from every job he had except newspaper reporting. The latter was for a small paper at $15 per week, which he quit. He has been discharged from steamship job, garage job and waiter job. He is irresponsible not caring. He found it difficult to adjust to the recruit-training program "because of the regimentation and discipline."

Naval medical experts were careful to add that Kerouac had been "cooperative ever since his admission to this hospital," adding that he was, "well-dressed, neat, tidy and appears to be in excellent physical condition. Although alert and attentive most of the time, occasionally he appears somewhat manneristic [sic] and preoccupied. He gives all information readily and does not appear to be evasive, although a moderate amount of circumstantiality [sic] is noted."

The navy then turned its attentions to Kerouac's plans to embark upon a career as a writer:

Patient describes his writing ambitions. He has written several novels, one when he was quite young, another just prior to joining the service, and one he is writing now. Patient states he believes he might have been nervous when in boot camp because he had been working too hard just prior to induction. He had been writing a novel, in the style of James Joyce, about his own hometown, and averaging approximately 16 hours daily in an effort to get it down. This was an experiment and he doesn't intend to publish. At present he is writing a novel about his experiences in the Merchant Marine. Patient is very vague in describing all these activities. There seems to be an artistic factor in his thinking when discussing his theories of writing and philosophy. Patient believes he quit football for same reason he couldn't get along in Navy, he can't stand regulations, etc.

From an individual described as an "outside source," the navy learned more about Kerouac's complex character: "This patient has had marked conflicts about his religion. He is trying to resolve, according to his parents, a religious philosophy that will be satisfactory to himself. Also he tends to brood a good deal." Then, finally, on June 2, 1943, the navy's conclusions on Kerouac came to the fore. Stressing that Kerouac was still showing strong "schizoid trends," the official verdict and recommendation was summed up in twelve concise words: "He is considered unfit for the service and his discharge is recommended."

And thus ended the short military career of Apprentice Seaman John Louis Kerouac, United States Naval Reserve. But the life of Beat writer Jack Kerouac had barely begun. Kerouac's first novel, *The Town and the City*, was published in 1950. However, he is perhaps most widely identified with *On the Road*, which was published in 1957 and which went on to make Kerouac one of the most controversial and cherished writers of his era. But it was his classic *Big Sur* that brought to the fore Kerouac's infinitely complex character, and his many anxieties, hopes, dreams, and thoughts on women, religion, death, living life to its fullest, friendship, the nature and purpose of human existence, spirituality—and a whole lot more.

In *Big Sur*, Kerouac wrote: "My work comprises one vast book like Proust's except that my remembrances are written on the run instead of afterwards in a sick bed. Because of the objections of my early publishers I was not allowed to use the same personae names in each work. *On the Road, The Subterraneans, The Dharma Bums, Doctor Sax, Maggie Cassidy, Tristessa, Desolation Angels, Visions of Cody,* and the others including this book *Big Sur* are just chapters in the whole work which I call *The Duluoz Legend.* In my old age, I intend to collect all my work and reinsert my pantheon of uniform names, leave the long shelf of books there, and die happy."

Sadly, and perhaps inevitably, it was not to be. A keen lover of the grape at the best of times, by middle age Kerouac, once the proud, handsome, athletic football star that made the girls' hearts beat faster, had turned into an overweight alcoholic. Kerouac died prematurely in St. Petersburg, Florida, in 1969 at the age of forty-seven following a massive, alcohol-induced abdominal hemorrhage.

It is fitting to close this tale with the words of poet, novelist, and biographer, Aram Saroyan: "Jack Kerouac was the American hero in looks and deeds who dared to have a series of long, tender nervous breakdowns in the prose of his dozen or so books. His work at its best brought something of the luminous pleasures of the French Impressionists into American writing, and something too of the brooding syntactic circuitry of Proust. Above all, he was a tender writer. It would be hard to find a mean-spirited word about anybody in all his writing."

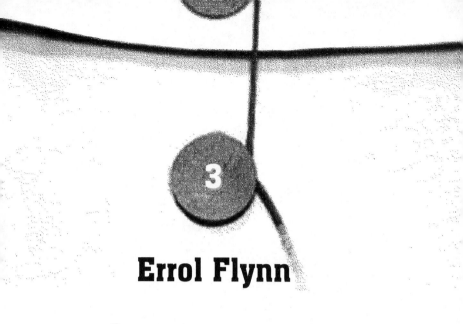

Errol Flynn

"He is generally regarded in
Hollywood circles as a 'wolf.' "

For people with a love and appreciation of cinematic history, the late actor, Errol Flynn, was the ultimate swashbuckling star of the 1940s. In movies such as *The Adventures of Robin Hood, Captain Blood, The Adventures of Don Juan*, and *The Charge of the Light Brigade*, Flynn earned his reputation as a force to be reckoned with in Hollywood, and became one of the most loved and admired screen stars of that bygone era. Behind the glossy, celluloid image that Flynn was careful to cultivate, however, there existed a far more intriguing, secretive, and controversial persona.

From the previously classified files of numerous government, intelligence, and military agencies, comes a truly astonishing body of data on Flynn that covers such controversial issues as allegations of rape, extortion attempts, Hollywood scandal, and most intriguing of all, links with both wartime Nazi spies and the Cold War-era activities of Cuba's Fidel Castro. It's no wonder that Flynn's FBI file alone runs to almost four hundred pages.

Los Angeles, California
September 21, 1940

Special Agent in Charge
San Francisco, California

Re: DR. HERMANN FREDERICK ERBEN
ESPIONAGE

Dear Sir:

Reference is made to report of Special Agent
dated New York City, March 18, 1940, in the
above captioned matter.

You were advised that through the assistance of
his agent, WALTER HERMER, and his attorney, OSCAR CUMMINS, ERROL
FLYNN, motion picture actor, was interviewed at the Warner Bros.
Studio, Burbank, California, by Special Agent in Charge R. B. HOOD.

Mr. FLYNN at the outset of the interview, admitted
being acquainted with DR. ERBEN and regarded him highly. They
have been acquainted for about ten years and have traveled extensively
together all over the world. They first met in Guinea. FLYNN
believes that DR. ERBEN has a very brilliant mind and is an excellent physician; that he is the type of person who would do
everything in his power to make it appear that he was in fact an
espionage agent. FLYNN was of the opinion that DR. ERBEN has the
propensity for getting into trouble.

Mr. FLYNN stated that heretofore ERBEN had been
very much opposed to Nazism and Communism and from what he,
FLYNN, knows of his background, he does not believe ERBEN would
now be a devout Nazi. FLYNN informed that he had several letters
in his possession from ERBEN which he would turn over to Mr. HOOD
for examination.

As evidence of ERBEN'S ability, FLYNN stated he had
gone to Australia about 1932 or 1934 as the head of an expedition
for the Rockefeller Institute, where he has seen the doctor work
twenty-four hours at a stretch entirely without compensation.
ERBEN recently advised FLYNN of his difficulties with the Immigration
Bureau and as a result thereof FLYNN communicated with Mrs. FRANKLIN
D. ROOSEVELT in an effort to have her do anything possible for
ERBEN.

INDEXED 65-682-76?

FEDERAL BUREAU OF INVESTIGATION
SEP 28 1940
U.S. DEPARTMENT OF JUSTICE

Errol Leslie Thomson Flynn was born on June 20, 1909. He arrived in Hollywood in the early part of 1935, having traveled from Tasmania via New Guinea, London, and New York. Even at that stage, Flynn was embroiled in controversy: his departure from New Guinea, for example, was hastened by the fact that a warrant had been issued for his arrest on charges of illegally procuring native labor. He was twenty-six years of age and in the prime of his life. Not surprisingly, for someone thrust into the Hollywood lifestyle of fame, fortune, and glamour, Flynn lived life to the fullest: wine, women, and adventure were the order of the day, both on and off screen.

At times, however, Flynn's adrenaline-driven lifestyle of non-stop parties, drugs, and booze went too far even for him. Declassified police records demonstrate that during the latter part of 1942, Flynn was accused of unlawful sexual intercourse with a striking seventeen-year-old blonde named Betty Hansen. According to Hansen, Flynn had raped her at the Bel-Air home of one of his friends, Freddie McEvoy. Hansen's graphic testimony was presented in Los Angeles County Court on January 14, 1943, along with that of another girl, Peggy LaRue Satterlee, who was also alleging rape by Flynn. But records show that the allegations were summarily thrown out, and Flynn lived to fight another day. His problems, however, had barely begun.

It was during this period in his life and career that Flynn received the first of two extortion notes that found their way to the FBI's Technical Laboratory. The first note, sent only weeks after the rape controversy had died down, advised Flynn that if he "valued [his] life and career" he was to "send ten thousand dollars in cash wrapped in a small package" to a particular drop-off point, which was a malt shop in San Bernardino, California. Obviously concerned, Flynn contacted the authorities, and the declassified records show that the FBI made a detailed study of both the letter and its contents. Not only that, but FBI agents and local police initiated a stakeout of this malt shop.

As demanded by the extortion note, a package was duly left at the malt shop on the day in question, and the FBI patiently waited for its quarry to come along. All involved in the entrapment were utterly amazed, however, when the person turned out to be a thirteen-year-old boy named Billy Seamster. According to the FBI's files, young Billy was a fan of Flynn's and he maintained, rather weakly, that he had really only wanted the movie star's autograph. For their part, both the FBI and the police decided not to prosecute Billy because of his young age. In April 1943, Flynn received yet another extortion note. This time, however, it bore all of the hallmarks of something far more serious than a schoolboy prank.

MR FLYNN!!!! If you know what is good for you, you will pay attention to the girls you raped. I know you did it. You cannot fool me, so you better fork over some dough. Put your answer in the BOSTON DAILY RECORD. Put it near WEINCHELL [sic] column and just say anything but give a hint you received this and in a week if you don't want trouble. Get what I mean chum. Be hearing from you don't forget a week from today. That will be April 29 and then I will send you your instructions on where and when to leave the money and how much. Do not worry it will not be over $15,000 for that's all I need to skip town.

Again, the FBI launched an extensive investigation through the bureau's Los Angeles office, with a wealth of assistance provided by FBI special agents in Boston, and by local police. Once more, the perpetrator was ultimately caught and revealed this time to be one Robert Street, a mental patient then on parole from the Medfield State Hospital. But far worse things were to come for Flynn.

Additional official memoranda of 1943 show that during this same time frame, none other than FBI boss J. Edgar Hoover was out for Flynn's blood. Hoover wanted him charged under the White Slave Traffic Act because of a trip to Mexico Flynn had made with an eighteen-year-old girl named Nora Eddington (who would later become his wife) that Hoover and the FBI felt was not entirely innocent in nature. As the FBI stated in a wonderfully antiquated style on August 27, 1943: "The Bureau files maintain fragmentary information in connection with National Defense cases which attributed to Flynn a rather depraved character. Information in these files reflect that he is generally regarded in Hollywood circles as a 'wolf' who delights in achieving intimacies with young innocent girls."

Once again, however, the Teflon-like Flynn succeeded in escaping prosecution, as the following memorandum to FBI headquarters made clear: "Flynn and the girl have returned from Mexico: it is pretty much of a personal escapade and that [*sic*] the girl went to Mexico in company with Flynn with the consent of her parents."

Hollywood scandal was one thing, but darker allegations linked Flynn with something far more sinister: namely, deep connections to wartime Nazi spies. Flynn authority Charles Higham has stated: "I spoke to Colonel William E. Williamson, former director of demilitarization procedures in Japan under General [Douglas] MacArthur. . . . Williamson had done his own research at the Pentagon and State Department and the CIA . . . and had learned that Errol was a spy for the Nazis on a major scale." Also, nightclub owner, and friend of Flynn's, Johnny Meyer told Higham: "I believe Errol was not merely in touch with the Nazis in San Francisco but was actively aiding and abetting them." And the alleged links do not end there.

It is a matter of official record that one of Flynn's girlfriends was Gertrude Anderson, a key Nazi agent who was the subject of deep FBI surveillance. According to Charles Higham, Flynn's friend Freddie McEvoy, at whose home Flynn was alleged to have raped Betty Hansen, had been under investigation as a possible collaborator with the Nazis. In the years leading up to the Second World War, he was involved in U-boat refueling operations. Interestingly, the government's files on Flynn include transcripts of telephone conversations between Flynn and McEvoy that were monitored by the wartime Office of Censorship.

Of particular note is a document that can be found within the Office of Censorship's files on Flynn that is dated December 14, 1942, and titled "American Film Actor Reported Associating with German Agent in Mexico." This document details the testimony of an unnamed informant who had provided the office with some intriguing material:

Writer, after telling of three weeks spent in Acapulco . . . adds, Errol Flynn came up to the hotel for drinks a couple of evenings bringing his girl along—Hilda Kruger, leading German spy here, arranged the date for him. An associate of hers, another Nazi suspect, gave Errol Flynn and Frederik McEvoy as references while spending time in California.

Most controversial of all, however, was Flynn's friendship with a certain Dr. Hermann Frederick Erben. Born on November 15, 1897, in Vienna, Austria, Erben was described in Lionel Godfrey's *The Life and Crimes of Errol Flynn*, as "a specialist in tropical diseases." Indeed, he was. However, he was much more, according to Flynn authority Charles Higham, who described Erben as "one of the most important and ingenious Nazi agents."

Erben had graduated from the State High School, Vienna, in 1915, and between that year and 1918 had served with the Austrian army, before being honorably discharged as a first lieutenant. Eight years later, Erben received a fellowship to study in the United States, and while there was granted an immigration visa. In 1927 he was licensed to practice medicine and surgery in Louisiana, and the following year he was also licensed for the state of Washington. But what of Erben's friendship with Flynn? The files of the Intelligence Detachment Screening Center make for eye-opening reading:

1932: [Erben] went via the Far East to New Guinea on another scientific expedition, which was financed by himself. On this trip he met the film star Errol Flynn and became a very close friend of same. 1937: [Erben] returned from South America and in the same year he and his friend Errol Flynn embarked in New York for London and went via Paris. Being in London [Erben] volunteered with a British ambulance unit, which was committed for the loyalists in Spain. Errol Flynn also went as a journalist and unofficial observer to Spain. After 20 days in Spain, subject went to Vienna and from there to Canton, China.

Erben had a darker side, too. American authorities were able to confirm that he *had* worked as a Nazi agent during the Second World War. Details of this startling fact can be found within the files of the Intelligence Detachment Screening Center, and specifically in the pages of a document titled *Subject Accepted the Job as German Intelligence Agent:* "[Erben] claims that he accepted the proposition to become a German intelligence agent, fully conscious of the fact that at the present, he was still an American citizen, and thus subject to the penalty of high treason. [Erben] admits that he was not forced or coerced to accept the job." Needless to say, because of his close friendship with Erben, Flynn was interviewed by FBI agents who subsequently prepared a two-page report, from which the following is extracted:

Mr. FLYNN at the outset of the interview, admitted being acquainted with Dr ERBEN and regarded him highly. They have been acquainted for about ten years and have traveled extensively together all over the world. Mr. FLYNN stated that heretofore ERBEN had been very much opposed to Nazism and communism and from what he, FLYNN, knows of his background, he does not believe ERBEN would now be a devout Nazi.

The FBI and the IDSC were not the only ones watching the activities of Flynn and Erben. The wartime Office of Strategic Services, a precursor to the CIA, was doing likewise. The OSS stated starkly in its files on the men that "Erben tried to return to the United States as a repatriate. We believe that if he had been successful in so doing, he would have been acting in the United States as an agent of the German government. Erben's only contact in the United States was Errol Flynn. We know of absolutely no other contact with Dr Erben there."

The British *Daily Telegraph* newspaper uncovered highly disturbing data, too, concerning Flynn's relationship with Erben: "Declassified files held by the CIA show that, in an intercepted letter in September 1933, Flynn wrote to Erben: 'A slimy Jew is trying to cheat me. . . . I do wish we could bring Hitler over here to teach these Isaacs a thing or two. The bastards have absolutely no business probity or honor whatsoever.' "

And as the *Daily Telegraph* added: "The letter, if genuine, certainly shows anti-Semitism, which was common at the time, but defenders say that Flynn, writing before he was famous and having lost money on a business deal, was not expressing a deep commitment to Nazism. Hitler had only just come to power and the true horror of his policies had yet to be revealed."

This may well be so. In December 2000, the *Daily Telegraph* revealed that it had learned that the British government's Home Office department possessed still classified documents "dispelling claims" that Flynn was a "Nazi sympathizer" and that, in reality, confirmed he had offered his services during the Second World War to British intelligence.

Harry Cohen, a Labor Member of the British Parliament, petitioned Jack Straw, then home secretary of the British government, to declassify the files. Cohen told the *Telegraph*: "I think there now has to be a great deal of doubt about suggestions that Flynn was a Nazi spy. On the contrary, I think he was probably used by the security services in this country. More likely he was taken up by the British security services towards the end of the war. I know the Home Office has documents on him, which should be released to the public."

Flynn authority Charles Higham uncovered data suggesting that the British government's files on Flynn had more to do with *perceived* pro-Nazi connections. In Higham's own words: "In early 1980, I was interviewed about Flynn for an American radio program. One of the callers who took part was a woman called Anne Lane. . . . She said that she had worked from 1946 to 1951 for the MI5 chief Sir Percy Sillitoe. . . . Lane had been in charge of the Flynn dossier, which she described clearly as a beige, red-ribboned [*sic*] concertina file stamped 'MOST SECRET.'

"The file," added Higham, "revealed that Flynn had been under surveillance by both MI5 and MI6 since 1934, when he made pro-Nazi remarks at a party in Mayfair. Flynn had also been monitored by British intelligence at a Paris meeting in 1937 with high-ranking German officials and the Duke of Windsor, a meeting clearly inimical to British interests. . . ."

So much for Flynn's still unresolved and decidedly mysterious wartime activities. But what of the final years of the man's life? Declassified files from the late 1950s that originated with the State Department, tell an intriguing story. By now, Flynn's roller-coaster lifestyle had completely and utterly ravaged his once healthy, athletic body. The heartthrob star of the late 1930s and 1940s had, by the 1950s, become a pathetic shadow of his former self. Racked with illness, a drug- and alcohol-dependent Flynn had lost his position as the number one Hollywood box office draw but not his uncanny knack for attracting controversy at an official level.

In 1959, the State Department recorded the details of its surveillance of Flynn's activities while he was on the island of Cuba:

Fidel Castro has asked Errol Flynn, movie actor, to suggest someone who might be able to take over the Sans Souci gambling casino. . . . Flynn is modestly displaying a minor leg wound these days which he says was inflicted by government bullets while he was roving with a rebel band last week. Flynn told a press conference here that he had been out three times since Christmas with rebel raiders in the service of Fidel Castro, whom he has known for eight years.

Only months later, Flynn's past finally caught up with him. On October 14, 1959, he died of a heart attack in Vancouver, Canada, at the all-too-young age of fifty. According to the coroner's report, Flynn's death was attributed to "coronary thrombosis of the arteries, degeneration of the liver and infection of the lower intestines."

Despite the fact that the many and varied files declassified by the FBI, the State Department, the Office of Strategic Services, the Office of Censorship, and the Intelligence Detachment Screening Center all throw intriguing light on Flynn's career, his wild times, his links with Nazi spies, his time spent covering the Spanish Civil War, his connections to Fidel Castro, and much more, it is fair to say that in some ways those same files, fragmentary as they are when it comes to stating with certainty that Flynn was in league with the Nazis, only serve to deepen the mystery of his truly extraordinary private life. Errol Flynn was, without doubt, enigmatic to the very end.

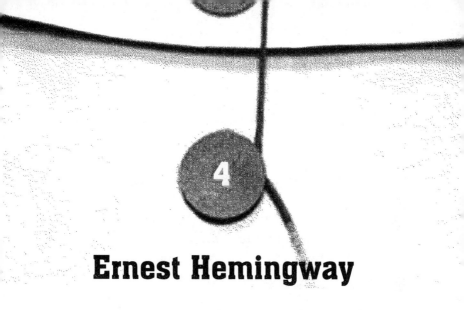

Ernest Hemingway

"His sobriety is certainly questionable."

Born in Oak Park, Illinois, in 1899, Ernest Hemingway began what would be a phenomenal career as an internationally acclaimed writer, on a Kansas-based newspaper at the age of seventeen. After the United States entered the First World War, Hemingway joined a volunteer ambulance unit in the Italian army, and, while serving at the front, was wounded and subsequently decorated by the Italian government. After his return to the United States, Hemingway became reporter for a variety of Canadian and American newspapers and was soon sent back to Europe to cover various events, including the Greek Revolution.

During the 1920s, Hemingway became a member of a group of expatriate Americans living in Paris, an episode he described in what was arguably his first important work, *The Sun Also Rises*, published in 1926. Equally successful was Hemingway's widely acclaimed A *Farewell to Arms* that was published three years later and told the story of an American ambulance officer's disillusionment with the war, as well as his role as a deserter. Hemingway

CONFIDENTIAL

Havana, Cuba
October 8, 1942

Director,
Federal Bureau of Investigation,
Washington, D. C.

Re: ERNEST HEMINGWAY

Dear Sir:

DECLASSIFIED BY

     The writer desires to acquaint the Bureau, in detail, with a relationship that has developed under the direction of the Ambassador with Mr. ERNEST HEMINGWAY.

     As the Bureau is aware, HEMINGWAY has been resident in Cuba almost continuously during the past two years, occupying his private finca at San Francisco de Paula about 14 miles east of Havana.

     Mr. HEMINGWAY has been on friendly terms with Consul KENNETH POTTER since the spring of 1941; recently he has become very friendly with Mr. ROBERT P. JOYCE, Second Secretary of Embassy, and through Mr. JOYCE has met the Ambassador on several occasions. It is the writer's observation that the initiative in developing these friendships has come from HEMINGWAY, but the opportunity of association with him has been welcomed by Embassy officials.

     At several conferences with the Ambassador and officers of the Embassy late in August 1942, the topic of utilizing HEMINGWAY'S services in intelligence activities was discussed. The Ambassador pointed out that HEMINGWAY'S experiences during the Spanish Civil War, his intimate acquaintances with Spanish Republican refugees in Cuba, as well as his long experience on this island, seemed to place him in a position of great usefulness to the Embassy's intelligence program. While this program is inclusive of all intelligence agencies and the Embassy's own sources of information, the fact is that the Ambassador regards the Bureau representation in the Embassy as the unit primarily concerned in this work. The Ambassador further pointed out that HEMINGWAY had completed some writing which had occupied him until that time, and was now ready and anxious to be called upon.

RECORDED & INDEXED

     The writer pointed out at these conferences that any information which could be secured concerning the operations of the Spanish Falange in Cuba would be of material assistance in our work, and that if HEMINGWAY was willing to devote his time and abilities to the gathering of such information, the results would be most welcome to us. It was pointed out to Mr. JOYCE, who is designated

-X JAN 4 1943

CLASS. & EXT. BY
REASON - FCIM 11, 1-
DATE OF REVIEW 10-24-89

CONFIDENTIAL

would use his experiences as a journalist during the Spanish Civil War in the 1930s as the background for his most ambitious novel, *For Whom the Bell Tolls.* Among his later works, the most outstanding was certainly *The Old Man and the Sea,* the 1952 tale of an elderly fisherman's journey, his long and lonely struggle with a fish and the sea, and his ultimate victory in defeat.

Equally of note is the fact that at the height of the Second World War, and while living on the island of Cuba, Hemingway's path crossed with that of the FBI after the author had offered his services to J. Edgar Hoover's crime-fighting agency. The relationship between the writer and the bureau boss was hardly cordial, however. In fact, it was downright fraught. An FBI document of 1942 gives an early indication of why Hoover would ultimately become so concerned about recruiting Hemingway as an intelligence-gathering asset:

While in Spain during the Spanish Revolution, Hemingway was said to have associated with Jay Allen, of the North American Newspaper Alliance. It has been alleged by a number of sources that Allen was a Communist and he is known to have been affiliated with alleged Communist Front organizations.

In the fall of 1940 Hemingway's name was included in a group of names of individuals who were said to be engaged in Communist activities. These individuals were reported to occupy positions on the "intellectual front" and were said to render valuable service as propagandists. According to the informant, those whose names were included on the list loaned their efforts politically as writers, artists and speakers and traveled throughout the country and supporting and taking part in Communist Front meetings and in the Program of the Party generally. Hemingway, according to a confidential source who furnished information on October 4, 1941, was one of the "heads" of the Committee for Medical Aid to the Soviet Union.

This informant alleged that the above-captioned committee was backed by the Communist Party.

As a committed anti-Communist, FBI boss Hoover had an instant, and inevitable, dislike of Hemingway from the very beginning. But it was a letter of October 8, 1942, sent to Hoover by R. G. Leddy, the FBI's legal attaché at Havana, Cuba, that really sent Hoover's blood pressure skyrocketing. Hoover learned that Hemingway, the hated alleged Red, had had the unmitigated and outrageous gall to offer his services to officials as an undercover spy. Leddy explained to Hoover the background to Hemingway's offer: "As the Bureau is aware, Hemingway has been resident in Cuba almost continuously during the past two years, occupying his private finca at San Francisco de Paula about 14 miles east of Havana. Mr. Hemingway has been on friendly terms with Consul Kenneth Potter since the spring of 1941; recently he has become very friendly with Mr. Robert P. Joyce, Second Secretary of Embassy, and through Mr. Joyce has met the Ambassador on several occasions."

Leddy then revealed that "at several conferences with the Ambassador and officers of the Embassy late in August 1942, the topic of using Hemingway's services in intelligence activities was discussed." Hoover further perused Leddy's report, which explained Leddy's justification for utilizing Hemingway's presumed skills in the field of espionage:

The Ambassador pointed out that Hemingway's experiences during the Spanish Civil War, his intimate acquaintances with Spanish Republican refugees in Cuba, as well as his long experience on the island, seemed to place him in a position of great usefulness to the Embassy's intelligence program. While this program is inclusive of all intelligence agencies and the Embassy's own sources of information, the fact is that the Ambassador regards the Bureau representation in the Embassy as the unit primarily concerned in this work. The Ambassador further pointed out that Hemingway had completed some writing, which had occupied him until that time, and was now ready and anxious to be called upon.

As much as Hoover hated to admit it, Hemingway's influential standing and position on Cuba *was* something that could, conceivably at least, be useful to American officials. And Leddy further informed Hoover that, while Hemingway wanted to get more involved with working in tandem with the FBI, he was *already* secretly undertaking covert tasks on behalf of the American embassy on the island:

Early in September 1942, Ernest Hemingway began to engage directly in intelligence activities on behalf of the American Embassy in Havana. He is operating through Spanish Republicans whose identities have not been furnished but which we are assured are obtainable when desired. [Hemingway] advised that he now has four men operating on a full time basis, and 14 more whose positions are barmen, waiters, and the like, operating on a part-time basis. The cost of this program is approximately $500 a month. Hemingway himself told me that he declined an offer from Hollywood to write a script for a "March of Time" report on the "Flying Tigers" in Burma, for which the compensation was to be $150,000, because he considers the work he is now engaged in as of greater importance. With specific reference to the conducting of intelligence investigations on the island of Cuba by Mr. Hemingway, the writer wishes to suggest that his interest thus far has not been limited to the Spanish Falange and Spanish activities, but that he has included numerous German suspects.

Although Leddy was seemingly amenable to having Hemingway on board, he was somewhat less enamored by the writer's unique and quirky sense of humor, particularly after Hemingway had introduced Leddy to one of Hemingway's friends as "a member of the Gestapo." It goes without saying that this was yet another reason for the decidedly humorless J. Edgar Hoover to hate Hemingway's guts. Another memo from Leddy to Hoover on Hemingway suggested that the writer's espionage activities were destined for the eyes of none other than the commander in chief, President Roosevelt:

It is now understood that one Gustavo Duran is being sent from Washington for the special purpose of assisting Mr. Hemingway in this work. Mr. Hemingway advised the Ambassador that Duran had been active with him in intelligence work on the Republican side of the Spanish Civil War, and recommended his abilities very highly.

Of further interest in this matter is a visit of Mrs. Ernest Hemingway (the former Martha Gellhorn) to Washington during the week commencing October 12, 1942. Mrs. Hemingway is to be the personal guest of Mrs. Roosevelt during her stay in Washington, and the Ambassador outlined to her certain aspects of the intelligence situation in Cuba, that she might convey the same, in personal conversation, to the President and Mrs. Roosevelt.

The debate over using Hemingway as an intelligence asset continued until December 1942, by which time Hoover could contain himself no longer. In a memorandum to Assistant Director Edward A. Tamm and D. M. Ladd of the bureau's Domestic Intelligence Division, Hoover stated:

In regard to . . . the use of Ernest Hemingway by the United States Ambassador to Cuba, I of course realize the complete undesirability of this sort of a connection or relationship. Certainly Hemingway is the last man, in my estimation, to be used in any such capacity. His judgment is not of the best, and if his sobriety is the same as it was some years ago, that is certainly questionable.

However, I do not think there is anything we should do in this matter, nor do I think our representatives at Havana should do anything about it with the Ambassador. The Ambassador is somewhat hot-headed and I haven't the slightest doubt that he would immediately tell Hemingway of the objections being raised by the FBI. Hemingway has no particular love for the FBI and would no doubt embark upon a campaign of vilification.

In addition, thereto, you will recall that in my conference recently with the President, he indicated that some message had been sent to him, the President, by Hemingway through a mutual friend, and Hemingway was insisting that one-half million dollars be granted to the Cuban authorities so that they could take care of internees. I do not see that this is a matter that directly affects our relationship as long as Hemingway does not report directly to us or we deal directly with him. Anything which he gives to the Ambassador which the Ambassador in turn forwards to us, we can accept without any impropriety.

It appears that one other, key reason why Hoover was so adamantly against having anything to do with Hemingway in a spying capacity was because, according to bureau records of the same time period, "It will be recalled that recently Hemingway gave information concerning the refueling of submarines in Caribbean waters which has proved unreliable." As far as Hoover was concerned at least, Hemingway's espionage activities were hardly of G-man standards. This led the bureau director to dismiss his work as being of little or no value to the FBI.

Among Hemingway's apparent failures was a case in late 1942 involving Prince Camilo Ruspoli, the Italian Fascist leader who had been interned by Cuban authorities, and who was confined to a clinic due to ill health. On this matter the FBI prepared the following, summary report:

In December 1942, Hemingway reported that Ruspoli had attended a public luncheon in honor of the new Spanish Charges d'Affaires, Pelayo Garcia Olay at the Hotel Nacional. This report greatly disturbed the Ambassador; there was an immediate check at the Hotel Nacional by the Legal Attaché and no substantiation of the public luncheon or the presence of Ruspoli could be found either from the hotel management and employees or from two of the guests alleged to have been present. The ambassador was so advised and later Hemingway wrote a memorandum asking that his source, a waiter at the hotel, not be "grilled" by the FBI as this would destroy his usefulness; he also asked to see our proof's regarding the absence of Prince Ruspoli from this public luncheon.

Another apparent failure of Hemingway's usefulness as an intelligence asset caught the attention of the FBI in January 1943:

Mr. Joyce of the Embassy asked the assistance of the Legal Attaché in ascertaining the contents of a tightly wrapped box left by a suspect at the Bar Basque under conditions suggesting that the box contained espionage information. The box had been recovered from the Bar Basque by an operative of Hemingway. The Legal Attaché made private arrangements for opening the box and returned the contents to Hemingway through Mr. Joyce. The box contained only a cheap edition of the "Life of St. Teresa." Hemingway was present and appeared irritated that nothing more was produced and later told an Assistant Legal Attaché that he was sure that we had withdrawn the vital material and had shown him something worthless. When this statement was challenged by the Assistant Legal Attaché, Hemingway jocularly said he was only joking but that he thought something was funny about the whole business of the box.

Hoover became further enraged by Hemingway's activities after he learned, from his contacts at the embassy on Cuba, that the author had been saying some highly unflattering things about Hoover's beloved organization:

In personal relations Hemingway has maintained a surface show of friendship and interest with representatives of the FBI. Through statements he has made to reliable contacts of the Legal Attaché, however, it is known that Hemingway and his assistant, Gustavo Duran, have a low esteem for the work of the FBI which they consider to be methodical, unimaginative and performed by persons of comparative youth without experience in foreign countries and knowledge of international intrigue and politics. Both Hemingway and Duran, it is also known, have personal hostility to the FBI on an ideological basis, especially Hemingway, as he considers the FBI anti-Liberal, pro-Fascist and dangerous as developing into an American Gestapo. Although Hemingway's opinions coincide with those of some Communists in this regard, he has repeatedly asserted that he is anti-Communist and that he was as much opposed to the Communist influence in the Spanish war as he was to the Fascist.

Nonetheless, some officials *were* impressed by Hemingway's spying activities. Ladd informed Hoover of one such example: "At the present time [Hemingway] is alleged to be performing a highly secret naval operation for the Navy Department. In this connection, the Navy Department is said to be paying the expenses for the operation of Hemingway's boat, furnishing him with arms and charting courses in the Cuban area." Another document, dated

June 23, 1943, elaborates on Hemingway's secret work with the navy and states: "He is on a special confidential assignment for the Naval Attaché chasing submarines along the Cuban coast and keeping a careful observance on the movements of Spanish steamers which occasionally come to Cuba."

But the FBI remained completely unimpressed, as a note from Assistant Director Tamm attached to the same document made very clear: "The Bureau has by careful and impartial investigation from time to time disproved practically all of the so-called Hemingway information. I don't care what his contacts are or what his background is—I see no reason why we should make any effort to avoid exposing him for the phony that he is."

To the great relief of the FBI, on April 21, 1943, the Cuban attaché advised Hoover that: "Hemingway's organization was disbanded and its work terminated as of April 1, 1943." Hoover exhibited even more relief that Hemingway's services with American intelligence had been terminated when, only six days later, there was a further development in the story:

Hemingway has been connected with various so-called Communist front organizations and was active in aiding the Loyalist cause in Spain. Despite Hemingway's activities, no information has been received which would definitely tie him with the Communist Party or which would indicate that he is or has been a Party member. His actions, however, have indicated that his views are "liberal" and that he may be inclined favorably to Communist political philosophies. These data were almost without fail valueless.

Hoover might have been done with Hemingway, but Hemingway was not done with the FBI, much to Hoover's regret. Somewhat outrageously and amusingly, on August 13, 1943, Hemingway informed R. G. Leddy that he was planning to write a book "on his experiences in intelligence work."

Hemingway states that all of the people whom he has known during the last year in Cuba in connection with intelligence work will appear in his book, including Ambassador Braden. We are not yet informed as to what role the representatives of the FBI will play, but in view of Hemingway's known sentiments, will probably be portrayed as the dull, heavy-footed, unimaginative professional policeman type.

A note from Hoover, which was attached to the document, stated: "We ought to try and keep close to this development." Weeks later, however, Hoover's concern was somewhat lessened, after he was advised by his colleagues on Cuba that Hemingway "does not intend to use these plots until the War is over." And that, "If he wrote anything as a result of his present experiences, he would limit it to a fictional story based on anti-submarine work."

In the immediate and postwar years, the bulk of the entries contained within the FBI's file on Ernest Hemingway continued to focus upon his alleged Communist affiliations. However, without doubt the most bizarre entry in the document collection concerned a challenge of a "duel" that was made to Hemingway by one Edward "Ted" Scott, a British subject and a New Zealand native, who was a columnist for the Cuba-based English-language newspaper, the *Havana Post*.

FBI files of August 26, 1954, reveal the way in which the events developed:

Scott has always outwardly been very friendly with Hemingway and frequently has made laudatory references to him in his daily column called "Interesting If True." Several weeks ago Scott in his column reported a conversation that he had had with Hemingway's wife, Mary, in which the latter stated that lion steaks were very delectable. Scott said he took issue with Mrs. Hemingway on this question and she retorted that he was a "stupid British colonial." Scott went on to say in his column that from a woman he could take this but he would never stand still for it if it had come from her husband.

When an outraged Hemingway, in turn, took issue with Scott, the FBI noted that "Scott challenged Hemingway to a duel." The FBI continued to pay close attention to the rather farcical affair:

On 8–30–54 Scott exhibited a letter dated 8–28–54 and written by Dr. Pedro Sanchez Pessino, Scott's representative in the matter of the duel. In his letter, Dr. Pedro Sanchez Pessino quoted verbatim a letter, date not shown, written to him by Hemingway.

In the letter Hemingway advised Dr. Sanchez Pessino that he had no intention of fighting a duel with Mr. Scott, giving as his reasons the fact that he is in ill health and "has a lot of writing to do." Hemingway further stated that he felt sure that a court of honor would not consider this cowardice on his part.

Scott advised that although he was not satisfied with Hemingway's answer he did not know what else he could do about the matter.

Fortunately for all parties involved, Scott decided to pursue the matter no further, and it was largely forgotten about. And, for the most part, the FBI took little further interest in Ernest Hemingway, whose health was failing and which ultimately led to a relatively early death for the author in 1961. While history has shown that Hemingway was certainly one of the most gifted writers of the twentieth century, to the FBI at least, he was certainly no James Bond.

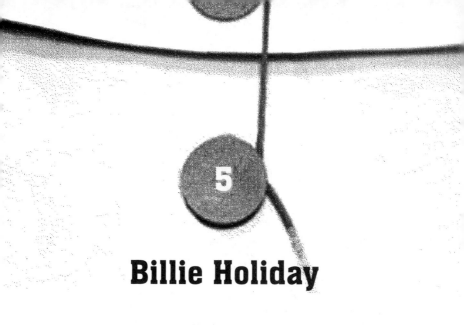

Billie Holiday

"She attempted to destroy makeshift opium pipe."

Rightly recognized by one and all as the "First Lady of Jazz," Billie Holiday's contribution to the world of music is unlikely to ever be eclipsed. However, it is her brushes with government officials that are of chief relevance to us. At the age of nine, the young Holiday had been sent to a reform school, was incarcerated on New York's notorious Welfare Island at fifteen, and in 1947, when her career was at its peak, she was arrested on a drugs charge and sentenced to a year and a day at a federal reformatory for women in West Virginia.

According to writer and Holiday researcher Julia Blackburn, "Two narcotic agents involved in the case, [said] Holiday was 'chosen' simply because she was a 'very attractive customer' whose arrest (but not her singing) got her into all the white tabloid newspapers and provided an organization like the Federal Bureau of Narcotics with exactly the kind of law enforcement publicity they were looking for. Apparently the drugs were not really the problem, but there was anger about her insistence on singing the

574

FEDERAL BUREAU OF INVESTIGATION
U. S. DEPARTMENT OF JUSTICE
COMMUNICATIONS SECTION

JAN 27 1949

TELEMETER

Mr. Tolson
Mr. Clegg
Mr. Glavin
Mr. Ladd
Mr. Nichols
Mr. Rosen
Mr. Tracy
Mr. Egan
Mr. Gurnea
Mr. Harbo
Mr. Mohr
Mr. Tamm
Mr. Nease
Miss Gandy

WASHINGTON FROM SFRAN S2   1-27-49   12-33 PM

DIRECTOR   ROUTINE   -REPEAT-

ATTENTION - INSPECTOR JOHN MOHR

BILLIE HOLIDAY, NARCOTICS MATTER. REMYTEL JAN. TWENTY FIVE LAST.

A SQUIB APPEARING IN COLUMN OF HERB CAEN, LOCAL GOSSIP COLUMNIST

OF SAN FRANCISCO CHRONICLE, ISSUE OF JAN. TWENTY SEVEN READS

"CHANTOOSE BILLIE HOLIDAY, OUT ON BAIL AFTER BEING NABBED ON A

NARCOTICS CHARGE SAT., HAD A PACKED HOUSE AS USUAL AT CAFE

SOCIETY UPTOWN TUES. NIGHT -- BUT THE CUSTOMER WHO MUST-VE IN-

TRIGUED HER MOST WAS A GENT WHO SAT AT RINGSIDE THROUGH TWO

SHOWS AND EVEN MADE A COUPLE OF REQUESTS.   COL. GEORGE

H.   WHITE, BOSS OF THE FEDERAL NARCOTICS BUREAU HERE.."

KIMBALL

ALL INFORMATION CONTAINED
HEREIN IS UNCLASSIFIED
DATE 1/29/81 BY SPSCCI/eBG   SE 28

RECORDED - 80   12 - 1728 - 2

62 FEB 11 1949

anti-lynching song 'Strange Fruit,' even when she was warned against it. . . ."

Similarly, when asked if Holiday's insistence on performing "Strange Fruit," a song that she made a point of singing for European audiences in an effort to enlighten them on racial issues in the United States, made her vulnerable to investigation by the official world, Holiday biographer Farah Griffin stated: "She did it at a time . . . when many black artists and intellectuals were making agreements not to be critical of the United States abroad. Billie Holiday was already so followed and tracked down and harassed by federal agents and local police that it would have been hard for them to do anymore than they had already done. Although earlier in her career, what brings her to the attention of the FBI was not her narcotics use at all. It is her singing a song called 'The Yanks Aren't Coming,' which would have been a follow up to 'Strange Fruit.' That is when they first take notice of her."

And take notice of Billie Holiday the FBI certainly did, particularly on January 25, 1949. Under cover of a memo marked "Extremely Urgent: Billie Holiday, Narcotics Matter," J. Edgar Hoover was informed of the circumstances surrounding the arrest of the singer three days earlier, on January 22:

Source states that Holiday and Levy are known users of narcotics and have been under close observation by Federal Bureau of Narcotics during their tour of Utah and California. Raid led by District Supervisor, Federal Bureau of Narcotics. Raid took place at the Motel Mark Twain, 345 Taylor, Room 602, San Francisco. Holiday was intercepted as she attempted to destroy makeshift opium pipe and bundle of opium in toilet bowl of her room. A portion of the pipe, which consisted of a rubber hose and a glass jar was recovered on the floor of the bathroom and the bundle of opium from the bowl. This raid was made on Holiday and Levy when it was known by the Narcotics Bureau at San Francisco that they were living together at instant [*sic*] hotel.

Narcotics Bureau possessed no definite information of any narcotics in their possession but presumed that since they were together they probably possessed some narcotics, and accordingly they requested the assistance of the San Francisco Police Department in conducting this raid because of more liberal state laws covering searches and seizures. Because of the importance of Holiday it has been the policy of this Bureau to discredit individuals of this caliber using narcotics. Because of their notoriety it offered excuses to minor users. Raid was a legitimate raid based on above and that claimed quote frame-up unquote was as much for publicity purposes as it was to avert the suspicion of guilt from her inasmuch as she was caught in possession of the makeshift pipe. Head of Special Services Detail [was] contacted and advised substantially the same information as set forth above. Holiday is charged with possession of opium and is being tried in Municipal Court. Her hearing is set for February 2 next.

As the affair progressed, the FBI was careful to monitor what the media was saying about the arrest of Billie Holiday. On January 27, 1949, the FBI office at San Francisco recorded the latest developments in a document titled "Billie Holiday, Narcotics Matter":

A squib appearing in column of Herb Caen, local gossip columnist of San Francisco Chronicle, issue of Jan. 27 reads: "Chantoose Billie Holiday, out on bail after being nabbed on a narcotics charge sat., had a packed house as usual at Café Society uptown tues. night. But the customer who must've intrigued her most was a gent who sat at ringside through two shows and even made a couple of requests.

According to columnist Caen, the "gent" in question was none other than "Colonel George H. White, boss of the Federal Narcotics Bureau." Interestingly, FBI files reveal that only days later, on February 9, 1949, a popular actress of the time, Tallulah Bankhead, wrote a passionate letter to J. Edgar Hoover, imploring officials to go easy on Holiday. "Dear Mr. Hoover," she began,

> I am ashamed of my unpardonable delay in writing to thank you a thousand times for the kindness, consideration, and courtesy, in fact all the nicest adjectives in the book, for the trouble you took re our telephone conversation in connection with Billie Holiday. I tremble when I think of my audacity in approaching you at all with so little to recommend me except the esteem, admiration and high regard my father held for you. I would never have dared to ask him or you a favor for myself but knowing your true humanitarian spirit it seemed quite natural at the time to go to the top man. As my Negro mammy used to say—"When you pray you pray to God don't you?" I have met Billie Holiday but twice in my life but admire her immensely as an artist and feel the most profound compassion for her as I do the unfortunate circumstances of her background. Although my intention is not to condone her weaknesses I certainly understand the eccentricities of her behavior because she is essentially a child at heart whose troubles have made her psychologically unable to cope with the world in which she finds herself. Her vital need is more medical than the confinement of four walls. However guilty she may be, whatever penalty she may be required to pay for her frailties, poor thing, you know I did everything within the law to lighten her burden.
>
> Bless you for this.

Hoover replied just forty-eight hours later. Although courteous, he was very careful to avoid giving any impression whatsoever to Bankhead that authorities would be giving Holiday an easy ride. In fact, Hoover avoided any mention of Holiday at all: "Dear Tallulah, I have received your kind letter of February 9 and was very glad indeed to hear from you. Your kind comments are greatly appreciated, and I trust that you will not hesitate to call on me at any time you think I might be of assistance to you."

We may never really know if the actions of Tallulah Bankhead had any real bearing on the outcome of the case against Billie Holiday, but on June 5, 1949, the FBI reported, she was found innocent on all charges: "Billie Holiday, blues singer, has been declared innocent of charges of possessing opium. A jury of six men and six women returned a not guilty verdict yesterday, after hearing Miss Holiday testify that her manager, John Levy, thrust a package of narcotics into her hand just before her hotel room was raided by federal agents. The defense contended Levy turned informer on Miss Holiday to avoid marriage."

Three weeks later, FBI files reveal that an unnamed agency was apparently *still* aggrieved that she had successfully avoided prosecution and requested that Hoover supply it with "any information you may have concerning Miss Holiday." Hoover accorded with its wishes: "Enclosed herewith are two copies of the Identification Record of Billie Holiday as it appears in the files of the Identification Division under FBI#-4855389."

Holiday continued to have brushes with government personnel, the last time being in 1959 when she was arrested while in the hospital. But Holiday realized the inevitability of this. As she noted to trumpeter Buck Clayton, FBI agents—"young ones with crew-cuts"—would come up to her and say: "We know everything you're doing and when the time comes, we're going to get you!"

Sadly, like many gifted artists, Billie Holiday died from the ravaging effects of an overindulgence in alcohol and drugs on July 17, 1959. Her influence on the world music scene, however, lives on.

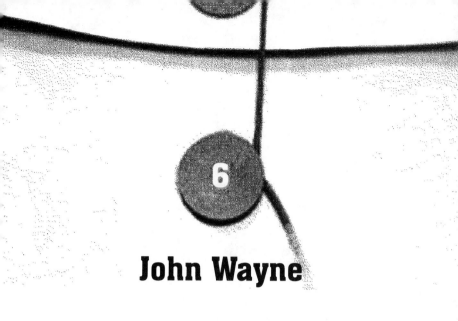

John Wayne

"If it is for the FBI, I will do anything for them."

While the FBI certainly had a very antagonistic relationship with Billie Holiday, Ernest Hemingway, and Errol Flynn, the exact opposite was the case when it came to actor John Wayne. In fact, the bureau's many dealings with the actor could almost be seen as a lovefest. Born Marion Michael Morrison on May 26, 1907, John Wayne went on to become one of the true cornerstones of the American movie industry of the mid-twentieth century. Whether he was storming the beaches in military garb, or riding into town on the back of his horse and blasting outlaws with his six-shooter, the six-foot-four college-football-playing Wayne always projected an image that embodied the all-American hero. His films, including *Stagecoach*, *True Grit*, *Sands of Iwo Jima*, *Flying Tigers*, and *The Man Who Shot Liberty Valance*, among many others, earned "the Duke" a place and image in Hollywood history that is unlikely to be eclipsed for many years, if at all. And like so many other stars and starlets of Hollywood, John Wayne also earned himself a place within the archives of the FBI.

Transmit the following in _____ AIRTEL _____

(Type in plain text or code)

Via _____ AIR MAIL _____

(Priority or Method of Mailing)

TO: DIRECTOR, FBI

FROM: SAC, LOS ANGELES (94-558)

RE: CRIMDEL - CRS

E.H. ~~Greenberg~~

Actor JOHN WAYNE Linked
with Alleged Revolt in Panama

Los Angeles newspapers today headline the state-
ments attributed to Panamanian Presidential Press Secretary
SALUSTIANO CHACON, linking the motion picture actor, JOHN
WAYNE, with a suspected revolt under direction of ROBERTO
(TITO) ARIAS, son of a former President of Panama and now
a lawyer in that country.

The "Hollywood Citizen News" quotes CHACON as
saying letters and documents found in a suitcase abandoned
by ARIAS, allegedly in a flight from Panama while being
sought, included an envelope bearing the name and return
address of JOHN WAYNE. Inside the envelope was said to be
an interoffice memorandum to WAYNE from a ROBERT D. WEESNER,
dated 4/9/59, outlining a "schedule of funds totalling
$682,850 given to or drawn by Tito Arias in connection with
his Panamanian operations in which you are involved."

CHACON continued there was "nothing here to implicate WAYNE. But the fact that the memorandum mentions
$525,000 turned over to Arias personally, apparently without
supporting documents to satisfy Mr. Weesner, seems a little
strange."

REC- 58   63-4296

3 - Bureau
2 - Los Angeles

LJL:pk
(5)   66 MAY 5 1959   FX-113   APR 25 1959

cc-SIX
cc-Week

Approved: _____   Sent _____ M
Special Agent in Charge

The earliest FBI involvement in the life and career of John Wayne is still unconfirmed; it's something the bureau refuses to discuss publicly and has yet to relinquish its files on the subject, namely a Soviet-planned assassination of the vehemently anticommunist actor. As incredible as this may sound, the allegation appears to have a basis in fact. According to Michael Munn, a noted film historian, he had got the story in 1983 from renowned moviemaker, Orson Welles. Munn stated that Welles informed him that Soviet premier Joseph Stalin had personally ordered the assassination of Wayne, after Russian filmmaker Sergei Gerasimov had attended a peace conference in New York in 1949 and learned of Wayne's absolute hatred of communism. Munn further revealed that Wayne had personally told him that his friend, the stuntman Yakima Canutt, had "saved his life once."

After questioning Canutt about this intriguing statement, Munn added: "Yakima told me that the FBI had discovered there were agents sent to Hollywood to kill John Wayne. He said the FBI had come to tell John about the plot. John told the FBI to let the men show up and he would deal with them." Furthermore, according to the story, Wayne apparently then hatched his own plot with his scriptwriter at the time, Jimmy Grant, to abduct the assassins, drive to a beach, and stage a "mock execution to frighten them." Munn stated that he did not know exactly what transpired but did hear that the two assassins stayed in the United States "to work for the FBI."

Is this strange and incredible story true? Michael Munn believes it is. He insists that Orson Welles had offered the story without prompting and that his sources were excellent: "Mr. Welles was a great storyteller, but he had no particular admiration for John Wayne. I am quite convinced that it was not propagated by John or his inner circle."

The earliest *confirmed* FBI interest in John Wayne's activities occurred on September 22, 1959. The FBI noted on that date that Los Angeles newspapers had broken a story that Wayne was involved "with a suspected revolt under direction of Roberto "Tito" Arias, son of a former president of Panama and now a lawyer in that country." The memo continues, "The *Hollywood Citizen News* quotes Chacon as saying letters and documents found in a suitcase abandoned by Arias, allegedly in a flight from Panama while being sought, including an envelope bearing the name and address of John Wayne. Inside the envelope was said to be an interoffice memorandum to Wayne from a Robert D. Weesner, dated 4/9/59, outlining a 'schedule of funds totaling $682,850 to or drawn by Tito Arias in connection with his Panamanian operations in which you are involved.' "

The FBI noted that the media had recorded Chacon stressing that there was "nothing here to implicate Wayne." As was also recorded in FBI files, however: "The fact that the memorandum mentions $525,000 turned over to Arias personally, apparently without supporting documents to satisfy Mr. Weesner, seems a little strange." Wayne, the FBI learned, was quick to play down his involvement in this strange saga and maintained that it was all just a big mistake:

Wayne is quoted as saying, in an interview in Hollywood, that he was shocked to hear reports Arias and his wife, Dame Margot Fonteyn, premier British ballerina, had been named as connected with a plot to overthrow the government, and he describes such accusations as "ridiculous." According to the news articles, Wayne said, "I have been in business with the Arias family for a long time. A group of us are in several business ventures, including a shrimp import company. Roberto never talked politics, and I never heard him say anything about overthrowing the Panamanian Government." The news articles state the alleged evidence was discovered at Santa Clara, a Pacific beach resort 73 miles from Panama City and a residential resort area where many retired Americans have homes.

Despite Wayne's assertions to the effect that any suggestions that he, Arias, or Fonteyn were linked with a planned overthrow of the Panamanian government were patently "ridiculous," additional files demonstrate that Fonteyn was detained in a Panamanian jail on April 20, as a direct result of suspicions that she was indeed a part of a plan to oust President Ernesto de la Guarda from power. Moreover, it was only because of the quick intervention of British Ambassador Sir Ian Henderson that Fonteyn was freed and flown out of the country. The FBI was informed that: "The British public did not appreciate having seen her in the role of the swan, then seeing her in the role of a decoy duck."

Further data reached the FBI to the effect that Arias had set off around the nineteenth on a fishing trip in the Gulf of Panama aboard a boat called the *Nola*, and had planned to jump onto a shrimp boat, then storm the national guard barracks at La Chorrera, Panama. According to interviews with local fishermen, Arias had reportedly asked them to raise a buoy from the ocean that had been previously loaded with machine guns and grenades that were to be used in the planned raid.

The attempt failed, however, and Arias took refuge in the Brazilian embassy in Panama City, ultimately deciding to fight the government by more legitimate means, which led to a seat in elections for Panama's National Assembly in 1964. Tragedy struck, however, when, after his election, Arias was crippled by gunshots fired by a former political associate. Nevertheless, after being treated at Britain's Stoke Mandeville Hospital, Arias resumed his political career in 1967. For someone who, according to John Wayne, "never talked politics," and never said "anything about overthrowing the Panamanian Government," Arias was certainly full of big surprises of both a political and a revolutionary nature.

It must be said that the curious references to various documents that had been "found in a suitcase abandoned by Arias," and that specifically referred to John Wayne and the "Panamanian operations" of Arias in which the actor was "involved," do not exactly inspire very much faith in the idea that this was really just related to the intricacies of the shrimp industry, as John Wayne so anxiously wanted everyone to believe.

Evidently, this episode did not cause problems for Wayne at an official level. In the following year, he was, somewhat unusually, asked by the FBI to take part in a photo shoot for inclusion in an article on the bureau that would appear in an issue of *National Geographic Magazine*. According to the relevant documentation, on June 2, 1960, various staged pictures were taken at the FBI's Los Angeles office, including "a group of agents before a blackboard containing a diagram of an area surrounding an extortionist's home," "a photograph of a clerical employee in the closed files section," and "the aftermath of a bank robbery." In addition, another picture displayed "an agent interviewing movie star John Wayne on the set of the movie 'Go North,' which is a story of early Alaska. This places an agent in modern day business attire in an unusual setting and adds to the scope of activities which agents are involved in daily throughout the country. A rugged looking agent approximating John Wayne's size was chosen for this particular photograph."

Hoover was informed that "Mr. Wayne was extremely enthusiastic about being of assistance in connection with being photographed with an agent. He has long been an outspoken foe of Communists in the film industry generally and when approached with the proposal for this photograph, he said in effect, 'If it is for the FBI, I will do anything for them.' Wayne also said that he would like to extend his regards to the Director and said, 'Tell Mr. Hoover I am on his side.' Wayne spent considerable more time in connection with the photograph which was desired than might be expected of him and was extremely courteous and friendly."

The FBI continued to look on with glowing approval when, on July 21, 1961, Wayne's name surfaced in a report titled "Defense Movie on Reds Ready":

The Defense Department has completed the filming of its official narrative on communism to replace several other training films formerly used by the armed forces, some of which have become involved in controversy. Work on the script for the new film "Challenge of Ideas" intended to explain the ideological background of communism, was started more than a year ago under the direction of the Pentagon's troop information and education experts, with civilian advisers. Meanwhile the services withdrew from use at least two films which had been produced by non-defense organizations and about which complaints have been made—"Operation Abolition" and "Communism on the March." Production of "Challenge of Ideas" cost about $20,000, a spokesman said. The Army has ordered 200 copies; the Navy and Marine Corps 184; and the Air Corps 275. Cooperating in the preparation of the film were Edward R. Murrow, now Chief of the United States Information Agency, Hanson Baldwin of the New York Times, Television-Radio commentator Lowell Thomas, and actors John Wayne and Helen Hayes. The Defense spokesman said the civilians donated their services.

The new film is one of several planned for production. A second, based on youth organizations, is still in the script-writing stage.

Five years later, on June 9, 1966, in a report titled "ABC TV Series, Suggested Narrator During 1966-67 Season," Hoover expressed deep interest in employing Wayne's skills in a narration capacity for ABC's Quinn Martin series, *The FBI*. Nevertheless, the bureau did have concerns about the actor's known links with the ultraright John Birch Society:

Mr. James Stewart was initially considered to handle the narration for our forthcoming television season; however, he regretfully declined. QM Productions has now requested our consideration of John Wayne, the well-known actor, to handle this commitment. Bufiles [Bureau files] reflect that in 1960 [*he*] was a member and past President of the anti-communist Motion Picture Alliance. It was reported by the Los Angeles Office in 1960 that Wayne was a member of the John Birch Society, along with a number of other well-known actors and personalities in the movie industry.

While there is no indication of current activity on the part of John Wayne with regard to the John Birch Society it is felt that in order to prevent any possible criticism of the Bureau using someone with known John Birch Society connections we should have Inspector Kemper determine Wayne's present association. This can be easily done through [Deleted], all of whom are very close to the Bureau.

The report recommended that an investigation be initiated to determine "whether John Wayne has any present or widely-known association with the John Birch Society." Established officially in 1958 to combat what was viewed as nothing short of widespread Communist infiltration of the United States, the John Birch Society was founded by Robert H. W. Welch, who named the society after a Baptist missionary who had been killed by Chinese Communists in 1945. Although the group began with only eleven members, it quickly drew a huge amount of support from rich conservatives, and by the early 1960s, the society had an annual income of no less than $5 million and a membership that had blossomed to an impressive figure estimated to be somewhere between sixty thousand and one hundred thousand. Those whom the John Birch Society targeted as "dedicated conscious agents of the Communist conspiracy" included none other than President Dwight D. Eisenhower, CIA Director Allen Dulles, and Chief Justice Earl Warren.

We may never know to what extent John Wayne's associations with the John Birch Society were seen as problematic to the FBI, but the actor ultimately did not provide the narrative for Quinn Martin's *The FBI*. Still, the relationship between the FBI and John Wayne remained cordial, even downright friendly and intensely personal at times. As evidence of this, on March 19, 1970, Hoover wrote to offer his sincere condolences to Wayne after he learned of the recent death of the actor's mother:

> I was indeed sorry to learn of the passing of your Mother and want to extend my heartfelt sympathy to you. While words are most inadequate at a time like this, I hope you will derive some measure of comfort from the knowledge that your friends share your grief.
>
> Sincerely Yours,
> J. Edgar Hoover.

In an internal memorandum generated as a result of his letter of sympathy, Hoover noted that, "Mr. Wayne is on the Special Correspondents List." In response to Hoover's letter, Wayne replied: "My deep thanks for your note of sympathy to me and my family in our time of grief."

In the following month, Hoover was full of praise for Wayne after the screen star won an Oscar for his role in *True Grit*: "Heartiest congratulations on your winning an 'Oscar' as best actor of 1969. This is indeed a well-deserved and splendid tribute to you and your ability, and you have my very best wishes for continued success."

Again, Wayne was quick to reply: "Naturally I was pleased to receive the 1969 Oscar, but what delighted me more was the goodwill that has been shown me by friends and acquaintances throughout the country. I thank you for your thoughtful note."

Eight years later, and six years after Hoover had finally shuffled off this mortal coil, John Wayne's name was still turning up in FBI files, but this time in relation to threats of extortion, blackmail, and perhaps even murder. It was December 13, 1978, and the FBI learned from a source identified in the declassified files only as "Hassett" that the life of Wayne and several other well-known personalities in the entertainment business were potentially in very grave danger.

On December 13, 1978, Bob Corwin, Director, Broadcast Facilities, NBC, Burbank, California, advised [that] Hassett [had] telephoned Hope Enterprises, California, December 11, 1978, left name, telephone numbers and address in Long Island, New York. Hope's secretary returned call. Hassett stated [he had] made contacts in Harlem, New York, over last two years and developed plan whereby famous personalities such as Bob Hope, Johnny Carson, John Wayne, etc., could help change corrupt government, poverty, crime and drug abuse by speaking out publicly. Hassett composed letter, copies of which he mailed to Hope, Wayne and Carson. On December 10, 1978, he spoke before Harlem based people in Greenwich Village and handed out copies of letter mailed to Hope, Carson and Wayne.

This was all very laudable, but things did not quite go the way Hassett had planned: "Hassett said superstars would not help cause because they may be involved in shady business deals, drugs, etc., and fear retaliation by blackmail if they were to speak out." This, the FBI learned, resulted in a colleague of Hassett's identified in the bureau's files as "Unsub" threatening to do bodily harm, and worse, to Wayne and Co., if they failed to lend their support to Hassett's plans:

Unsub said he had "Army" at disposal if [Hassett] would name names of superstars contacted concerning cause but who were not cooperative. Said superstars would be taken care of. Unsub said, "If you name the names that's all it takes. If you don't have any remorse." Unsub also said, "You've been doing this for a year and a half. You're getting your head banged against a wall and you're not accomplishing anything. Tell me two names of people that you will contact within a week and be able to get back with information from or that they will give information for." When Hassett gave him names of Bob Hope, John Wayne and Johnny Carson, Unsub said, "Okay, get in touch and get back to us or they will get back to us; and if it doesn't happen you are not to worry about any innocent people getting hurt because we are professionals." Hassett said he took that statement to mean that if he was not able to get back to Unsub with a valid reason why Hope, Wayne and Carson did not speak out, that they would be harmed.

Forty-eight hours later, Hassett was personally interviewed by agents of the FBI, who, on December 15, 1978, prepared a document titled "Bob Hope—Victim; Johnny Carson—Victim; John Wayne—Victim; Extortion." It read as follows:

Hassett advised two years ago he met an individual who told him that he has control over a well-trained army who would kill whoever Hassett designated. [The individual] requested the names of prominent individuals from Hassett who did not cooperate with him. Hassett advised that he furnished no names. Subsequently, on Sunday, 12/10/78, he furnished the names of Bob Hope, John Wayne and/or Johnny Carson to an individual whom he assumes is associated with Unsub, as individuals who have not cooperated. Hassett advised that he was frightened of this individual when he furnished the names and he, subsequently, has attempted to contact Bob Hope, Johnny Carson and John Wayne to alert them that this individual may do them bodily harm. In view of the above, [Deleted] should be considered armed, dangerous and suicidal and should be approached with extreme caution.

Ultimately, the affair was brought to a swift and satisfactory conclusion—albeit in a fashion that is not entirely clear to us, since the FBI's files on its resolution remain substantially blacked out to this day. However, the trio of Wayne, Hope, and Carson *were* safe and the threat *was* nullified.

As someone who embodied the image of the all-American hero, and who was a strong and passionate supporter of the military war machine, it is somewhat sad, indeed ironic even, that John Wayne's death from cancer only months later on June 11, 1979, was almost certainly the direct result of the secret activities of that same war machine. In 1955, Wayne, portraying none other than Genghis Khan, was on location in Utah filming *The Conqueror* with Susan Hayward and Agnes Moorehead. Although Utah was seen as a suitable stand-in for Mongolia, no one at the time could have anticipated the fatal outcome of director Dick Powell's decision to film in the blistering heat of Utah's Snow Canyon.

Unknown to the cast and crew, the town of St. George and Snow Canyon, where they spent much of their time, was barely 100 miles downwind from the Nevada test site where, in 1953, a number of atomic bombs had been tested by the Atomic Energy Commission. No one within the government or the military thought to warn in advance those working on the movie of the disturbing and life-threatening fact that they would be spending three months filming in a location that was still saturated by killer radiation. The result?

By 1980, *People* magazine learned, no fewer than ninety-one members of the cast and crew of *The Conqueror* had contracted cancer, including John Wayne, Susan Hayward, Agnes Moorhead, and director Dick Powell. And furthermore, in the years that followed, a truly staggering number of residents of St. George also contracted cancer. Had John Wayne known in advance before he agreed to star in *The Conqueror* that deadly radiation hung ominously in the air over the deserts of Utah back in 1955, he might just still be with us today. He could take on KGB assassins, but not even the Duke could beat the power of the atom.

Office Memorandum · UNITED STATES GOVERNMENT

TO : DIRECTOR, FBI   DATE: June 28, 1955

FROM : SAC, LOS ANGELES

SUBJECT: AUDIE MURPHY,
(OO:Los Angeles)

ALL INFORMATION CONTAINED
HEREIN IS UNCLASSIFIED
DATE _____ BY _____

    Rebulet June 21, 1955 in regard to above captioned individual.

    From New York letters to Bureau dated June 6 and 9, 1955, it is noted that during recent interviews with ▓▓▓▓▓▓▓▓▓▓

    For the completion of the Bureau's files, Los Angeles indices reflect that AUDIE MURPHY, film actor, who has been described as the most decorated serviceman in World War II, was listed in the "Daily People's World" of October 28, 1947 as one of approximately 50 Hollywood film personalities who appeared on a radio program on October 27, 1947 which was sponsored by the "Committee for the First Amendment" to protest the hearings being held in Washington, D. C. to probe the extent of alleged Communist infiltration into the film industry.

    The California Committee on Un-American Activities, in its 1948 report on Communist Party front organizations, cited the "Committee for the First Amendment" as a Communist front. It may be noted, however, that a great many non-Communist people in Hollywood associated themselves with the First Amendment Committee who subsequently disavowed any sympathy with or intention to further the interests of the Communist Party.

    SA ▓▓▓▓▓▓▓▓ was present at a public meeting and forum sponsored on March 31, 1948 by "Motion Picture Alliance for the Preservation of American Ideals" (MPA) which was held at American Legion Hall in Hollywood. MPA was and continues to be a very anti-Communist organization formed in 1944 by a number of Hollywood film producers, writers, actors, and labor leaders. At the MPA meeting, Hollywood columnist HEDDA HOPPER was one of a number of speakers and introduced AUDIE MURPHY, World War II hero. MURPHY thereafter made a few remarks about the efforts of the Communists to infiltrate veterans' organizations.

RECORDED - 94

(4)
Registered
cc:New York (Info)

EX-122

17 JUL 5 1955

60 JUL 11 1955

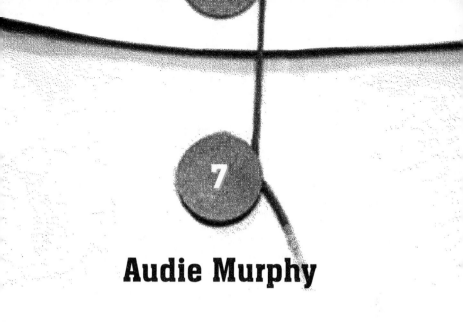

Audie Murphy

"Murphy was 'a social loner.'"

Audie Leon Murphy, the son of poor Texas sharecroppers, was born on June 20, 1924, and rose to international fame as the most decorated American soldier of the Second World War, after having participated in seven major battle campaigns: Tunisia, Sicily, Naples-Foggia, Rome-Arno, Southern France, the Rhineland, and Central Europe. According to his FBI file, Murphy was "credited with killing, wounding or capturing 240 Germans." In addition, he was awarded the highest military decoration of the United States, namely the Congressional Medal of Honor, and also received no fewer than twenty-three additional decorations, including the Distinguished Service Cross, the Silver Star with an oak leaf cluster, the Legion of Merit, the Bronze Star, the EAMA Campaign Ribbon with seven Battle Stars, a Presidential Citation Ribbon, the Expert Infantryman's Badge, the French Legion of Honor Chevalier, the French Croix de Guerre with Palm, and a Purple Heart with two oak leaf clusters.

Murphy left the army on September 21, 1945, and, only days

later, his photograph appeared on the cover of *Life Magazine* and he received an invitation to Hollywood from actor James Cagney. Audie Murphy's new career was about to begin. For a while at least, Murphy personified the image of the ultimate struggling actor (he was even forced to sleep in a local gymnasium when his finances were slim), but he finally succeeded in realizing his dream with his first starring role in the 1949 movie, *Bad Boy.*

Twelve months later, Murphy signed a contract with Universal that led to starring roles in no fewer than twenty-six movies for the company, and a best-selling autobiography titled *To Hell and Back.* As evidence of the box-office appeal of the former war hero during the 1950s, the 1955 cinematic version of *To Hell and Back* held the record as the highest grossing Universal Pictures movie of all time until the release of *Jaws*, a full twenty years later.

Despite living in the heart of Hollywood, Murphy never forgot his humble roots in the Lone Star State and was renowned as someone who always looked after his family, his friends, and just about anyone and everyone he thought deserved help. But behind the glamour and glitz lifestyle of Hollywood, the fame, the money, and the movies, lay a distinctly tortured soul who had been devastated by his wartime experiences. Murphy recognized this and, to his credit, was not above discussing in public his complex and ever present struggles with what was known at the time as "battle fatigue." Today, that condition is widely known to the medical community as post-traumatic stress disorder (PTSD), and nowhere else is Murphy's struggle with PTSD more graphically highlighted than within the pages of his FBI file.

As David Kinchin reveals in his book *Post Traumatic Stress Disorder: The Invisible Injury*, sleep disturbances, nightmares, harrowing flashbacks, sudden intense anger, and hypervigilance are all classic symptoms of PTSD. And, as the FBI learned, they were all facets of the infinitely complex character that was Audie Murphy.

But why would the ultimate warrior, patriot, and American hero, who went on to become a major Hollywood actor of the late

1940s and 1950s, and whose wartime experiences easily surpassed John Wayne's on-screen portrayals, be the subject of an FBI file at all? To some extent, that question remains unanswered to this day. However, the declassified portions of his FBI file do hint at the story.

The FBI's interest in Murphy essentially began on July 26, 1968, when a bureau memorandum recorded that the White House had "requested investigation of Murphy, position for which being considered not stated." We can speculate, however, that perhaps the undefined position was related to Murphy's wartime heroics, and that he was possibly being groomed as a spokesman for the army's recruitment office. Given the vehement opposition to the Vietnam War that existed at the time in the United States, it would make perfect sense from the government's perspective to have someone like Murphy on board to try and redress the balance.

As a result of this White House request for data on Murphy, the FBI's response was twofold: it began to carefully search its older files for data on the actor, and it initiated inquiries with just about anyone and everyone who was acquainted with Murphy, in an effort to determine if he was a suitable candidate for the unnamed White House job. From the beginning, the investigation was steeped in controversy, as a document from 1947, uncovered as part of the 1968 study of Murphy, makes clear.

On October 28, 1947, the FBI sat up and took keen notice when the *Hollywood Reporter* published an article titled "Hollywood Fights Back" that referred to a variety of movie stars who were "disgusted and outraged by the continuing attempt of the House Committee on Un-American Activities to smear the Motion Picture Industry." The article continued that a spokesperson for the actors in question had stated very vocally that "Any investigation into the political beliefs of the individual is contrary to the basic principles of our democracy." Moreover, the same spokesperson added: "Any attempt to curb freedom of expression and to set arbitrary standards of Americanism is in itself disloyal to both the spirit and the letter of our Constitution." The FBI noted that, "the name of Audie Murphy is included in the list as supporting the above 'Committee for the First Amendment.' "

Since the work of the House Committee on Un-American Activities was focused, in part, upon outing Communists in Hollywood, the FBI viewed anyone who was critical of the work of the House committee to be a potential subversive, or worse still, a Communist themselves. Of course, Murphy was merely supporting the right of the individual to believe whatever they wanted to believe. But, the revelation that the actor had allied himself with those who were critical of the House committee ensured that the FBI kept a very close watch on Murphy and his ensuing activities. Two decades later, the bureau recorded its reasons why Murphy's support of the Committee for the First Amendment was seen as such a disturbing factor—in Hoover's eyes, at least:

The Guide to Subversive Organizations and Publications, prepared by the House Committee on Un-American Activities, cites the Committee for the First Amendment as "A recently created Communist front in the defense of Communists and Communist fellow travelers. Its immediate purpose is to create favorable public opinion for the Communists who refused to testify before the House Committee. . . ."

Nevertheless, the FBI *did* eventually concede that Murphy's associations with the Committee for the First Amendment could have been relatively innocent in nature: "It may be noted that a great many non-Communist people in Hollywood associated themselves with the First Amendment Committee [and] subsequently disavowed any sympathy with or intention to further the interests of the Communist Party."

On July 29, 1968, the Dallas FBI informed Hoover that, two years previously, "a judgment was filed against Murphy for $7454.34 plus ten per cent interest in the 134th Judicial District

Court, Dallas." This would not be the only time the FBI would learn of Murphy's financial woes. But in their effort to determine his character and background, the bureau began secretly speaking with colleagues and associates of Murphy in Hollywood about the actor's many and varied character traits, some good and some not so good. The previously secret files paint a picture of an incredibly generous man, but one who was tortured by his wartime inner demons, which would manifest themselves in violence, out-of-control gambling, and a hair-trigger temper.

One source interviewed by the FBI had nothing but good words to say about Murphy. Indeed, that same source revealed a little-known and heartwarming story full of festive cheer that sounded almost too good to be true:

The interviewee considers Murphy to be one of the most humble and conscientious persons he has ever known. He has used much of the money he has made in Hollywood to aid his family and to aid others who were in need of assistance. . . . He stated one of the facts that impressed him most about Murphy was that while he had been a movie star in Hollywood, he had never "gone Hollywood" and does not socialize very much and is a family man and a "home boy." He gave as an example of the humility and responsibility of Murphy an incident which occurred on Christmas Eve around 1954. He stated he and Murphy were walking downtown in the city of McKinney, Texas, and it was snowing and quite cold. As they walked along the street, they passed a youth who appeared to be 12 or 13 years old. He was shabbily dressed, had long unkempt hair, and was obviously cold. He stated Murphy saw him as they walked by, and when they had progressed a few feet, Murphy stopped and told him to wait a moment. Murphy returned to the youth and asked him if he was cold. The youth replied he was. Murphy then took the boy into a nearby dry good store and purchased a complete set of clothing for him, including a warm coat. Then, he took the boy to a barbershop and gave him the money to get a hair cut. He stated he watched Murphy while doing this and at no time did Murphy tell the clerks who he was. He then left the boy and has never seen him again. Murphy cannot forget the fact that he was once poor and is always attempting to help those who are obviously in need of help.

A second source interviewed in the same time frame, however, claimed that Murphy was "presently broke." Perhaps his charity had gone too far. Or perhaps it was Murphy's rumored heavy gambling that was to blame. Files reflect that the FBI was quite interested in Murphy's many betting sprees, as well as in his overall character. Details of both were discussed on August 5, 1968, with a third acquaintance of Murphy:

On August 5 1968 interviewee described Murphy as a heavy gambler but noted that he always provided for his family first and gambled with whatever money remained. He observed that Murphy has a fatalistic philosophy toward life and believes living for today with the expectation that tomorrow will take care of itself. He did not mean to imply that the appointee was of reckless character, but only that he felt no concern for himself. It was this same attitude which possibly led to the appointee's exploits during the war and enabled him to achieve so many military honors.

The FBI then began digging deeper into the Hollywood world as it sought to provide a full report on Murphy for the White House. On August 6, 1968, the Los Angeles FBI office noted that, "Most former employees at movie studios comment favorably concerning Murphy's character, associates, reputation and loyalty. Universal Pictures advised that he is in poor financial condition and is considering the advantages and disadvantages of declaring bankruptcy." In fact, the comments made by Hollywood insiders were all carefully logged by FBI agents, who further recorded that, "several directors and producers at Universal Pictures advised Murphy had a reputation for being volatile in nature and a difficult person to work with."

An FBI document of August 21, 1968, gives a good indication of the early struggles that Murphy was having with post-traumatic stress disorder in the postwar era. From a source whose identity the FBI still protects to this day, Murphy was described as having "emotional problems," was "moody, introverted, and close-mouthed," and had "domestic trouble" with his first wife, Wanda Hendrix. And the actor's personal problems were also confirmed by another, independent source: "Murphy has had some marital difficulty with his current wife, Pamela, which he believes is based upon Pamela's rigid religious attitude and her desire to raise their sons in a strict religious atmosphere, while Murphy desires to give the boys a little more freedom."

More serious to the FBI, however, was the following report from another interviewee, which demonstrated what the FBI perceived to be further evidence of Murphy's more unfortunate character traits:

Murphy seemed normal at the start of his career in 1949; however, he seemed to develop serious trouble as the years passed. Murphy became increasingly difficult to work with and sometimes refused to work after all the movie picture's cast, crew, and technicians were assembled to commence filming. This refusal on the part of Murphy caused great financial problems to the studio. On the basis of the foregoing, he considers Murphy as emotionally unstable and of poor character and reputation. He concluded that he would not recommend Murphy for any position of trust and confidence. He does not believe Murphy should be held up as an example to the American youth based on his emotional instability and in view of his unfavorable moral reputation.

Murphy's apparent fascination with guns did not go unnoticed by the FBI either, and this was made very clear to Hoover on August 5, 1968:

On one occasion while Murphy was filming the movie entitled "Seven Ways From Sundown," Murphy had such a violent disagreement with George Sherman, who was one director of the picture that Mr. Sherman had to be replaced in order to proceed with the picture. . . . Murphy threatened this director with physical violence. . . . Murphy is "a nut about guns" and always carried guns on his person while making his pictures. . . . The fact that Murphy always carried these guns and was always practicing made many people apprehensive in dealing with Murphy.

As further evidence of what was without doubt a classic case of post-traumatic stress disorder, the FBI recorded that another source had revealed information to its agents that Hoover knew the White House would find extremely disconcerting:

Murphy would be "normal" for several days and then he would become "irascible and contrary. . . ." [Source] pointed out that Murphy carried loaded guns and that he frequently would put on a shooting demonstration, which demonstration was considered by some individuals to be of "questionable taste. . . ." It is his belief that Murphy was "a social loner" and that he did not mix too well with people. He stated that, because Murphy was undiplomatic and was outspoken and irascible, he cannot recommend him for a position involving trust and confidence as well as one that would undoubtedly require tact and discretion.

And, again, there was the firm conclusion from the interviewee that "undoubtedly much of Murphy's problem as pertains to his argumentativeness, unreliability, and unpredictability is attributable to his war history." But most graphically revealing of all with respect to Murphy's psychological state was an August 1968 document generated by the Veterans Administration records that can be found within the FBI's declassified records on Audie Murphy:

This record reveals that as of August 12, 1949, the appointee filed his supplemental claim for bronchial dissemination of calcified tuberculosis and gastric ulcers. . . . The file does reveal that the appointee had a physical examination conducted on June 17, 1947, by the Veterans Administration. During the course of this examination, it was noted that Murphy has episodes lasting for approximately one week during which time he has headaches and vomiting spells in the morning. The record states that during these episodes, the appointee's sleep is disturbed by a variety of nightmares and that he primarily dreams of combat. This record also states that the appointee complained of having to take sleeping pills to avoid these nightmares.

Although brief, this record perfectly captures the harrowing mental and physical effects of PTSD. And still more data continued to reach the FBI that did not paint the sort of picture that the FBI had hoped to provide to the White House. As the FBI continued to prowl around Hollywood in search of any and all data on Murphy, it learned from a colleague of his who had costarred with the war hero in the 1952 movie, *Posse From Hell*, that during filming one day Murphy had "overstayed lunch period considerably and returned to studio in apparent bad mood. He looked briefly at script for afternoon and then described it with an indecent four-letter word. He then threw script into air."

The FBI's informant told agents that he admonished Murphy

for using "such language in front of women," at which point Murphy "flew into a rage," grabbed the man by the arms, and pushed him headlong into a camera. The source advised the FBI that although he was not injured, he was most certainly "shocked" by the whole experience, and from thereon considered Murphy to be "mentally unbalanced." Notably, the same source expanded that Murphy "insisted on having all windows locked in any rooms in which he slept, and he had a gun under his mattress when sleeping," and that, "Murphy was addicted to driving at excessive speeds and kept a gun handy in his car."

After completing its investigation into Murphy, the FBI sent a lengthy report to the White House that summed up the situation:

While Murphy was generally recommended by those interviewed, a number of persons declined to recommend him, indicating he is blunt, outspoken, and undiplomatic at times. It was also stated Murphy is a compulsive gambler and his many debts are the result of his gambling activities. In October, 1947, his name appeared among a group of Hollywood motion picture people who protested the actions of the House Committee on Un-American Activities. No one interviewed questioned Murphy's loyalty.

Perhaps inevitably, the potential White House career for the actor did not come to fruition. But the FBI continued to watch Murphy's activities closely. As evidence of this, Hoover was apprised of the facts when the *New York Daily News* of September 10, 1968, reported that "Audie Murphy, Broke, Can't Pay." Then, on September 17, 1970, the FBI's Special Investigation Division revealed to Hoover that Murphy's gambling was causing him problems again: "Audie Murphy admits to placing $10,000 horse bets from Los Angeles. . . . And having lost $37,000 in a month."

Murphy's spiraling gambling activities, and sadly, his life, came to an end on May 28, 1971, when he was killed at the age of forty-six, after the private plane he was aboard slammed into the side of a mountain near Roanoke, Virginia, while trying to negotiate thick fog. Ten days later, Murphy was buried with full military honors in Arlington National Cemetery. His gravesite, near the Memorial Amphitheater, is the cemetery's second most visited gravesite. The honor of most-visited grave goes to that of President John F. Kennedy.

Federal Bureau of Investigation
United States Department of Justice
Newark 2, New Jersey

JLD:vml   February 10, 1944

Director, FBI

Re: FRANK ALBERT SINATRA
SELECTIVE SERVICE

Dear Sir:

Reference is made to the telephone message from
Mr. Christopher Callan at the Seat of Government on February 8,
1944 concerning the receipt by the Bureau of an anonymous letter
alleging, in effect, that $40,000 had been paid to the doctors who
examined FRANK ALBERT SINATRA and thereafter gave an opinion that
SINATRA had a perforated eardrum and was unsuitable for military
service.

In accordance with instructions, the investiga-
tion was limited to an examination of SINATRA's Selective Service
File in order to obtain from that file certain information as set
forth below. On February 9, 1944, the file was examined by
Special Agent _____ at Local Draft Board #19 for Hudson   b7C
County, Room 308, 26 Journal Square, Jersey City, New Jersey. The
Chief Clerk of this board is Mrs. MAE E. JONES.

(1) PRESENT CLASSIFICATION: 4F as of December 11, 1943.

(2) REASON FOR THAT CLASSIFICATION: D.S.S. Form #221, "Report
    of Physical Examination and Induction", carries under Section 4,
    "Physical Examination Results", the following certification:
    "78. I certify that the above-named registrant was carefully
    examined, that the results of the examination have been cor-
    rectly recorded in this form, that to the best of my knowledge
    and belief: . . . (a) FRANK ALBERT SINATRA is physically and/or
    mentally disqualified for military service by reason of:
    1. chronic perforation lt. tympanum; 2. chronic mastoiditis."

This was supported by the stamped name, "J. WEINTROB, Captain,
M.C., Assistant Chief Medical Officer". Immediately following
is:

"79. . . . (b) FRANK ALBERT SINATRA was on this date rejected
for service in the Army of the United States."

COPIES DESTROYED 2-12-60

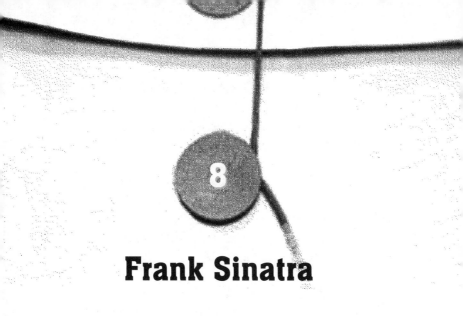

Frank Sinatra

"Sinatra has the 'Hoodlum Complex.'"

Francis Albert Sinatra was born on December 12, 1915, the son of a Sicilian father who was a fireman and an amateur boxer, and a mother who dabbled in politics and who, according to FBI rumors, was reputed to be a backstreet abortionist. With his laid-back, drink-in-hand style, tough-guy looks, Mob links, women falling at his feet, and his now legendary Vegas shows with Rat Pack buddies Dean Martin, Sammy Davis Jr., and Joey Bishop, Sinatra epitomized what it meant to be cool in the 1950s and 1960s and became a true twentieth-century icon of both the stage and screen. But to the FBI, Sinatra was anything but cool: he was trouble. Big trouble.

The bureau's file on Frank Sinatra spans no less than fifty years. As with the singing legend himself, the most interesting material contained within the document collection covers the period when Sinatra's celebrity career was at its peak: namely the mid-1940s to the late-1960s. As might be expected for someone who, at the time, moved effortlessly within Mafia circles and appeared regularly on the Vegas strip, the file contains some priceless pieces of gossip.

The beginnings of the fraught relationship between J. Edgar and the singer were largely seeded following an investigation of Sinatra that began when controversial rumors began to circulate to the effect that Ol' Blue Eyes had secretly paid off a doctor in a devious attempt to avoid wartime service in the United States military. FBI documents show that the controversy began on December 30, 1943, when the broadcaster and columnist Walter Winchell (who was himself the subject of a 3,908-page FBI dossier) received the following anonymous letter, a copy of which Winchell quickly provided to the bureau:

I don't dare give you my name because of my job but here is a bit of news you can check which I think is front page. The Federal Bureau of Investigation is said to be investigating a report that Frank Sinatra paid $40,000.00 to the doctors who examined him in Newark recently and presented him with a 4-F classification. The money is supposed to have been paid by Sinatra's business manager. One of the recipients is said to have talked too loud about the gift in a beer joint recently and a report was sent to the FBI. A former schoolmate of Sinatra's from Highland, N.J., said recently that Sinatra has no more eardrum trouble than Gen. McArthur. If there is any truth to these reports I think that it should be made known. Mothers around this section who have sons in the service are planning a petition to Pres. Roosevelt asking for a re-examination of the singer by a neutral board of examiners. You'll probably read about this in the papers within a few days unless you break the story first. I wish I could give you my name but I would lose my job within 24 hours if I did. You'd probably recognize it immediately if I did because I have sent you numerous items in the past which appeared in your column.

By February 1944, the FBI had launched an investigation of the allegation that Sinatra was a draft-dodger and recorded that a special agent of the bureau had examined Sinatra's Selective Service file, which was housed at the local draft board for Hudson County, New Jersey. The file noted very clearly and concisely the conclusions of the examining doctor, Captain J. Weintrob, the assistant chief medical officer: "To the best of my knowledge and belief Frank Sinatra is physically and/or mentally disqualified for military service by reason of Chronic perforation left tympanum [and] Chronic mastoiditis. Also: emotional instability."

FBI agents noted that, "On its face the file appeared to be in regular order. [The] Local Board had been particularly careful not to afford Sinatra special treatment and where any question of importance arose, the Board would immediately communicate with the State Headquarters for advice in view of the 'position' held by Sinatra."

The FBI *did* note what it described as one "inconsistency" as a result of its investigation, however. In the section of his Selective Service Questionnaire titled *"Physical Condition"* that was executed on December 17, 1940, Sinatra quite clearly wrote: "To the best of my knowledge, I have no physical or mental defects or diseases." The fact that Sinatra's military medical examination demonstrated very different results and showed "chronic" ear problems as well as "emotional instability," however, led some within the FBI to think that this discrepancy might indeed be evidence that Sinatra had taken steps to avoid war service. And so the investigation continued.

On February 24, 1944, the FBI learned some illuminating and surprising facts from the military about Sinatra's state of mind that also had a direct bearing upon its decision to declare him both physically and mentally unfit for service:

During the psychiatric interview the patient stated that he was neurotic, afraid to be in crowds, afraid to go in elevator, makes him feel that he would want to run when surrounded by people. He had somatic ideas and headaches and has been very nervous for four or five years. Wakens tired in the A.M., is run down and undernourished. The examining psychiatrist concluded that this selectee [sic] suffered from psychoneurosis and was not acceptable material from the psychiatric viewpoint. The diagnosis of psychoneurosis, severe was not added to the list. Notation of emotional instability was made instead. It was felt that this would avoid undue unpleasantness for both the selectee [sic] and the induction service.

The reference to the military wishing to "avoid undue unpleasantness" for Sinatra if details of his highly strained psychological state became public was undoubtedly evidence that some official, at least, *was* willing to cut the singer a break of sorts, even if the allegations that Sinatra had paid off the military to avoid wartime service were false, as the FBI eventually came to believe.

It was the singer's notorious ties with the criminal elite of the underworld, however, that kept the FBI busiest for years. A February 26, 1947, confidential document on Sinatra titled "Miscellaneous, Information Concerning 'Association with Criminals and Hoodlums' " sets the scene for what would ultimately amount to several decades of intense surveillance, as well as mountains of paperwork for the bureau on this aspect of Sinatra's private life:

During the course of inquiries made by the Newark Field Division in connection with the crime survey program, information was received from Captain Matthew J. Donohue of the Bergen County Police, Hackensack, New Jersey, that Willie Moretti of Hasbrouck Heights, New Jersey, has a financial interest in Frank Sinatra. It should be mentioned that Frank Sinatra's residence is also in Hasbrouck Heights, New Jersey. Moretti is reported to control the numbers rackets, horse racing, and gambling throughout Bergen County, New Jersey. The Newark Office has advised that Moretti is a close associate of Frank Costello, well-known gambler of New York City, and that during 1933 Moretti, while visiting the Arlington Hotel, Hot Springs, Arkansas, was in the company of Lucky Luciano.

And things did not look at all good for Sinatra when the FBI was informed on the same day of yet further examples of the singing star's underworld links:

The New York Field Division in August, 1946, was advised by Frances Duffy, clerk of local Selective Service Board Number 180, New York City, that she, Duffy, resides in a home owned by Mrs. Mary Fischetti, the mother of Charles Fischetti, who was considered a key figure by the Chicago Field Division in the investigation of the case entitled "Reactivation of the Capone Gang." Miss Duffy disclosed that Sinatra accompanied Charles Fischetti to the home of Fischetti's mother and spent the evening there in about June of 1946. During the course of the above-mentioned investigation, the Chicago Field Office advised that Charles Fischetti was requested to get in touch with his brother, Joe Fischetti, for the purpose of contacting Sinatra in New York, to expedite room reservations for a football game to be played around November 7, 1946. It was indicated that the reservations for the hotels were desired by the Fischettis as they intended to take in the Notre Dame-Army football game. In addition, it was reported that Fischetti forwarded two-dozen shirts to Frank Sinatra in Hollywood.

The same document then turned its attention to the fact that Sinatra was also associated with two of the most infamous figures in organized crime and racketeering during this period:

In connection with the case entitled "Benjamin 'Bugsy' Siegel, with aliases, miscellaneous information concerning, crime survey", the Los Angeles Office reported that "Bugsy" Siegel arrived in Los Angeles on December 18, 1946, from Las Vegas, Nevada, for the purpose of contacting Lana Turner, Jimmie Durante, and Frank Sinatra in order to have these individuals attend the opening at the Flamingo Hotel, which is operated by Siegel. In the investigation of the same case, the Los Angeles Office advised that Mickey Cohen, a well-known gambler and racketeer in Los Angeles, California, had been in contact with Sinatra on occasions. Information received from a technical source reflected that Cohen desired to contact Sinatra to make "a deal."

A somewhat amusing, and curiously brief, reference is made in an April 17, 1947, document to a prostitute who was apparently complaining about the fact that Sinatra was refusing to pay her for her sexual services. The fact that the hooker was so out of it on booze at the time that Sinatra received no satisfaction at all, however, appeared not to faze her in the slightest when it came to wanting payment: "Assistant-Special-Agent-in-Charge A.H. Belmont advised that a well known prostitute, stated through arrangements made by 'Toots' Shor, she paid a professional visit to Sinatra in his room in the Waldorf Astoria on April 11, 1947. She advised, however, that due to her drunken condition, she was unable to fulfill her engagement, but nevertheless expected to be paid a fee of $100."

But what perhaps enraged FBI boss Hoover more than anything else was an offer that Sinatra made in September 1950 to actually undertake undercover work on behalf of the bureau. As the following document demonstrates, Hoover, adamant that no personal buddy of the Mob would ever be tied to his beloved organization, nixed the idea from the very beginning:

Sinatra had first considered contacting the CIA, but on the advice of a CIA representative had contacted the Bureau. Sinatra denied any subversive affiliations but felt that as a result of the publicity which he had received connecting him with subversive elements, he might be able to be of service. The Director noted his agreement with Mr. Tolson's comment that "We want nothing to do with him."

Also in 1950, the allegations of Mafia and gangster-style connections to Frank Sinatra just kept growing, much to Hoover's satisfaction, one suspects:

According to an informant of unknown reliability, Frank Sinatra is a nephew of Ralph Capone, well-known Chicago gambler. According to this informant the Capones brought Sinatra out of obscurity by buying him a nightclub job and paying representatives of the press for favorable publicity. Robert C. Ruark, newspaper columnist, reported that Frank Sinatra associated with Charles "Lucky" Luciano, notorious underworld character, who was deported from Cuba to Italy in the spring of 1947, while Sinatra spent a four-day vacation in Havana, Cuba, during February 1947. When Luciano was arrested in Rome, Italy on July 7, 1949, his address book included the name of Frank Sinatra. On June 13, 1948, Allan Smiley, notorious Los Angeles underworld character who was with "Bugsy" Siegel the night he was murdered, claimed to know Frank Sinatra quite well.

Things got even darker for Sinatra when the bureau began looking into very serious claims, which were never substantiated, to the effect that he was actively running drugs for the Mob, as a document titled "Allegations Of Being A Dope Racketeer" shows:

The interviewee sent a letter to the Attorney General under date of June 10, 1947, claiming that he had quite a bit of information concerning vice rackets, narcotics and jewel thieves. When he was interviewed by Bureau agents he reported, among other items, that Frank Sinatra handled dope on the West Coast for "Bugsy" Siegel, Allan Smiley and George Raft, the movie actor. He alleged that Sinatra maintained his headquarters in one of the bigger hotels in Hollywood, either the Roosevelt or Hollywood Hotel. Lee Mortimer of the New York "Daily Mirror" conferred with Mr. Tolson on May 13, 1947, to inquire for information concerning Frank Sinatra. Mortimer advised that when Colonel Fain Dorsey, alias Charles Conley was arrested in the spring of 1946 for smuggling narcotics from Mexico to the United States he was driving a station wagon which belonged to Sinatra. He indicated that Sinatra had made no effort as of that time to secure repossession of his station wagon.

And it was not just the FBI that Sinatra had problems with. An interagency FBI memo of October 25, 1954, clearly reveals that there was serious friction between the singer and elements of the United States military, too:

George Murphy called from Hollywood. Abe Last[f]ogel of the William Morris Agency has been in touch with him since Murphy has played an active role in recent years in sending troops of actors to the various parts of the world where members of the armed forces are congregated. Murphy has been handling such assignments since he at one time was President of the Screen Actors Guild.

Last[f]ogel told Murphy that some weeks ago Frank Sinatra volunteered to go to Korea but the Army turned him down and indicated there was something against him in the Department of Justice and that as best as he, Last[f]ogel, could determine, it was based upon a column written by Westbrook Pegler to the effect that Sinatra went to Cuba to see Lucky Luciano. Murphy stated that the top military people, according to Last[f]ogel, had told Sinatra nothing could be done as long as this was being held up in the FBI and the Department of Justice. Murphy further stated he had a call in for the Attorney General.

I told Murphy he did not have the complete report; that the matter of determining what actors were to visit the various theaters was one for the determination of the Defense establishment and the various branches of the armed services. I further told him we had heard rumbles of this previously and it was our understanding the Army had taken the action which they took based upon their own records. I told Murphy it seemed to me if he was interested in straightening out this matter, he should go to the Army. Murphy then asked me confidentially if there were any suggestions I could offer. I told him, of course, there had been numerous news stories about Sinatra, his various connections, not just with Lucky Luciano, but with front organizations and the American Youth for Democracy; that it appeared these were untrue, but the thing for Sinatra to do would be to answer them and furnish full facts. I told, Murphy, however, this was not a matter within the Bureau's jurisdiction. George stated he would cancel his call for the Attorney General and get out of this.

Sinatra vigorously and repeatedly denied any such Communist "front" affiliations, but the damage was already done in the eyes of the military. Indeed, the FBI had been quietly collecting data on Sinatra's alleged dabbling in Communism for years. On February 28, 1955, J. Edgar Hoover was told that, "In 1945, an informant described as reliable stated that he had heard from other CP [Communist Party] members that Sinatra was a member of the CP." A summary document was prepared for Hoover that expanded upon these controversial claims:

Sinatra has been associated with numerous groups cited by the Attorney General, the House Committee on Un-American Activities (HCUA), or [the] California Committee on Un-American Activities as a sponsor or as a speaker. In 1946, he was elected as one of the vice-chairmen of the Independent Citizens Committee of the Arts, Sciences and Professions (ICCASP) in New York City. The ICCASP has been cited by the House Committee on Un-American Activities. A review of Bureau files from 1950 to date reflected that Sinatra was reported in 1950, by a source of unknown reliability, to have taken $1,000,000 cash to Luciano in Italy, and to have attended a Mafia meeting in 1951 in Cuba. Newspaper articles indicate Sinatra is now anti-Communist.

Despite these newspaper articles, the FBI's surveillance of the singer on this specific issue continued unabated. On January 23, 1957, more incriminating data was added to the secret Sinatra file concerning his alleged interest in communism:

Allegations concerning his contacts with the Communist Party and numerous communist front groups came to the Bureau's attention for a number of years and were included in a memorandum sent to the State Department in December, 1954, on their request for a name check on Sinatra. In view of a sworn affidavit that he had never been a member of the Communist Party or of any organization of a subversive character, the State Department requested an investigation by the Bureau to determine whether prosecution was warranted against Sinatra for making a false statement in the application.

History has shown that Sinatra was not prosecuted. His fraught relationship with government agencies continued, however. Additional FBI documents of 1957 reported on further Mob ties that the singer was cultivating:

The records of the Clerk County, Nevada, Sheriff's Office at Las Vegas as of July 25, 1955, lists Frank Sinatra as one of the twelve major stockholders in the Sands Hotel, a gambling establishment in Las Vegas. According to information developed by the Salt Lake City Office, many of the stockholders of record in this particular operation are actually working for notorious gamblers and racketeers. Included among the more prominent of the latter are [Abner] "Longie" Zwillman and Joseph "Doc" Stacher, both notorious gangsters from New Jersey.

And as a new decade dawned, Sinatra was still courting controversy. Throughout March 1960, the FBI recorded the details of a wealth of rumors and stories on the star that it was closely monitoring—at least two of which linked him with future president John F. Kennedy. On the third of the month, the following tidbit reached the desk of J. Edgar Hoover: "Sinatra was to be the master of ceremonies on the occasion of [Soviet President] Nikita Krushchev's visit to a motion picture sound stage in Hollywood, California, to observe movie making."

Then, on March 22, 1960, "an informant" of the FBI had advised the bureau that *Confidential* magazine was, "investigating rumors concerning an indiscreet party held in Palm Springs, California, which was allegedly attended by Senator John Kennedy of Massachusetts, Kennedy's brother-in-law and business partner of Sinatra, Peter Lawford, and Sinatra. It was reported that on his last visit to California, Senator Kennedy stayed at Sinatra's home in Palm Springs."

And on the matter of Sinatra's relationship to John F. Kennedy, additional FBI files of March 1960 reflect that "someone" described as being "very close to the Communist Party" was "trying to promote Sinatra, Sammy Davis, Jr., the Negro star and their crowd as 'fair-haired boys' known to Senator Kennedy in case the Senator gets to the White House. It was further speculated that Sinatra may, through Peter Lawford and Lawford's wife, have been able to get Senator Kennedy to take a financial interest in Sinatra's film producing enterprise."

The matter of the connections between Sinatra and JFK was of keen interest to Hoover. On April 1, 1960, FBI agents reported to Hoover that *Confidential* magazine was still digging into the Sinatra-Kennedy story. In an attempt to ascertain where this would lead, FBI personnel were cultivating a relationship with a man described as a "notorious private investigator," who had some knowledge of *Confidential*'s inquiries, and who had recently "participated in a conversation with Senator Kennedy's campaign manager." The report to Hoover revealed some highly controversial facts: "The campaign manager bewailed Kennedy's association with Sinatra, stating something to the effect that the Senator is vulnerable to bad publicity only because of his associations with Sinatra. This worried man added that there are certain sex activities by Kennedy that he hopes never are publicized. . . . These parties involving the Senator and Sinatra occurred in Palm Springs, Las Vegas and New York City."

Hoover also noted with some concern that Belden Katelman, a prominent Las Vegas investor, had "made the point that Kennedy had stayed at the Sands with Sinatra while in Las Vegas." On this issue, Hoover's files add that, "Katelman said it is a known fact that the Sands is owned by hoodlums and that while the Senator, Sinatra and Lawford were there, show girls from all over town were running in and out of the Senator's suite."

And the wild parties continued unabated for Sinatra, as the FBI was fully aware. On November 15, 1963, a confidential contact in the office of the Ventura County district attorney informed Los Angeles-based FBI agents that the attorney's office was aware of a number of "pot parties" that had taken place at a particular private Hollywood residence from 1959 to 1962. Notably, the source added that, "On three or four occasions" Frank Sinatra was there, "accompanied by a large male Negro whom he called Johnny." The document stated in closing: "[Source] also advised saw Joan Crawford at some of the pot parties."

But it was the ever present allegations of deep-running Mafia links that continued to plague Sinatra, as a November 20, 1964, FBI document demonstrates:

In early 1964 an informant, who has furnished reliable information in the past regarding general criminal activities in the United States, indicated among other things that Paul "Skinny" [D'] Amato, operator of the 500 Club, Atlantic City, New Jersey, and a business partner with Sinatra in Nevada, was a hoodlum and a member of the La Cosa Nostra syndicate. The informant stated that although Sinatra was not a member of the syndicate, he was big enough and close enough to the organization to obtain any favors he desired.

In 1966, files reflect that Sinatra was still seething over the fact that, more than a decade previously, the military had denied him permission to entertain troops overseas:

On 3/30/66, Colonel John R. Elting, (U.S. Army), G-2, Military District of Washington, advised that on 3/25/66, Joseph F. Goetz, (Colonel, U.S. Air Force, Retired), contacted him and informed him that he had been commissioned by Frank Sinatra, the entertainer, to determine the identity of the "S.O.B" who had "tagged" Sinatra as a "Commie." Colonel Elting explained that in 1950, 1952, and 1954, Sinatra had offered his services for entertainment of military troops overseas. In each instance, he was not cleared by Army because of his reported affiliation with subversive organizations. Elting added that Sinatra was later cleared in 1962 to entertain troops overseas but that this clearance expired in 1966 without the clearance having been used.

The FBI took some secret satisfaction in informing Elting and Goetz that: "Information was developed or received previously indicating that Sinatra reportedly had been associated with or lent his name to 16 organizations which have been cited or described as communist fronts." The FBI continued to watch this controversy with much interest:

Inquiry was made of Colonel Elting by Liaison Agent as to why Sinatra, at this late date, wanted to pursue this matter. According to Elting, Goetz stated that Sinatra is a very temperamental, vindictive and moody individual and he has periods where he dwells on his past life. Goetz added that he has known Sinatra for many years and he has noticed several occasions where Sinatra, in retrospect, has made derogatory comments concerning individuals who have hurt him in the past. Elting advised that he gave Goetz no satisfaction other than to state that Sinatra was recently cleared to entertain troops overseas. Goetz informed Elting that he was going to counsel Sinatra to drop the matter.

More than a decade after Sinatra's antics involving Vegas showgirls and JFK were creating high-level anxieties for both the FBI and Kennedy's political team, the singer's name was referenced in FBI files alongside that of another president, namely Richard Nixon. However, Nixon was less taken by the legend of Sinatra than was Kennedy:

On 1/26/73 . . . Frank Sinatra was being his usual charming self. . . . [W]hile attending the inauguration of President Nixon he approached a female columnist, and in a loud vulgar voice, called her a $2 whore and ended the conversation by throwing $2 in her drink, spilling it all over, and leaving her table. . . . [A]s a result of this and many other obnoxious conversations and activities of Sinatra, President Nixon severely reprimanded Vice President Agnew because of his close association with Sinatra. . . . Vice President Agnew spends considerable time with Sinatra flying across the country in his jet and playing golf at country clubs throughout the world. . . . Vice President Agnew has spent many weekends at Sinatra's Palm Springs home and as such this is upsetting President Nixon. . . . Ted Kennedy and Sinatra have been traveling extensively together and feels that Sinatra is playing both sides of the fence as far as politics is concerned.

FBI records after the early 1970s reveal nothing further concerning Sinatra's Mob ties or sexual intrigue; the bulk of the remainder of the files focused largely upon death threats made to Sinatra and extortion-style letters sent to his management. The golden years of Sinatra's career were over, as was, for all intents and purposes, the FBI's deep surveillance of the man. In November 1986, Sinatra underwent an emergency operation to remove a foot-long piece of his large intestine, and in March 1994, he collapsed on stage from heat exhaustion in Richmond, Virginia, midway through "My Way" and was hospitalized briefly. He was again admitted to the hospital on November 1, 1996, for what his publicist insisted was nothing more than a pinched nerve. However, rumors circulated widely about heart problems and pneumonia, and on May 14, 1998, at the age of eighty-two, Ol' Blue Eyes was no more.

Frank Sinatra certainly changed the course of popular music at the height of his career, and he was undoubtedly one of the most charismatic performers of his era, but a comment made by a confidential FBI informant aptly sums up what Hoover thought of the celebrity crooner: "Sinatra has the 'hoodlum complex.' "

FBI

Date: 5/25/65

Transmit the following in _____
(Type in plaintext or code)

Via AIRTEL _____
(Priority)

Mr. Beh
Mr. Mo
Mr. Del
Mr. Ca
Mr. Cu
Mr. C.
Mr. Fel
Mr. Gal
Mr. Ro
Mr. Su
Mr. Ta
Mr. Tre
Tele. Ro
Miss H
Miss G

TO: DIRECTOR, FBI (145-2961)

FROM: SAC, DETROIT (145-420)(P)

UNSUB; 45 r.p.m.
Recording "Louie Louie"
POSSIBLE ITOM
(OO: DETROIT)

Re FBI Laboratory letter to Detroit dated 5/17/65, and Detroit
letter to Bureau dated 4/22/65.

For the information of the New York Office, the FBI Laboratory
advised Detroit by referenced letter that the Department of
Justice has ▓▓▓▓▓▓▓▓▓▓▓▓▓▓▓▓ a copy of the record, "Louie
Louie" from ▓▓▓▓▓▓▓▓▓▓▓▓▓▓▓▓▓▓ with a
request that it be reviewed to determine if it was an obscene
matter. The Department advised that they were unable to
interpret any of the wording in the record and, therefore,
could not make a decision concerning the matter. Also, that
the AUSA at Tampa, Fla. and Hammond, Indiana, have declined
prosecution.

Also, for the information of the New York Office, the FBI
Laboratory advised that because the lyrics of the recording,
"Louie Louie" could not be definitely determined in the
Laboratory examination, it was not possible to determine
whether this recording is obscene.

Referenced Detroit letter requested New York to contact the
Wand Co. regarding "Louie Louie" record in an effort to
obtain the lyrics in this recording. New York is requested
to expedite this investigation.

SA ▓▓▓▓▓▓▓▓▓▓▓▓▓ of the Detroit Office discussed the
case with AUSA ROBERT J. GRACE, EDM 839 Federal Bldg., Detroit,
as to the Laboratory report in this matter. He stated he would
defer his prosecutive opinion in this case regarding the recording
"Louie Louie" until completion of investigation by the New York O

3 - Bureau
2 - New York
1 - Detroit
(6)   Special Agent in Charge   Sent ___ M ___ Per ___

REC 27 145-2961-10

MAY 28 1965

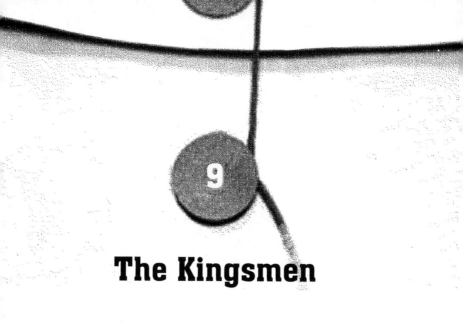

The Kingsmen

"How can we stamp out this menace???"

Formed in Portland, Oregon, in 1959, the Kingsmen will forever be associated with their monster-sized hit record of 1963, "Louie Louie." Astonishingly, the song, along with another number, "Haunted Castle," was the group's first ever attempt at a professional recording, which was undertaken at Portland's Northwestern, Inc. for the sum of $36.

Northwest music fans were already familiar with "Louie Louie," as there had been a number of previous recordings of the song made by various artists for the label, including Richard Berry in 1956, and the Wailers in 1961. And only days after the Kingsmen made their now historic version, yet *another* recording was made: this one by Paul Revere and the Raiders, and in the same studio, no less. The Kingsmen fought it out with the Raiders on local radio for a few months, with the Kingsmen's version ultimately finding its way to the East Coast, where it was regularly played by a wealth of Boston radio stations, and generated a huge, positive response from listeners. As a result, record producer Jerry

Dennon entered into an agreement with New York's Wand Corporation for immediate mass pressing and distribution of the Kingsmen's record across the entire United States.

To everyone's delight, Wand worked the record endlessly and "Louie Louie" rapidly broke out in several markets, climbing the charts rapidly. When sales eventually began to drop, however, a controversy regarding the lyrics began to spread throughout America, something that saw the record summarily banned from both record stores and radio stations in Indiana. And that controversy had another effect, too: it caught the attention of the FBI. On February 7, 1964, a concerned mother contacted Attorney General Robert F. Kennedy with an impassioned plea:

Who do you turn to when your teenage daughter buys or brings home pornographic or obscene materials being sold along with objects directed and aimed at the teen age market in every City, Village and Record Shop in this nation? My daughter brought home a record of 'LOUIE LOUIE' and I, after reading that record had been banned from being played on the air because it was obscene, proceeded to try to decipher the jumble of words. The lyrics are so filthy that I cannot enclose them in this letter. This record is on the WAND label #143 and recorded by The KINGSMEN 'a Jordan production by Ken Chase and Jerry Dennon' and there is an address 1650 Broadway, New York, N.Y. I would like to see these people, the 'Artists', the record company, and the promoters prosecuted to the full extent of the law. We all know there is obscene materials available for those who seek it, but when they start sneaking in this material in the guise of the latest teen-age rock & roll hit record these morons have gone too far. This land of ours is headed for an extreme state of moral degradation what with this record, the biggest hit movies and the sex and violence exploited on T.V. How can we stamp out this menace???

Were the Kingsmen really a countrywide "menace," peddling "filthy" pornography and "obscene" produce to innocent cherubs? Of course they weren't. But the FBI assumed the worst, and with numerous similar letters on file, many of which bordered upon the hysterical, FBI agents quickly swung into action. Amusingly, declassified FBI memoranda demonstrate that the FBI was faced with a major problem when it initiated Operation Louie Louie. Try as it might, what was perhaps the most powerful law enforcement agency on the planet at the time, simply could not decipher the lyrics to "Louie Louie," sung in the Kingsmen's own, unique style. To their credit, however, the FBI's finest *did* do their best to try and understand what on earth it was that the Kingsmen were going on about.

While this episode might have entertained the younger and less staid members of the FBI who were in tune with the pop culture of the time, it was a singular failure, as the Detroit Office of the bureau noted on May 25, 1965:

For the information of the New York Office, the FBI Laboratory advised Detroit by referenced letter that the Department of Justice has [deleted] a copy of the record, "Louie Louie" with a request that it be reviewed to determine if it was an obscene matter. The Department advised that they were unable to interpret any of the wording in the record and, therefore, could not make a decision concerning the matter. Also for the information of the New York Office, the FBI Laboratory advised that because the lyrics of the recording, "Louie Louie" could not be definitely determined in the Laboratory examination, it was not possible to determine whether this recording is obscene.

While the distinctly surreal image of endless groups of FBI agents sitting in their offices, tapping their toes, and endlessly blaring "Louie Louie" out of the speakers of a plethora of stereo systems almost beggars belief, sometimes truth really is stranger than fiction. FBI papers show that several "versions" of the lyrics to "Louie Louie" were filed by bureau agents seeking to unravel this controversy of distinctly less-than-epic proportions. The first version, found in the FBI's records, went:

Oh, Louie, Louie, Oh, No,
Get her way down low.
Oh, Louie, Louie, Oh, Baby,
A fine little girl awaiting for me
She's just a girl across the way
Well I'll take her and park all alone
She's never a girl I'd lay at home
(Chorus Repeat)
At night at 10 I lay her again
Fuck you girl, Oh, all the way
Oh, my bed and I lay here there
I meet a rose in her hair.
(Chorus Repeat)
Ok, Lets give it to them, right now!
She's got a rag on I'll move above
It won't be long she'll slip it off
I'll take her in my arms again
I'll tell her I'll never leave her again
(Chorus Repeat)
Get that broad out of here!

Then, after much FBI head scratching, came version two, which also surfaced from the bureau's archives:

There is a fine little girl waiting for me.
She is just a girl across the way.
Then I take her all alone,
She's never the girl I lay at home.

(Chorus)
Tonight at ten I'll lay her again
We'll fuck your girl and by the way
And . . . on that chair I'll lay her there.
I felt my bone ..ah.. in her hair.
(Chorus)
She had a rag on, I moved above.
It won't be long she'll slip it off.
I held her in my arms and then
And I told her I'd rather lay her again.

And then number three, also from FBI files:

Fine little girl waits for me to get your thrills
across the way girl I dream about is all alone
she never could get away from home
Every night and day I play with my thing
I fuck your girl all kinds of ways.
In all night now meet me there
I feel her low I give her hell
Hey you bitch. Hey lovermaker now hold my
bone, it won't take long so leave it [illegible]
Hey Senorita I'm hot as hell I told her I'd
never lay here again

Needless to say, all three versions could not possibly have been correct, and so steps were taken to interview members of the Kingsmen themselves in an effort to try and determine the full and unexpurgated facts. On September 7, 1965, the FBI at Chicopee, Massachusetts, filed the results of its interviews:

[Deleted] Washington, was advised as to the identity of the interviewing agent, that he could consult with an attorney before making any statement, that he did not have to make any statement, and that any statement he did make could be used against him in court.

[Deleted] identified himself as a member of the "Kingsmen." He said he was aware of the widespread complaint that the "Kingsmen" had spoken obscene words in their recording of the song "Louie Louie". [He said] he would swear that this was not deliberately true and that he and the others selected a standard lyric for recording, changed it not at all, and after short practice recording it at Seattle, Washington around January 1963. He said the record sold on the west coast primarily for several months without criticism and was later put on the Wand label in New York in an exact duplication of the earlier record since it was recorded only once.

For several months on the Wand label nothing was said of the obscenity which some claim to hear, or at least nothing of the complaint had come to their attention, until it was banned from radio and public performance by the Governor of Indiana. He said the "Kingsmen" and their management have attempted to counter the charge but apparently the more said about it the more talk of the obscenity spreads.

[He] does not admit to complaints that the words exist even accidentally because he does not believe that they do and contended that those who want to hear such things have apparently interpreted an unintelligible sounding of words which were honestly inserted for harmony.

On the same day, the FBI interviewed another member of the Kingsmen:

The original recording sold poorly for several months on the west coast and was later recorded on the Wand label in New York. Some months after that label went on sale, the talk of obscenity in the recording arose. He said to put an end to this and establish their own position, the Wand Corporation forwarded a record to the Federal Communications Commission at Washington, D.C., and it is his belief that the Commission replied they observed no obscenity in the unintelligible wording. The Corporation later offered a $1000 reward to anyone who could substantiate the reported obscenity.

[He said] there was no deliberate attempt to include any obscenity in the recording and it is his belief only those who want to hear such things can read it into the vocal. He said he has heard others point out where the suggested obscenity exists in the recording but cannot make out what they suggest appears.

And so the bizarre controversy over what the Kingsmen were, or were not, singing about rumbled on until a weary FBI eventually gave up the chase and conceded that, with the lyrics remaining undecipherable, there was no chance of the case ever coming to trial, even if such action was ultimately considered warranted by the FBI.

Inevitably, this stimulated even more controversy and interest. And, recognizing that controversy sells, Wand reissued the record in 1964, 1965, and, 1966. It would reach number two in *Billboard* and number one in *Cash Box*. The Kingsmen also became the number one touring band in the United States for a time, and in 1965, during a series of one-night events, set fifty-six consecutive attendance records in colleges, ballrooms, arenas, state fairs, and community dances all across the country.

A note to all aspiring bands: if you want a hit song, ensure that your lyrics are vastly open to interpretation and get your publicist to mail a copy of the CD to the FBI. You are guaranteed to go a long way. You may even become the subject of a secret government file.

And here finally are the *real* lyrics to *Louie Louie* that so baffled the nonhipsters and squares of the 1960s at the FBI. These lyrics appear in a declassified FBI document of 1965 that related them word-for-word:

Louie, Louie . . . Oh yea, a-way we go
Yea, Yea, Yea, Yea, Yea
Louie, Louie . . . Oh, Baby, a-way we go
A fine little girl—she wait for me
Me catch the ship—a-cross the sea
I sailed the ship—all a-lone
I never think—I'll make it home
Louie, Louie—a-way we go
Three nights and days we sailed the sea
Me think of girl constant-ly
On the ship—dream she there
I smell the rose—in her hair
Louie, Louie—a-way we go
Me see Ja-mai-ca—moon a-bove
It won't be long—me see me love
Me take her in arms and then
I tell her I never leave her a-gain
Louie, Louie . . . Oh yea, a-way we go

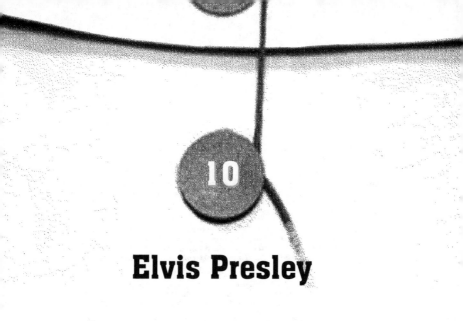

Elvis Presley

"Juvenile acts of lust and perversion will follow his show."

Considering the fact that the FBI's file on Elvis Presley runs to more than six hundred pages, a person would be forgiven for assuming that it is packed with all sorts of hot gossip and titillating scandal on the dead singer. In fact, the exact opposite is the case. Most of the file focuses its attention upon scams, cons, extortion attempts, and criminal activity of a truly mind-numbingly tedious nature, all of which were carefully designed to financially exploit Presley, or his estate, after his "expiration-on-the-can" in 1977. Nevertheless, a close and careful perusal of the file does reveal a few notable gems of data.

For example, on May 16, 1955, when the King's hip-swiveling career was arguably at his peak, his onstage activities were causing teenage girls to hyperventilate, and the more hysterical elements of society were insisting on his imprisonment, the FBI received a vitriolic letter from a source described as a "former member of Army Intelligence Service." According to the letter writer, who worked for the Wisconsin-based *La Crosse Register*, the official competent to address large groups but much rather prefers small gatherings in community centers and the like, where he makes himself accessible for talks and discussions regarding the evils of narcotics and other problems of concern to teenagers and other young people.

Following their tour, Presley privately advised that he has volunteered his services to the President in connection with the narcotics problem and that Mr. Nixon had responded by furnishing him an Agent's badge of the Bureau of Narcotics and Dangerous Drugs. Presley was carrying this badge in his pocket and displayed it.

Presley advised that he wished the Director to be aware that he, Presley, from time to time is approached by individuals and groups in and outside of the entertainment business whose motives and goals he is convinced are not in the best interests of this country and who seek to have him to lend his name to their questionable activities. In this regard, he volunteered to make such information available to the Bureau on a confidential basis whenever it came to his attention. He further indicated that he wanted the Director to know that should the Bureau ever have any need of his services in any way that he would be delighted to be of assistance.

Presley indicated that he is of the opinion that the Beatles laid the groundwork for many of the problems we are having with young people by their filthy unkempt appearances and suggestive music while entertaining in this country during the early and middle 1960's. He advised that the Smothers Brothers, Jane Fonda, and other persons in the entertainment industry of their ilk have a lot to answer for in the hereafter for the way they have poisoned young minds by disparaging the United States in their public statements and unsavory activities.

Presley advised that he resides at 3764 Highway 51, South, Memphis, Tennessee, but that he spends a substantial portion of his time in the Beverly Hills, California - Las Vegas, Nevada, areas fulfilling motion picture assignments and singing commitments.

He noted that he can be contacted anytime through his Memphis address and that because of problems he has had with people tampering with his mail, such correspondence should be addressed to him under the pseudonym Colonel Jon Burrows

- 2 -

CONTINUED - OVER

newspaper of the diocese of La Crosse, Presley was nothing less than a "definite danger to the security of the United States." Commenting on, or rather, ranting about an adrenaline-charged performance that Presley had given in La Crosse two nights previously, the outraged man informed the FBI:

Eyewitnesses have told me that Presley's actions and motions were such as to rouse the sexual passions of teenaged youth. One eye-witness described his actions as "sexual self-gratification on the stage,"—another as "a strip-tease with clothes on." Although police and auxiliaries were there, the show went on. Perhaps the hardened police did not get the import of his motions and gestures, like those of masturbation or riding a microphone.

Indications of the harm Presley did just in La Crosse were the two high school girls (of whom I have direct personal knowledge) whose abdomen and thigh had Presley's autograph. They admitted they went to his room where this happened. It is known by psychologists, psychiatrists and priests that teenaged girls from the age of eleven, and boys in their adolescence are easily aroused to sexual indulgence and perversion by certain types of motions and hysteria—the type that was exhibited at the Presley show.

There is also gossip of the Presley Fan Clubs that degenerate into sex orgies. I would judge that he may possibly be both a drug addict and a sexual pervert. I am convinced that juvenile acts of lust and perversion will follow his show here in La Crosse.

I do not report idly to the FBI. My last official report to an FBI agent in New York before I entered the U.S. Army resulted in arrest of a saboteur (who committed suicide before his trial).

Though the writer was certainly entitled to his opinion, his highly descriptive and emotional response to what were simply minor onstage antics designed to hype up the audience of largely teenage girls, strongly suggests that the writer himself had a few sexual hang-ups that needed addressing. And the man most certainly did not do himself any favors at all by stating that "It is known by priests that . . . boys in their adolescence are easily aroused."

Four years later, when Presley was in Germany with the United States Army (where he ultimately reached the rank of sergeant), both the Pentagon and the FBI took note when they learned that Presley's manager, Colonel Tom Parker, had received a letter to the effect that a "Red Army soldier in East Germany" was planning to kill the singer. A concerned military speculated on whether or not this was an undercover Commie plot designed to assassinate the U.S. military's most famous and idolized soldier. But the truth was apparently less sensational.

While the FBI and the military were running around frantically trying to uncover Red spies and paid-for-hire assassins, Colonel Tom merely scoffed at the whole saga and asserted that, in his opinion, the letter was probably just the latest in a long line of many from a woman in Ohio whom the Colonel described firmly and concisely as "nuts." Officials in the army were not so sure. But when no assassination attempt occurred, senior sources within the military breathed a collective sigh of relief and went back to their normal business of saving the world from the threat posed by the Soviet Union.

Perhaps the oddest episode of Presley's military career occurred in late 1959, when he began receiving dermatological care from a South African homosexual who had provided the King certain, ahem, "treatments." Not only that, but after Presley fired the man on Christmas Eve 1959 for "embarrassing" him, the outraged zit exterminator threatened to reveal certain photographs that showed Presley in what was intriguingly and tantalizingly described as "compromising situations." One does not have to be a genius to figure out that it would not have been good for Presley's singing career if this episode had been made public. Both the army and the FBI prepared memoranda on the events for its records that spelled out the full picture, as the following report written on February 3, 1960, by Major Warren H. Metzner, chief of the Army's Investigations Branch, demonstrates:

1. Elvis Presley was interviewed on 28 December 1959 concerning his complaint that he was the victim of blackmail by a Mr. Laurenz Johannes Griessel-Landau, of Johannesburg, South Africa. Griessel-Landau represents himself to be a doctor specialist in the field of dermatology. Griessel-Landau is not a medical doctor.

2. Copies of letters from Griessel-Landau to Presley's private secretary were obtained on loan basis so that they could be photographed.

3. On or about 27 November 1959, Griessel-Landau appeared at the residence of Elvis Presley in Bad Nauheim, Germany and began his treatments. These treatments took place in Presley's quarters in the presence of two female secretaries (both U.S.). The treatment involved Presley's shoulders and face.

4. Presley reported that Griessel-Landau made several homosexual advances to some of his enlisted friends. Griessel-Landau also is alleged to have admitted to Presley that he is bi-sexual. His first homosexual experience took place early in his life in the orphanage in which he was brought up.

5. On 24 December 1959 Presley decided to discontinue the skin treatments. At the time that he told Griessel-Landau of this decision he also thoroughly censured Griessel-Landau for embarrassing him as a result of the improper advances that he (Griessel-Landau) had made to his (Presley's) friends. Griessel-Landau immediately went into a fit of rage, tore up a photo album of Presley's, and threatened to ruin his singing career and to involve Presley's American girl friend (a 16 year old daughter of an

Air Force captain). Griessel-Landau further threatened to expose Presley by photographs and tape recordings which are alleged to present Presley in compromising situations. Presley assures that this is impossible since he never was in any compromising situations. Presley contends that Griessel-Landau is mentally disturbed. This is based upon the fits that Griessel-Landau has had and his statements concerning the shock treatments he has been taking.

6. By negotiation, Presley agreed to pay Griessel-Landau $200.00 for treatments received and also to furnish him with a $315.00 plane fare to London, England. Griessel-Landau agreed to depart to England on 25 December 1959 at 1930 hours from Frankfurt, Germany. Griessel-Landau did not leave as agreed, rather returned and demanded an additional $250.00, which Presley paid. A day later, Griessel-Landau made a telephonic demand for 2,000 F and for the loss of his practice which he closed in Johannesburg, South Africa prior to his departure for Bad Nauheim to treat Presley.

7. Griessel-Landau finally departed Rhein-Main Air Field, Frankfurt, Germany at 1600 hours, 6 January 1960 on Flight 491, British European Airways for London, England under the name of Griessel. He is alleged to be seeking entry into the United States. No contact between Presley and Griessel-Landau has been reported since 5 January.

Although Presley was seemingly both highly embarrassed and angered by his experience with Griessel-Landau, it seems decidedly odd that he would have paid the dermatologist's $315 airfare all the way to England, as well as an additional $250. Perhaps Presley just wanted to get rid of the man. Certainly, the army wanted a swift conclusion to the affair, as the FBI noted on February 19, 1960: "Information concerning the subject was furnished to this office by the Provost Marshal Division, Headquarters, U.S.

Army, Europe, with the indication that they wished to avoid any publicity in this matter since they did not want to involve Elvis Presley nor put him in an unfavorable light since Presley had been a first-rate soldier and had caused the Army no trouble during his term of service." If there is anything more to this admittedly curious episode, it has yet to surface from the files of any government agency.

For the most amusing link between Presley and the FBI, we have to jump forward to 1970, when astonishing amounts of prescribed medication, artery-clogging peanut-butter-and-jelly sandwiches, ridiculous white suits, onstage martial arts, and the decadent delights of Las Vegas were all looming on the horizon for the King. It was December 30, 1970, and J. Edgar Hoover's secretary was advised that Presley and his ever-present entourage of helpers and hangers-on were in town and wanted a favor:

The well-known entertainer Elvis Presley and six other people in Presley's party inquired concerning the possibility of a tour of our facilities and an opportunity to meet and shake hands with the Director tomorrow, 12–31–70. Morris indicated to Mr. Casper that Presley had just received an award from the President for his work in discouraging the use of narcotics among young people and for his assistance in connection with youth problems in the Beverley Hills, California, area.

Bufiles reflect that Presley has been the victim in a number of extortion attempts which have been referred to the Bureau. Our files also reflect that he is presently involved in a paternity suit pending in Los Angeles, California, and that during the height of his popularity during the latter part of the 1950's and early 1960's his gyrations while performing were the subject of considerable criticism by the public and comment in the press.

But Hoover was most definitely not up for meeting the King on FBI turf:

Presley's sincerity and good intentions notwithstanding he is certainly not the type of individual whom the Director would wish to meet. It is noted at the present time he is wearing his hair down to his shoulders and indulges in the wearing of all sorts of exotic dress.

Nevertheless, Presley and his entourage *were* afforded a tour of the headquarters of the crime-fighting agency on New Year's Eve, 1970:

Presley advised that he wished the Director to be aware that he, Presley, from time to time is approached by individuals and groups in and outside of the entertainment business whose motives and goals he is convinced are not in the best interests of this country and who seek to have him lend his name to their questionable activities. In this regard, he volunteered to make such information available to the Bureau on a confidential basis whenever it came to his attention.

Presley indicated that he is of the opinion that the Beatles laid the groundwork for many of the problems we are having with young people by their filthy unkempt appearances and suggestive music while entertaining in this country during the early and middle 1960's. He advised that the Smothers Brothers, Jane Fonda, and other persons in the entertainment industry of their ilk have a lot to answer for in the hereafter for the way they have poisoned young minds by disparaging the United States in the public statements and unsavory activities.

Sadly, Presley, who had started his career in the 1950s as a young, vibrant, and rebellious soul, was by the dawn of the 1970s an overweight shadow of his former self, seemingly content to spend his time complaining and griping about the "suggestive music" of bands such as the Beatles, as well as the "problems" that America's youth posed to the country. The King had become little more than the Court Jester.

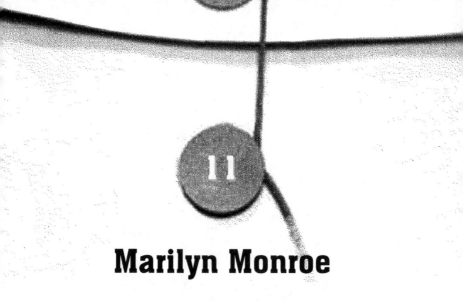

Marilyn Monroe

"Monroe feels like a negated sex symbol."

Born Norma Jean Mortensen on June 1, 1926, in Los Angeles, Marilyn Monroe had a spectacular career that spanned sixteen years, during which time she made thirty movies, experienced numerous emotional highs, suffered a devastating wealth of lows, and finally, and many said inevitably, came to a tragic end at the all-too-young age of thirty-six.

On July 23, 1946, Monroe signed a contract with Twentieth Century Fox and opted to use the last name of her maternal grandmother: Gladys Monroe. Numerous movies followed, including *The Asphalt Jungle, Gentlemen Prefer Blondes, Clash by Night,* and *Niagara.* Perhaps best known for the production *Bus Stop* and the hysterical comedy classic *Some Like It Hot,* in which she starred with Jack Lemmon and Tony Curtis, Monroe was a sad, insecure, and fragile character, albeit one that was also highly intelligent, quick witted, and possessed of superb memory skills and a deep appreciation of world politics. Unfortunately, she also had an all-consuming dependency on prescription drugs, including barbiturates and tranquilizers,

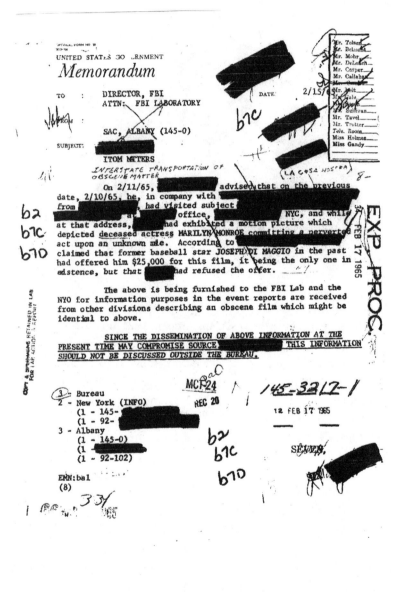

OPTIONAL FORM NO. 10

UNITED STATES GOVERNMENT

Memorandum

TO : DIRECTOR, FBI
ATTN: FBI LABORATORY

DATE: 2/15/65

FROM : SAC, ALBANY (145-0)

SUBJECT: ████████

ITOM MATTERS
INTERSTATE TRANSPORTATION OF
OBSCENE MATTER

On 2/11/65, ████████ advised that on the previous
date, 2/10/65, he, in company with ████████
from ████████ had visited subject ████████
at ████████ office, ████████ NYC, and while
at that address, ████████ had exhibited a motion picture which
depicted <u>deceased</u> actress MARILYN MONROE committing a perverted
act upon an unknown male. According to ████████
claimed that former baseball star JOSEPH DI MAGGIO in the past
had offered him $25,000 for this film, it being the only one in
existence, but that ████████ had refused the offer.

The above is being furnished to the FBI Lab and the
NYO for information purposes in the event reports are received
from other divisions describing an obscene film which might be
identical to above.

SINCE THE DISSEMINATION OF ABOVE INFORMATION AT THE
PRESENT TIME MAY COMPROMISE SOURCE ████████ THIS INFORMATION
SHOULD NOT BE DISCUSSED OUTSIDE THE BUREAU.

3 - Bureau
2 - New York (INFO)
  (1 - 145-
  (1 - 92-
3 - Albany
  (1 - 145-0)
  (1 - ████
  (1 - 92-102)

EMN:bal
(8)

Mr. Tolson
Mr. Belmont
Mr. Mohr
Mr. DeLoach
Mr. Casper
Mr. Callahan
Mr. Conrad
Mr. Felt
Mr. Gale
Mr. Rosen
Mr. Sullivan
Mr. Tavel
Mr. Trotter
Tele. Room
Miss Holmes
Miss Gandy

145-3212-1

12 FEB 17 1965

SENT.

many of which were provided to her by Dr. Ralph Greenson, a noted psychoanalyst to the Hollywood glitterati.

High-profile marriages to well-known left-wing playwright Arthur Miller and to baseball star Joe DiMaggio, as well as numerous affairs with some very influential and powerful characters in entertainment and politics, including the Kennedy brothers, John and Robert, were all part and parcel of the life of the woman who loved to be loved.

Monroe would also become the subject of FBI files that, collectively, reached no fewer than three figures in number. Appropriately, like Monroe herself, the FBI's file on the actress is a veritable steaming-hot potato of sex, political intrigue, rumor, innuendo, and, ultimately and with complete and utter finality, death.

The first real inkling of official interest in Marilyn Monroe on the part of Hoover's all-powerful agency came about in August 1955. On the fifteenth of the month, in an FBI document titled "Visit of Soviet Farmers to the U.S., 1955," Monroe is said to have received an invitation to attend a reception at the Soviet embassy, "in honor of the Soviet Agricultural Delegation," which was making a planned visit to the United States later that month.

If the idea of one of America's most well-known and glamorous celebrity figures being invited to the Soviet embassy was not enough to irk the Red-hating J. Edgar Hoover, the events of four days later certainly were. It was on August 19 that, in Hoover's eyes, the actress committed the ultimate sin of all sins: she requested a visa to visit Communist Russia. Never one to ignore anything of a Soviet nature, the FBI swung into action, and the frantic tapping of typewriters resonated around the walls of FBI headquarters as bureau agents sought to quickly ascertain and record the facts and to distribute them to other, senior sources within the Intelligence community, including Dennis A. Flinn, the director of the Office of Security at the State Department; William F. Tompkins, the assistant attorney general; and none other than the director of the Central Intelligence Agency (CIA).

The Soviets were keeping the matter of Monroe's application "under consideration," according to the FBI. Seventy-two hours later, the FBI issued a document concerning Monroe's activities, the contents of which are unfortunately, but nevertheless intriguingly, completely blacked out under provision B1 of the Freedom of Information Act. Notably, B1 is a piece of legislation that specifically covers national security issues. And thus was born the FBI's secret surveillance file on Marilyn Monroe.

What began as a folder containing just a few scant pages eventually grew into a packed dossier on the star and her regular links to the Communist world. Indeed, Monroe's fraught relationship with officials of the U.S. government was hardly improved when, in April 1956, Hoover learned, much to his consternation, that the screen star had been seen in New York in the company of Milton Greene, a photographer, who the FBI believed to be a "party member."

FBI documentation of that period details a wealth of background data on Greene and his career, as well as his friendship with Monroe, all evidence of the fact that the FBI was not only watching Monroe's every move, but the movements and activities of those she worked with, met with, and socialized with. There can be absolutely no doubt that at least a part of the reason why Monroe was placed under official surveillance by the FBI was because of her June 29, 1956, marriage to noted playwright, Arthur Miller. A November 2, 1956, FBI document reveals detailed background data on Miller:

Arthur Asher Miller was born on October 17, 1915, in New York, New York. Miller, a playwright, is the author of the play "Death of a Salesman." On June 29, 1956, he was married to Marilyn Monroe, motion-picture actress. Miller has been reported to have been a member of the Communist Party (CP) in the 1940's and to have been associated with numerous communist-dominated organizations from 1946 to

1950. He testified before a subcommittee of the Committee on Un-American Activities, United States House of Representatives, Washington, D.C., on June 21, 1956. Miller admitted having attended 5 or 6 meetings of CP writers in 1947 but denied having been under CP discipline. In response to a question concerning whether he had signed an application to join the CP Miller testified that in 1939 or 1940, he had signed what he thought to be an application for a study course in Marxism but that he did not know the exact nature of the application. He refused to discuss activities of any other individuals and was, therefore, on July 25, 1956, cited for contempt of the House of Representatives, United States Congress. Contempt of Congress is an offense subject to criminal prosecution.

On August 12, 1958, the nation learned that the "full nineman bench of the United States Court of Appeals today reversed the contempt of Congress conviction of playwright Arthur Miller, husband of actress Marilyn Monroe." Even though the very first entry in the FBI's file on Monroe makes it abundantly clear that it was secretly sharing its data on the actress with the CIA, today the agency emphatically and officially denies having *any* data or documentation on file that pertains to the actress. Needless to say, with the director of the CIA himself listed on the distribution list of the FBI's records on Monroe as far back as 1955, this is a manifestly and truly laughable stance for the CIA to take. At an unofficial level, however, there is intriguing evidence at our disposal suggesting that the CIA was not only intimately aware of Monroe's activities, but, in the late 1950s, had even considered utilizing her considerable sexual skills in a bizarre psychological warfare operation.

Anthony Summers, a noted authority on Monroe has stated that: "During the shoot of *Bus Stop*, in 1956, Marilyn had met the Indonesian president, Achmed Sukarno. . . . She would tell her friend Robert Slatzer that she and Sukarno had 'spent an evening together.'" On the issue of official interest in Marilyn Monroe, Summers has revealed that, "Whatever occurred at the original meeting, it had not gone unnoticed at the Central Intelligence Agency. In those years, Indonesia loomed as large as Vietnam in Washington's view of Asian priorities. In 1957 and 1958, the record shows, the CIA had engaged in all sorts of skullduggery aimed at dislodging Sukarno, who was seen as responsible for his country's drift toward communism.

"Later, however, when the United States needed to curry favor with Sukarno, the CIA dreamed of using sex—in the shape of Marilyn Monroe—to make the dictator feel honored."

While the true story of the CIA's relationship to Marilyn Monroe in the late 1950s remains unresolved, over at the FBI the surveillance continued unabated. On March 6, 1962, FBI personnel reported to Hoover that Monroe was vacationing in Mexico with some distinctly controversial characters:

MARILYN MONROE, the movie actress, was recently in Mexico on vacation and while in Mexico associated closely with certain members of the American Communist Group in Mexico (ACGM). Source characterized the ACGM as a loose association of a predominantly social nature of present and/or past members of the Communist Party, USA, and their friends and associates who share a common sympathy for Communism and the Soviet Union.

Imagine the look of consternation that must surely have crossed the face of J. Edgar Hoover when he learned that Monroe and an unnamed individual directly tied to the ACGM were developing a "mutual infatuation" that quickly "arose" between the two. Whoever the lucky lefty was, his relationship with the star reportedly caused "considerable dismay" to her entourage, "and also among the ACGM." Marilyn Monroe, the definitive American sex symbol, having sex with a commie? Not only that, but one who had "sympathy" for the Soviet Union? Inevitably, while Monroe was in Mexico, the secret surveillance of her activities increased both suddenly and dramatically. And practically her every movement, and those of her entire entourage, were carefully scrutinized by the hidden eyes of the FBI, as the following document makes clear. It also implicates some noted and powerful figures in the saga, too:

On 2/21/62 [Deleted] visited Monroe in her suite (#110) at the Hotel Continental Hilton at 5:00 P.M. The visit was arranged through New York friends and was based on his former friendship with ARTHUR MILLER, her former husband. He stayed about an hour and she agreed to go with [him] on 2/23/62 to Toluca, Mexico, for the day. Monroe arrived in Mexico on 2/19/62 from Miami. Her entry into Mexico reportedly was arranged by FRANK SINATRA through former President MIGUEL ALEMAN. She was accompanied by an agent, a hairdresser, and an interior decorator. The latter was identified as EUNICE CHURCHILL, a widow about 65 from Los Angeles. . . . She is a part time interior decorator and also claims to be an assistant of Dr. WEXLEY, Monroe's analyst. According to CHURCHILL, Monroe was much disturbed by ARTHUR MILLER's marriage on 2/20/62 and feels like a "negated sex symbol." CHURCHILL said that subject "has a lot of leftist rubbed off from MILLER." Monroe reportedly spent some time with ROBERT KENNEDY at the home of the PETER LAWFORDs in Hollywood. Monroe reportedly challenged Mr. KENNEDY on some points proposed to her by MILLER.

But it was the revelation that Monroe was developing a serious relationship with an unnamed member of the ACGM that really concerned the FBI:

On 2/25/62, EUNICE CHURCHILL said that Dr. WEXLEY did not like what was happening in the relationship between Monroe and [Deleted] and said that Monroe must get out with other people at once. She said Monroe is very vulnerable now because of her rejection by ARTHUR MILLER and also by JOE DI MAGGIO and FRANK SINATRA.

Churchill further advised that Monroe had telephoned Sinatra while in Mexico, but that he had declined to "come and comfort her," which is decidedly odd; most men would surely have immediately jumped at the chance to "comfort" Marilyn Monroe. The document then continues with a wealth of data on various parties and functions that Monroe had attended during her overseas trip, including "a reception for Princess [sic] Antonio de Braganza of Portugal." FBI agents closed the document, noting that: "Information copies of this communication are being directed to Los Angeles and New York as it contains information on activities of possible interest to those Divisions."

Although the FBI has been very careful to deny us access to the name of the Mexican individual Monroe was so enamored with, Anthony Summers states that the man was Jose Bolanos, a Mexican scriptwriter ten years Monroe's junior, who would shortly thereafter accompany the screen star to Hollywood for the Golden Globe Awards, and where she deservedly received a Golden Globe under the World Film Favorites category.

Of particular concern to Hoover and the FBI was the fact that just as Monroe was moving in circles with a heavy Communist bent, she was getting closer and closer to the Kennedy brothers, John and Robert, or as they were better known, the president of the United States of America and the attorney general. This is borne out in a document of July 18, 1962, in which two unnamed informants confidentially advised the bureau that not only had Monroe recently met the president, but that the issue of American politics was an integral part of the meeting:

Monroe said she had luncheon at the PETER LAWFORDs [*sic*] with President KENNEDY just a few days previously. She was very pleased, as she asked the President a lot of socially significant questions concerning the morality of atomic testing and the future of the youth of America. EUNICE MURRAY [Monroe's assistant] was in constant attendance upon Monroe. MURRAY is noncommittal politically but does not care how politically involved with leftist movements other persons with whom she associates may be and encourages Monroe toward "political consciousness." She says Monroe still reflects the views of ARTHUR MILLER.

What is particularly illuminating about this document is that it not only describes Monroe as "very positively and concisely leftist," but it also reveals that some within the FBI believed that Monroe was being "actively used by the Communist Party." Of course, if Monroe had been either an unwitting or witting player in a covert Communist-based plot, the motivation behind which was to get close to the president and potentially uncover some of the United States' most guarded secrets, as intelligence agents certainly feared was the case, then this could have led to a disaster of unmitigated proportions. As a result, twenty-four hours later, the FBI's Domestic Intelligence Division also began voicing its concerns about Monroe's associations with President Kennedy, as well as her "leftist" views. Whatever the truth of the matter, a month later, it no longer mattered.

Marilyn Monroe died on August 5, 1962. The circumstances and theories surrounding the death of the actress are as multifaceted as are the circumstances and theories surrounding the death of JFK himself, a little more than a year later.

Whatever the real picture, the FBI was keenly aware of rumors suggesting a sexual relationship between RFK and the actress. Robert Kennedy had himself acknowledged the rumors, if not the affair, in the following document generated by the FBI on August 20, 1962, and only days before the death of the actress:

The Attorney General was contacted and advised of the information we have received alleging he was having an affair with a girl in El Paso. He said he had never been to El Paso, Texas, and there was no basis in fact whatsoever for the allegation. He said he appreciated our informing him of it; that being in public life the gossipmongers just had to talk. He said he was aware there had been several allegations concerning his possibly being involved with Marilyn Monroe. He said he had at least met Marilyn Monroe, since she was a good friend of his sister, Pat Lawford, but these allegations just had a way of growing beyond any semblance of the truth.

Down to earth assertions suggest that the death of the always emotionally fragile actress was merely the result of a tragically inevitable suicide, and nothing else. In the wake of the controversial death of Monroe, however, the FBI file on her continued to grow and grow. Almost twelve months later, a document titled "PHOTOPLAY ARTICLE CONCERNING MARILYN MONROE'S DEATH" was prepared for the attention of former bureau assistant director, Cartha DeLoach. It began: "Walter Winchell's column in the July 8, 1963, issue of the 'New York Mirror' contained the statement, 'Photoplay's current article on the man who 'killed' Marilyn practically names him.' "

The FBI document simply presents a summary of Winchell's article, the key points of which were that the man "responsible" for Monroe's untimely end was, "happily married and has children; you can see him in a crowd and reach out and touch him; he is a great man, famous, known the world over; that he can be seen on television and in movie theaters; people look up to him and consider his wife and children lucky; he is mentioned almost daily in newspapers and magazines; and he is considered a 'truly honorable man.' "

The FBI added that, "The article states that she telephoned

the man on Sunday night, August 5, 1962, and when he said he would not leave his wife and could not see Miss Monroe 'any more,' she swallowed a 'handful' of sleeping pills. The article claims she later called the man again, implying that she told him of having taken the pills, only to have him hang up on her and states that the last sound she heard was the 'buzzing of the receiver in her hand,' after the man broke the telephone connection."

The FBI report concluded by stating that Monroe's second husband, Joe DiMaggio, "is the only one who remains faithful and that the man who killed Miss Monroe is still at large and can never be arrested. But, the article asserts, 'Wherever he goes, whatever he touches, whomever he sees; he thinks of Marilyn. His guilt never leaves him, his fear has become his friend.' "

In internal memoranda, the FBI noted that, in reality, the article came "no way near identifying anyone." However, for many people the references to the unnamed person being "a great man, famous, known the world over," who could be "seen on television and in movie theaters," and who was "mentioned almost daily in newspapers and magazines," *did* lead to intense and widespread speculation that the person concerned was none other than Robert F. Kennedy, the attorney general of the United States. In fact, rumors of a link between Monroe and RFK continued to reach the FBI on a regular basis. On January 20, 1965, for example, a resident of Winter Haven, Florida, contacted the FBI to say that they had read a "pamphlet" titled "Suicide or Murder?" "pertaining to the death of Marilyn Monroe and connecting her name with the former Attorney General." And while J. Edgar Hoover was quick to advise the letter writer that he could not comment at all on the allegations contained within the pamphlet, an internal memo generated as a result of the inquiry stated that "An alleged relationship between the Attorney General and Marilyn Monroe has come to the Bureau's attention previously."

Another document that alleged a link between the attorney general and the Hollywood star, and that had been written by an unidentified source, surfaced shortly after the *Photoplay* article, and was subsequently sent to the FBI by a "former Special Agent, who is currently Field Representative, Appointment Section, Governor's Office, State of California."

Paul Kirton, who worked as a private investigator in Los Angeles in the 1950s and 1960s, claims that the document in question was actually prepared by a "Hollywood investigator who had been hired by CIA" to look into "the people Marilyn was mixing with." While the FBI's field representative in California stated that he was not in a position to "evaluate the authenticity" of the three pages of the raw material, it certainly makes for illuminating reading. Given the fact that, according to Paul Kirton, the lengthy document was officially prepared for unknown sources within the CIA and relates what is purported to be the true story concerning Monroe's affair with RFK, as well as the supposedly real circumstances surrounding her early demise, its contents are reproduced in full below:

Robert Kennedy had been having a romance and sex affair over a period of time with Marilyn Monroe. He had met her, the first date being arranged by his sister and brother-in-law, Mr. and Mrs. Peter Lawford. Robert Kennedy had been spending much time in Hollywood during the last part of 1961 and early 1962, in connection with his trying to have a film made of his book dealing with the crime investigations. He used to meet with producer Jerry Wald. He was reported to be intensely jealous of the fact that they had been making a film of John F. Kennedy's book of the PT boat story.

Robert Kennedy was deeply involved emotionally with Marilyn Monroe, and had repeatedly promised to divorce his wife to marry Marilyn. Eventually Marilyn realized that Bobby had no intention of marrying her and about this time, 20th Century Fox studio had decided to cancel her contract. She had become very unreliable, being late for set, etc. In addition, the studio was in financial difficulty due to the large expenditures caused in the filming of "Cleopatra".

The studio notified Marilyn that they were canceling her contract. This was right in the middle of a picture she was making. They decided to replace her with actress Lee Remick. Marilyn telephoned Robert Kennedy from her home at Brentwood, California, person-to-person, at the Department of Justice, Washington, D.C. to tell him the bad news. Robert Kennedy told her not to worry about the contract—he would take care of everything. When nothing was done, she again called him from her home to the Department of Justice, person-to-person, and on this occasion they had unpleasant words. She was reported to have threatened to make public their affair. On the day that Marilyn died, Robert Kennedy was in town, and registered at the Beverly Hills Hotel. By coincidence, this is across the street from the house in which a number of years earlier his father, Joseph Kennedy, had lived for a time, common-law, with Gloria Swanson.

Peter Lawford [deleted] knew from Marilyn's friends that she often made suicide threats and that she was inclined to fake a suicide attempt in order to arouse sympathy. Lawford is reported as having made "special arrangement" with Marilyn's psychiatrist, Dr. Ralph Greenson, of Beverly Hills. The psychiatrist was treating Marilyn for emotional problems and getting her off the use of barbiturates. On her last visit to him, he prescribed [illegible] tablets, and gave her a prescription for 60 of them, which was unusual in quantity, especially since she saw him frequently.

Her housekeeper put the bottle of pills on the night table. It is reported the housekeeper and Marilyn's personal secretary and press agent, Pat Newcombe, were cooperating in the plan to induce suicide. Pat Newcombe was rewarded for her cooperation by being put on the head of the Federal payroll as top assistant to George Stevens, Jr., head of the Motion

Pictures Activities Division of the U.S. Information Service. His father, George Stevens, Sr., is a left-wing Hollywood director, who is well known for specializing in the making of slanted and left-wing pictures. One of these was the "Diary of Anne Frank".

On the day of Marilyn's death, Robert Kennedy checked out of the Beverly Hills Hotel and flew from Los Angeles International Airport via Western Airlines to San Francisco, where he checked into the St. Francis Hotel. The owner of this hotel is a Mr. London, a friend of Robert Kennedy. Robert Kennedy made a telephone call from St. Charles Hotel, San Francisco, to Peter Lawford to find out if Marilyn was dead yet. Peter Lawford had called Marilyn's number and spoke with her, and then checked again later to make sure she did not answer. Marilyn expected to have her stomach pumped out and to get sympathy through her suicide attempt. The psychiatrist left word for Marilyn to take a drive in the fresh air, but did not come to see her until after she was known to be dead. Marilyn received a call from Joe DiMaggio, Jr., who was in the U.S. Marines, stationed at Camp Pendleton, California. They were very friendly. Marilyn told him she was getting very sleepy. The last call she attempted to make was to Peter Lawford to return a call he had made to her. Joe DiMaggio, Sr., knows the whole story and is reported to have stated when Robert Kennedy gets out of office, he intends to kill him. [Deleted] knew of the affair between Robert Kennedy and Marilyn.

While Robert Kennedy was carrying on his sex affair with Marilyn Monroe, on a few occasions, John F. Kennedy came out and had sex parties with [Deleted], an actress. Chief of Police Parker, of the Los Angeles Police Department, has the toll call tickets obtained from the telephone company on the calls made from Marilyn's residence telephone. They are in his safe at Los Angeles Headquarters. Florabel Muir, the columnist, has considerable information and knowledge of the Robert F. Kennedy and Marilyn Monroe affair. She personally saw the telephone call records. Marilyn Monroe's psychiatrist, although he knew she had taken the pills, did not come to her home until after she was dead. He made contact with the coroner and an arrangement was made for a psychiatric board of inquiry to be appointed by the coroner, an unheard of procedure in the area. This was so the findings could be recorded that she was emotionally unbalanced. It was reported this arrangement was to discredit any statements she may have made before she died.

During the period of time that Robert F. Kennedy was having his sex affair with Marilyn Monroe, on one occasion a sex party was conducted at which several other persons were present. Tape recording was secretly made and is in the possession of a Los Angeles private detective agency. The detective wants $5,000 for a certified copy of the recording, in which all the voices are identifiable.

The issue of who Marilyn Monroe called, as well as who called her on the night of her mysterious death, is still a matter of extreme controversy. Notably, according to *Crime Library,* "Marilyn received several more phone calls that evening, including one to her part-time lover, Jose Bolanos. Bolanos claimed that Marilyn revealed, 'something shocking to him that would shock the whole world' in a phone call at about 9:30 p.m. During the conversation, Marilyn laid down the phone without hanging up because she heard some kind of disturbance at her door. He never heard from her again."

On February 16, 1965, an FBI document was secretly prepared that contained some truly explosive data. Titled "Interstate Transportation of Obscene Materials" and marked for the attention of FBI director Hoover and the FBI's laboratory, its author, an FBI agent whose name now languishes in obscurity thanks to the

restrictions of the Freedom of Information Act, recorded some remarkable data:

On 2/11/65, Source advised that on the previous date,
2/10/65, he, in company with [an unidentified individual]
had . . . exhibited a motion picture which depicted deceased
actress MARILYN MONROE committing a perverted act on
an unknown male. According to Source, he claimed that former baseball star JOE DIMAGGIO in the past had offered
him $25,000 for this film, it being the only one in exis-
tence, but that Source had refused the offer. The above is
being furnished to the FBI Lab and the NYO [New York Of-
fice] for information purposes in the event reports are received from other divisions describing an obscene film which
might be identical to above. It is noted that . . . on February 9, 1965, agents of the Albany and New York Divisions
conducted a surveillance of him. The results of this surveillance bore out information furnished by source and further,
based on contact with source, the New York Division has
opened a new Potential Confidential Informant case in New
York City and personally acquainted with numerous high
ranking LCN members there. Since the dissemination of
above information at the present time may compromise
source this information should not be discussed outside the
Bureau.

Without doubt this was a wild story. But was it true, or was it
merely the result of someone planning a wild con? Astonishingly,
there are good indications that the film was indeed the real deal.
First, the reference, and the alleged response, of Joe DiMaggio rings
true; the man was without doubt fiercely protective of his wife's reputation and particularly so after her death. And the idea that he
would have been willing to pay out no less than $25,000 to protect
that same reputation seems not so strange at all. But perhaps most

notable was not so much the data that the FBI's source had imparted on the priceless footage, but the FBI's response to its investigation of the source of the sensational story himself. Noting that bureau agents had, "conducted a surveillance of him," the FBI came away highly impressed by the man, even suggesting that he be offered a position as a "new Potential Confidential Informant."

Evidently, the FBI had learned something about its mysterious source that led it to view him as a valuable and worthwhile asset whose identity and activities had to remain carefully protected. Ultimately, the movie did not surface. However, taking into consideration the fact that, to the less-than-liberated FBI of the 1960s, and based upon a study of a wide range of additional FBI documentation generated during that time, the term "perverted act" was a euphemism for that most dastardly and devilish of all acts, a blowjob, we are faced with the startling possibility that someone, somewhere, is still sitting upon this priceless piece of cinematic Hollywood-head.

Only five months later, on July 12, 1965, the FBI obtained further information that had a bearing on the multifaceted sex life of Monroe, and that once again implicated the brothers Kennedy in her life: "[Deleted], age 40, has considerable information concerning sex parties which took place at the Hotel Carlyle in NYC, and in which a number of persons participated at different times. Among those mentioned were the following individuals: Robert F. Kennedy, John F. Kennedy, Peter Lawford, Marilyn Monroe."

Eight years later, the death of Marilyn Monroe was still causing problems for the FBI, albeit not for Hoover, who had passed away in 1972. A document dated July 23, 1973, titled "Norman Mailer—Information Concerning" and prepared for the higher echelons of the FBI, revealed that author Mailer would be addressing the controversial death of Monroe in his "soon-to-be-published biography on the deceased actress."

Of particular concern to the FBI was the fact that Mailer was going to suggest in his new book, titled *Marilyn*, that " 'right-wing'

FBI and CIA Agents had a 'huge motivation' to murder Marilyn Monroe in order to embarrass the Kennedy family, claiming the FBI and CIA were furious with the Kennedys because following the Bay of Pigs invasion President Kennedy was moving to limit the power of these agencies. Mailer has admitted in recent press interviews concerning his book that he has no evidence to support his theory and that it is based on his 'writer's instinct' and on speculation."

The FBI also noted that a "second allegation purportedly contained in the book" was that, in 1962, "FBI Agents in Los Angeles went to the telephone company in Santa Monica, California, and removed a 'paper tape' of Marilyn Monroe's telephone calls, some of which according to Mailer, were presumably to the White House or White House staff on the night of her death." The FBI's records stressed that this was "false" and that "neither the files of the Los Angeles Office nor FBI Headquarters indicate the existence of any such tapes." Indeed, the FBI was not at all impressed by either Mailer or his claims:

Norman Mailer is an eccentric but well-known author, who in the past has won a Pulitzer Prize and a National Book Award. He admits to little or no research concerning his speculation about Marilyn Monroe's death. He states his motive in writing the book is his dire need for money. He admits having no evidence to support his theory of FBI or CIA involvement and uses it to sensationalize his book and to gain publicity. Mailer has even coined a new word which describes some of his speculative writing in "Marilyn." The "factoid" he defines as "an event which has no existence other than it has appeared in print."

Aside from a few scant pages, there ends the FBI's file on Marilyn Monroe. However, in addition to the officially declassified files on the actress, a number of *unauthenticated* documents have surfaced that claim to add significantly to the story of Marilyn

Monroe's relationship to the Kennedys and her knowledge of classified government secrets. By far the most controversial piece of questionable documentation concerning Marilyn Monroe surfaced at a press conference in 1995 from Milo Speriglio, an investigative author now deceased, who wrote three books on Monroe's death: *The Marilyn Conspiracy*; *Marilyn Monroe: Murder Cover-Up*; and *Crypt 33: The Saga of Marilyn Monroe*. Incredibly, according to the document, allegedly leaked by a government insider to a California-based researcher of UFOs named Timothy Cooper, President John F. Kennedy had guardedly informed Monroe that he had secret knowledge of the notorious "crashed UFO" incident at Roswell, New Mexico, in July 1947. "I had [the document] probably about two months before I did anything with it. I looked at it and said, 'Marilyn Monroe and aliens, no way,'" explained Speriglio at the press conference.

The bulk of the document's contents focuses its attention upon telephone conversations between Howard Rothberg, the former owner of a New York-based antique store, and Dorothy Kilgallen, the well-known celebrity gossip columnist of the 1950s and 1960s, who was herself the subject of a 167-page FBI file. According to Speriglio: "[Rothberg] also dealt with a lot of photographers who used to film Marilyn. He got a lot of information about her from them, and he would feed it to Dorothy Kilgallen." The document, dated only two days before Monroe's death on August 5, 1962, tells the whole, remarkable story:

Rothberg discussed the apparent comeback of [Marilyn Monroe] with Kilgallen and the break up with the Kennedy's. Rothberg told Kilgallen that [Monroe] was attending Hollywood parties hosted by Hollywood's elite and was becoming the talk of the town again. Rothberg indicated in so many words, that [Monroe] had secrets to tell, no doubt arising from her trysts with the President and the Attorney General. One such "secret" mentioned the visit by the President at a secret air base for the purpose of inspecting things from outer space. Kilgallen replied that she knew what might be the source of the visit. In the mid-fifties Kilgallen learned of a secret effort by US and UK governments to identify the origins of crashed spacecraft and dead bodies, from a British Government official. Kilgallen believed the story may have come from the New Mexico area in the late forties. Kilgallen said that if the story is true, it would cause terrible embarrassment for Jack [Kennedy] and his plans to have NASA put men on the moon.

[Monroe] repeatedly called the Attorney General and complained about the way she was being ignored by the President and his brother.

[Monroe] threatened to hold a press conference and would tell all.

[Monroe] made references to bases in Cuba and knew of the President's plan to kill Castro.

[Monroe] made reference to her "diary of secrets" and what the newspapers would do with such disclosures.

Donald Wolfe's book, *The Assassination of Marilyn Monroe*, presents this document as possible evidence that the government was watching Monroe to an extent that went far beyond that described within the pages of her declassified FBI file. Wolfe omits the UFO references in his book, but does state that "Rothberg was Kilgallen's interior decorator and . . . was a friend of Ron Pataki, a syndicated drama critic for the Scripps-Howard newspaper in Columbus, Ohio, where Pataki was a long-time friend of Robert Slatzer.

"Pataki . . . remembers two calls that Slatzer received from Marilyn shortly before she died. It may have been the last part of July or the first of August when Marilyn called, Pataki stated. 'I was at Bob's and answered the phone and they spoke for a long time. After Bob hung up I knew he was upset and I asked him what was wrong. He told me Marilyn was having trouble with the Kennedys.' "

The document continues to provoke controversy more than a decade after it surfaced, with some researchers believing it to be a smoking gun of cosmic proportions; while other investigators maintain that it is nothing more than an outrageous, albeit ingenious, hoax.

Three years after this document first appeared, controversial stories about Marilyn Monroe and secret files were still circulating. On March 16, 1998, Lawrence Cusack III was arrested and charged with mail fraud for selling papers that he said proved President John F. Kennedy had an affair with Marilyn Monroe. United States Attorney Mary Jo White unsealed the charges that alleged Cusack had defrauded dozens of investors from around the country of six to seven million dollars for ownership shares of letters and notes that purported to be in Kennedy's handwriting.

According to the story, Cusack claimed to have in his possession hundreds of documents relating to the Kennedy family, Monroe, and Chicago mob boss Sam Giancana, that he had found within the files of his father, Lawrence Cusack Sr. A lawyer who died in 1985, Cusack Sr. had handled the affairs of Monroe's mother, Gladys Baker, from 1980 to 1984, the year in which the latter had died. Cusack had provided acclaimed author Seymour Hersh with seemingly genuine looking documents demonstrating that Kennedy had secretly bought Monroe's silence about their alleged affair by setting up a trust fund for her mother. The documents were due to play a key role in Seymour Hersh's book, *The Dark Side of Camelot*, but Hersh deleted the chapter before publication because he felt the authenticity of the documents had been convincingly challenged.

Cusack's lawyer, Thomas Sargent, told CNN at the time: "My client expects to plead not guilty and the government still has to prove their claims." The Government's claims *were* proven, and on October 15, 1999, United States District Judge Denise Cote of

New York sentenced Cusack to ten years in prison and ordered him to pay back the multimillion-dollar figure in restitution.

That then is both the official and unofficial story of Marilyn Monroe. We may never know for certain if the behind-closed-doors dalliances of the actress with the likes of JFK and RFK, and her links with the world of Communism, led to her downfall and ultimately to a state-sponsored murder, or if she simply died alone and tragically in a moment of depression. But of one thing we can be certain: the legend of the ultimate Hollywood bombshell will continue to live on for as long as gentlemen prefer blondes.

Rudolf Nureyev

"Interviewing agents noted a strong odor of cheap toilet water."

A Cold War tale that involves a Soviet defector, a cryptic message hidden in a Californian hotel room, secret agents, international espionage, sexual intrigue, and the involvement in the affair of a world-famous celebrity might sound like the perfect ingredients for a bestselling Robert Ludlum novel. But the strange events of early 1964 that implicated none other than the renowned Russian ballet dancer, Rudolf Nureyev, in the weird saga were far from fictional. In fact they were all too deadly real. It all began on April 8, 1964, when the San Francisco office of the FBI forwarded a document to Washington, D.C., titled "Nureyev—Espionage" that was marked for the attention of both Hoover and the bureau's Technical Laboratory. According to the document, an employee of the Hyatt House Hotel at Salinas, California, had found a hand-printed note hidden in a "heavy plaster wall plaque" in room 110 of the hotel on March 18.

The note, the FBI recorded, read:

F B I

Date: 4/28/64

Transmit the following in _____
(Type in plain text or code)

Via _____AIRTEL_____AIR MAIL_____
(Priority)

TO: DIRECTOR, FBI

FROM: SAC, LOS ANGELES (105-16578) (RUC)

RE: UNKNOWN SUBJECT;
           (FIRST NAME UNKNOWN) NUREYEV
           ESPIONAGE - X
           OO: San Francisco

           Re San Francisco airtel 4/8/64. (U)

           ████████████████████████████ Shrine Auditorium
Los Angeles, California, on 4/22/64 advised SA ████████
████████ that the British Royal Ballet appeared at the
Shrine Auditorium June 28, 29, and 30, 1963 and July 2
and 3, 1963. They appeared at the Hollywood Bowl July 5,
6, and 7, 1963 and were booked into the United States
by Hurok Productions, 427 West 5th Street, Los Angeles,
California. ████████ had no information concerning the
departure of the members of this group from Los Angeles,
but some of the members stayed at the Ambassador Hotel in
Los Angeles. ████████ stated that in some way he had heard
that RUDOLF NUREYEV is now in Canada. (U)

           On ████████ Hurok Productions (conceal identity as ████ is an
established source), advised SA ████████████ that the
British Royal Ballet was in Los Angeles on the dates
indicated by ████████████ advised that RUDOLPH NUREYEV,

3 - Bureau
1 - New York (Info) (AM)
2 - San Francisco
     (1 - 105-15785)
     (1 - 105-14151)
2 - Los Angeles
WCP:cem
(8)

REC- 51   65- 68730-4

12 APR 30 1964

ALL INFORMATION CONTAINED
HEREIN IS UNCLASSIFIED
DATE 4/23/97 BY SP2 ACM/eul

Approved: _____   Sent _____ M   Per _____
          Special Agent in Charge

72 MAY 8 1984

"Nureyev: I made contact with the agent at M.L.S. and he agreed that we should wait before we attempt to 3689Q01427. I hope you find the note as you requested I put it here on 7–19. I really don't approve of your hiding place, it is rather conspicuous."

The Hyatt House Hotel employee had advised the bureau that "she was taking a plaque, made of plaster cast material with figurine design, from the wall when the note fell to the floor. The back of the figurine area has indentations, which would afford a place to conceal and hold the paper." Recognizing that this was likely to be a reference to none other than Rudolf Nureyev, who had defected to the West in 1961 while in Paris, Hoover's finest quickly launched an investigation.

Things did not look good at all for the pirouetting marvel when Hoover was advised that the subject matter of the note was very possibly a highly sensitive military installation:

It is believed possible that the abbreviation M.L.S. refers to Monterey Language School which is a general term used frequently to refer to the Defense Language Institute—West Coast Branch (DLI), which was formerly known as the Army Language School at Monterey, California. This installation is located approximately 20 miles from the Hyatt House Hotel in Salinas, California. It is known that the Communist bloc intelligence agencies have in the past expressed an interest in the activities at the school.

This led Hoover to wonder if Nureyev's defection to the West was really as innocent as it seemingly appeared to be at first glance. Or, was the dancer, in reality, operating as a deep-cover agent, intent on uncovering classified American defense secrets for his Soviet masters back at the Kremlin? And, if so, was the secret penetration of the Defense Language Institute at Monterey

Nureyev's first, or worse still, *latest*, assignment? Hoover wanted answers, and he wanted them quickly.

The investigation was stepped up a notch and FBI special agents quickly returned to Salinas to speak with the employee that had originally found the coded note. Most frustrating to the FBI was the fact that the employee had told agents that, although the room in question was located "in a section of the hotel which is infrequently rented as it is near the highway and located in the building most distant from the hotel office," access to the room could have been made by "any present or past maid, bellboy, or other employee of the hotel."

The FBI was also advised of another issue that would make it very difficult to identify the person involved:

Many keys to the rooms have inadvertently or intentionally been kept by guests and it is highly possible that a previous guest failed to turn in the room key and still has a key in his possession. Also the hotel has run short on room keys on occasion and allowed guests to use pass keys without specifically being told that they had in their possession a pass key. It would be common knowledge for any guest or employee to realize that the building in question was almost never rented and, therefore, make it possible for a person with a key to go in and out of the room with very little fear of being seen.

The fact that practically anyone and everyone who had worked in the hotel, or who had stayed within the confines of the offending room, could have been the culprit, was both vexing and taxing to the FBI. But that was nothing compared to the consternation that circulated within the FBI after it was discovered that Nureyev *was* indeed in California in July 1963, the very month that the coded letter was supposedly left for him by his mysterious contact. The FBI noted this in a brief memo to Hoover: "By communication dated July 8, 1963, the Los Angeles Office advised that RUDOLF

NUREYEV had last danced with the Royal Ballet at the Hollywood Bowl, Los Angeles, California, on 7–5–63 and was scheduled to depart separately from other members of the troop for New York."

As a result of this very disturbing revelation, the FBI did its best to try and determine if the writer of the strange letter had left any telltale clues concerning his or her identity. As a result, the original letter was made available to experts at the FBI's laboratory, who made handwriting comparisons with known "suspects or subjects in espionage investigations," and took steps to ascertain when the note was written.

While staff at the FBI laboratory was kept busy on that particular task, Hoover ordered Los Angeles-based special agents to conduct an investigation at the Shrine Auditorium, "or the booking agency which handled the Royal Ballet visit to Los Angeles in June, 1963 in an effort to establish the itinerary of Rudolf Nureyev after he completed that engagement."

"It is of particular interest," Hoover added, "to know if Nureyev departed from Los Angeles en route to San Francisco by auto in July, 1963, as the Hyatt House Hotel is located on Highway 101 and might be a logical stop between the two cities." And Hoover had even more tasks lined up for his agents as he sought to get to the bottom of this potentially serious affair. He ordered his personnel to "identify the hotel where Nureyev stayed during his visit to the Los Angeles area and obtain any outgoing telephone calls made from his room between 6–29–63 and the date he left the Los Angeles area."

Hoover also decided to dispatch agents to speak to numerous people who were acquainted with Nureyev: "New York and Washington Field Divisions will contact any logical sources who might have knowledge of circumstances surrounding Nureyev's defection and interview them for observations as to the possibility that he may be involved in espionage activity."

By the end of April 1964, the FBI's laboratory had completed its study of the curious note. Unfortunately, the study of its makeup and content was a complete failure: "No indented writing was found; specimen was tested in an effort to determine the approximate date the note was hand printed with negative results. The age of this writing does not appear to be determinable by these means. No secret writing was found on specimen."

Hoover wasn't about to let a suspected Red spy get the better of him, however, and the investigation was taken to the next level. Five weeks later, the FBI had a lead, and agents returned to the Hyatt Hotel where the cloak-and-dagger events had kicked off months before and displayed for the chief informant a photograph of a source whom the FBI had determined (precisely how remains unknown) was potentially involved in the murky saga. Although this line of inquiry ultimately led nowhere, by mid-June, the FBI was following yet further leads. One heavily redacted document referenced a source who the FBI believed might have been none other than the person who had written the note:

[Source] was interviewed at his residence at [Deleted], California. At the outset he was queried concerning his knowledge of Rudolf Nureyev, a ballet dancer who defected from the Kirov (Leningrad) Ballet in Paris, France.

He stated he is most desirous in cooperating with the United States Government, and should he recollect further incidents which he feels to be of interest to the United States Government, he would bring them to the attention of the appropriate agency. He stated that he has never met Nureyev. He was shown the original copy of a note addressed to Nureyev which had been found at the Hyatt House Hotel in Salinas, California.

On seeing the note, he stated that the handprinting [sic] looked identical to his, but he said that he definitely did not write the note. He noted that up until recently he had used a Shaffer Cartridge Refill Pen, which wrote similar to the pen which was used in writing the note.

But, FBI agents quickly determined, there did seem to be nefarious duplicity at work, and Hoover was informed of this fact:

Interviewing agents noted, however, that in furnishing a sample of his handwriting [he] deliberately attempted to disguise his printing by printing in lower case letters, and he was requested to use capitals on the second specimens. The specimens were done by him in a relaxed manner and are probably the truest sample of his printing. He was obviously shaken on observing the note on the Hyatt House stationery and made the spontaneous statement that the printing thereon looked just like his. He stated that he is very fond of the Russian people but heartily disapproves of their system of government. He stated he would be receptive to further contact by representatives of the United States Government.

Potentially of some significance is the fact that the mysterious source provided the FBI with names that, he advised, might be able to assist in the investigation of what had really gone on that day at the Hyatt House Hotel. Interestingly, more than forty years after the affair began, the FBI refuses to make those names public, and it is specifically withholding them under exemption B1 of the Freedom of Information Act, which covers national security issues and American defense secrets.

Somewhat amusingly, Hoover was also advised that as far as the interviewing FBI agents were concerned, the man in question had some particular character traits that they felt honor bound to report to their master: "Interviewing agents noted that he was residing with another male in an apartment which had a strong odor of cheap toilet water. His manner appeared effeminate. When given an opportunity to indicate that he was or was not a homosexual, he evaded the issue. It was also noted that there was only one bed in the apartment shared by two males."

More serious, however, was the fact that by late June 1964, and despite the fact that the FBI now had a source who had, at least, provided a few potential leads, the whole saga still remained inconclusive. Worse, after a comparison was made between the handwriting on the letter found at the Hyatt Hotel and that of the unnamed interviewee, the FBI laboratory came to the conclusion that "the note may not have been written by [the interviewee]."

Since it now looked like the prime suspect in the case might not have been the letter writer after all, FBI special agents engaged in the case recommended to J. Edgar Hoover, in a document of September 1, 1964, titled "Recommendations," that the investigation should "be closed in the absence of significant information in Bureau files." And it was without Hoover being able to determine if Rudolf Nureyev was really a Soviet spy.

Though the investigation might have come to an end, the file on Nureyev certainly didn't. For example, an FBI report of June 7, 1972, contained within the Nureyev file and titled "Cossack Espionage" is almost completely deleted under U.S. national security laws, other than the sentence: "Source learned that Nureyev has a boyfriend and is a homosexual." Similarly, FBI files on Nureyev from 1975 are also almost completely blacked out, again specifically for national security reasons. That we do not have complete access to this material is both unfortunate and troubling. And, although many who knew Nureyev openly scoffed at the idea that the dancer was a Russian mole, it is intriguing that as far as the FBI was concerned, after the unresolved events of 1964 at the Hyatt House Hotel, Salinas, Hoover forever viewed the activities of Rudolf Nureyev with deep suspicion.

Rudolf Nureyev died in Paris on January 6, 1993, from the effects of AIDS at the age of fifty-four.

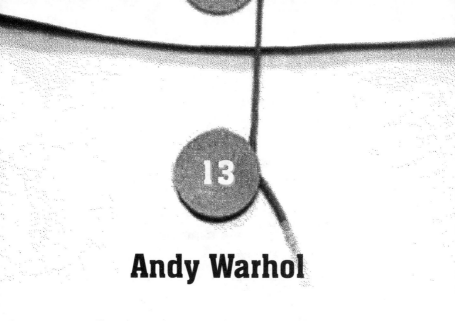

Andy Warhol

"A third male actor was trying to
stick his hat up her rectum."

Born in Pittsburgh in 1928 to Slovak immigrants, Andrew Warhola
would find both fame and fortune decades later as Andy Warhol.
After completing his high school education, the young Warhol
studied commercial art at the Carnegie Institute of Technology in
Pittsburgh, and having graduated in 1949, he relocated to New
York where he was employed as an illustrator for both *Vogue* and
Harper's Bazaar. In the 1950s, Warhol began dying his hair blond,
and in later years he took to wearing his famous blond and silver
gray wigs. His first one-man show was held at the Hugo Gallery in
New York in 1952, and four years later he had an important group
exhibition at the renowned Museum of Modern Art.

But Warhol really began to make his name when he formulated
plans for his now famous prints and designs of varied and sundry
items, including Campbell Soup cans and Coke bottles. And as
Warhol's stature grew, he became a celebrity figure on the New
York art scene, particularly when he started making silkscreen prints

1

Date_____ 2/21/68

_____ Oracle, advised that
he lives in Oracle, Arizona. He owns a horse. On January
27 or 28, 1968 he received a phone call from_____ in
Oracle, Arizona, asking if he had a horse that could be used
in a film that was being made at the Rancho Linda Vista
Guest Ranch at Oracle, Arizona. The movie company would pay
$10.00 for each horse. The movie company rented one horse
from him and two horses from_____

He and_____ arrived at the Rancho Linda Vista
Guest Ranch about 12 Noon. The movie cameras were all set up
at the corral at the guest ranch. He and_____ hung
around about one hour before they started to use their horses.

The first scene taken was at the corral where three
men rode in on the three horses. One man was sitting on the
corral fence. They had a pistol and a lever action rifle.
The second scene was of three different men on the same horses.
One man was sitting on the corral fence. Their conversation
was being recorded. They then went and ate.

About 3 PM another scene was being filmed at the
corral. This scene had a tall, slender blonde wearing tight-
fitting purple silk pants and blouse. She was riding on a____
_____ Bay horse. All of the men, about eight, were sitting
around on the ground on the bank of the wash. The girl on
the Bay gelding rode up among the men and said, "Get off my
ranch". She had a riding quirt. The men got up and pulled
the girl off the horse. They took off all of her clothes
consisting of a blouse, pants, boots, and panties. She had
no bra. She was naked. One man had her panties struck over
his hat and was wearing them.

A blond, curly headed male then unzipped and pulled
down his pants. This same man then performed an unnatural sex
act of Cunnilingus on the female. The other male individuals
held the girl down. She did very little struggling. She and
the male actors continued to use profane and vulgar words
during their sexual activity. The spontaneous conversation

-12-

On __2/15/68__ at __Oracle, Arizona__ File # __Phoenix 145-230__

by __SA _____ Date dictated __2/19/68__

of personalities and icons like Marilyn Monroe and Elizabeth Taylor. In 1962, Warhol founded the Factory, a New York art studio where he mass-produced his celebrated prints and posters.

Six years later, near tragedy struck when Warhol narrowly escaped death after being shot in the chest by a woman named Valerie Solanis, who had undertaken occasional work for him in the Factory. The founder, and indeed sole member, of a group known as SCUM, the wonderfully titled Society for Cutting Up Men, Solanis justified her actions when she was arrested by stating, "He had too much control over my life."

As someone whose life and career were often embroiled in controversy, it is not surprising that Warhol's actions attracted the attention of people in government, most notably in 1968 when his path crossed with that of none other than the FBI. It was the bureau's deep interest in Warhol that ultimately led it to generate some of the most bizarre and unintentionally hysterically amusing secret documents that ever found their way to the office of J. Edgar Hoover.

The weird story began when an attempt was made to get Warhol prosecuted on charges of "Interstate Transportation of Obscene Matter" after he drove from Arizona to New York with footage of a movie that he had begun producing in early 1968 called *Lonesome Cowboys*. The settings for this masterfully absurd piece of cinematic erotica were the eighty-acre Rancho Linda Vista Guest Ranch in the town of Oracle, Arizona, and Old Tucson, which, at the time, was still used for filming Westerns, including the *Death Valley Days* television series.

According to the FBI agents involved in the investigation of Warhol, on February 21, 1968, a source from the town of Ray, Arizona, whose name the FBI has deemed must remain withheld from public scrutiny to this day, had advised them that he had received a phone call at his home from an employee of the Rancho Linda Vista Guest Ranch at Oracle, Arizona, who stated that a movie was being made at the guest ranch, and that he should "come over and watch it because he couldn't believe what they were doing."

The man duly arrived at the guest ranch about 1:00 PM where, the FBI said, "Everyone was gathered around the corral area. They were taking various shots and poses. They had sound equipment recording all the conversation. The language was vulgar and 'hippish.' " The FBI files then became distinctly surreal in both nature and content, as the following extract makes abundantly and amusingly clear:

One fellow, described as a white male, American 5' 7", 145 pounds, 32 to 35 years of age, with receding hairline and a large head stated that he enjoyed sexual relations with a horse more than he did with a man or a girl. The man with the receding hairline and large head was on a horse and another man was up in a tree hanging by his feet and was kissing this large-headed man on the lips.

One might be forgiven for thinking that references to apparently deformed human beings with oversized heads that had a penchant for sex with animals were indicative of Warhol's attempts to make a low-budget precursor to *Deliverance*. Indeed, all that was seemingly missing were deranged banjo-playing freaks. But this was not the case. The FBI continued its report on the escalating sexual frenzy that Warhol had unleashed upon sleepy Arizona:

[A source] stated that one of the male actor's picture and VIVA's (last name unknown) picture appeared in the Phoenix paper about two or three weeks ago. VIVA, the man whose picture was in the paper, the bigheaded man and a fourth individual said to the spectators, "Give us the script, tell us what to do." The cameras were running and the film was in the lower part of the corral. The girl, VIVA, was wearing purple pants and shirt. The male actors in the film tackled the girl and threw her to the ground among the dirt, rocks and horse manure. One of the actors yelled, 'Strip her.' Three of the male actors took her clothes off. There were about thirty spectators around watching the filming. It was about 2PM in the afternoon.

In a typically humorless fashion, the FBI noted that, according to their informant, "One of the male actors was performing an act of cunnilingus on the girl, Viva, who was on the ground. A second man was licking her breasts. A third male actor was trying to stick his hat up her rectum. A fourth actor was exposing himself and had his trousers dropped to his knees and trying to have Viva perform an act of fellatio on him."

Precisely what J. Edgar Hoover, as well as the "thirty spectators" who had descended upon the ranch from the surrounding area to gleefully watch the afternoon's entertainment, thought of this rectal-probing-by-cowboy-hat saga remains mercifully unclear. In a similar matter-of-fact style, the FBI recorded that, "It appeared that all of the individuals, or some of them, had reached a sexual climax," while also carefully noting that "the men cooled off and wrestled among themselves."

Viva, said the FBI, "just sat on the ground alone, naked, for about five minutes. She then got up and got dressed and went into the house." Stressing that their informant had told them that Viva was "vulgar and foul in her talk," the FBI agents reported that, "During the time of the sexual acts she yelled so all the spectators could hear, 'I have fucked half of you here and none of you are a good fuck.' She then said, 'There is not enough of your prick to be a good fuck.'"

Born Susan Hoffman on August 23, 1938, in Thousand Islands, New York, Viva was raised with her eight siblings in Syracuse, where her father was an important criminal lawyer. She attended Marymount College, which was a Catholic college in Tarrytown, New York, and moved to Paris during her junior year to study art at the renowned Sorbonne. Viva first met Andy Warhol in 1963 at an art gallery opening, and at a time when, according to Warhol, she was "living with a photographer and trying to become a fashion illustrator." Then, in August 1967, Viva approached Warhol at a party given by fashion designer Betsey Johnson, and asked if she could be in his next movie: *The Loves of Ondine*. Warhol agreed, and the next day she was on set. Three more films followed quickly: *Bike Boy*, the truly excitingly titled *Tub Girls*, and *Nude Restaurant*. Then came *Lonesome Cowboys*, and the rest, as they say, is history.

Having advised Hoover of the apparently less-than-spectacular attempts of the male actors to satisfy Viva, the FBI agents concluded the document: "One of the actors had flown out from New York City to take a part in this movie. He had played in two or three other Warhol movies. He was a doorman at a theater in New York City. He stated that this was the 'most way out' of any of the Warhol films." With that statement, the FBI had no argument. But how had Warhol and his crew come to descend upon Oracle, Arizona? The FBI wanted the answers, and found them.

On March 22, 1968, agents recorded the background to how the controversy had kicked off in the first place:

[The co-owner of the] Rancho Linda Vista Guest Ranch, Oracle, Arizona . . . stated that the arrangements for the ANDY WARHOL films to come to their Guest Ranch was made through the University of Arizona Art Department, and she understood that it was to be a Swedish movie company. There was a total of 14 men and one girl, VIVA, who stayed at the Guest Ranch. But did not have a complete list of all 15 people but had a partial list furnished.

The woman added that in "cabin 33" were two men, one being Warhol, and the other unnamed individual, who she "believed to be lovers." Hoover was advised, "They both slept in the same bed." Indeed, the woman had much more to impart to the FBI, as the following report demonstrates:

[The man] who slept with Andy Warhol, acted like a big sissy
and did not take part in the movie. He wore ankle-strap
thongs. [Another] was a doorman somewhere in New York
City, New York, and belonged to a theatre group. [A third
man] was a sculptor. One of the men had a closet full of
women's clothing in his room. . . . She observed the girl,
VIVA, naked and several of the hippie-type cowboys dragging
her in the corral near the water tank. She became quite
upset and nervous over this incident.

Ankle-strap thongs, a big sissy who shared a bed with Warhol,
and hippie-type cowboys: the plot was definitely thickening.
Meanwhile, the FBI was doing a bit of corralling itself; it sought to
track down just about anyone and everyone at the ranch in an effort to shed as much light as possible on the day's events. As evidence of this, declassified FBI memoranda reveal that an
interview had been conducted with a source from the town of Oracle who was able to provide further pieces to the story, and who
had some direct input in Warhol's movie.

"He owns a horse," Hoover was informed. In fact, the horse became an integral part of both the movie and the FBI documentation,
particularly so when the horse displayed what was perceived to be apparent prudish outrage at certain "unnatural sex acts" taking place on
set. We might speculate that the FBI had in its midst an animal lover,
who was concerned by the predilection for bestiality on the part of
the "big-headed man," and desired to make Hoover aware of the fact
that the horse was definitely not having a happy time. The FBI supplied for Hoover the facts, as related by the man with the horse:

On January 27 or 28, 1968, he received a phone call asking
if he had a horse that could be used in a film that was being
made at the Rancho Linda Vista Guest Ranch at Oracle, Arizona. The movie company would pay $10.00 for each horse.
The movie company rented one horse from him . . .

He arrived at the Rancho Linda Vista Guest Ranch about 12 noon. The movie cameras were all set up at the corral at the guest ranch. He hung around about one hour before they started to use their horses. The first scene was at the corral where three men rode in on the three horses.

About 3PM another scene was being filmed at the Corral. This scene had a tall, slender blonde wearing tight fitting purple silk pants and blouse. She was riding on [a] Bay horse. All of the men, about eight, were sitting around on the ground of the bank of the wash. The girl on the Bay gelding rode up among the men and said, "Get off my ranch." She had a riding quirt. The men got up and pulled the girl off the horse. They took off all of her clothes consisting of a blouse, pants, boots, and panties. She had no bra. She was naked.

One of the men, the outraged FBI agents noted, "had her panties struck over his hat and was wearing them." The absolute decadence continued unabated:

A blonde, curly headed male then unzipped and pulled down his pants. This same man then performed an unnatural sex act of Cunnilingus on the female. The other male individuals held the girl down. She did very little struggling. She and the male actors continued to use profane and vulgar words during their sexual activity. The spontaneous conversation was recorded and their acts filmed. After about one minute the female got up and sat in the wash. She folded her arms over her bare chest. Somebody later threw her blouse and trousers over her back. She then put her trousers and blouse back on.

The FBI was always vigilant to ensure that nothing was omitted from this particular episode. The document noted that "The man continued to wear her panties over his hat." The fiend. Amusingly, the FBI's source was careful, and who knows, perhaps even proud, to stress to the FBI that "his horse broke loose about the time the unnatural sex acts took place." With the big-headed animal lover lurking, this was perhaps a wise move on the creature's part. And with the tale related to Hoover of how the sexually repressed horse had fled the scene, never to return, the FBI agents added matter-of-factly: "The men played with each other's rear ends. One had flowers sewed on the seat of his trousers in the shape of a diamond." The stern and straight-laced FBI special agents were most definitely not impressed.

The surreal and amusing aside, the matter became far more serious for Warhol when the FBI was able to determine that a number of minors were present on the set, as the following document of March 22, 1968, demonstrates:

[Source], 15 years of age, was contacted at his residence in Oracle, Arizona on March 18, 1968. He was contacted in the presence of his mother. He stated that he had been at the Rancho Linda Vista Guest Ranch on Sunday afternoon, January 28, 1968, and observed an obscene movie being filmed. He watched the entire thing and was alone. He stated that he desired to discuss the filming alone with the Interviewing Agent at his home. His mother agreed to this interview. He stated that he was not embarrassed to discuss what he had seen but did not wish to discuss it with his family. He had not told anyone what he had observed. He went around the corral at the Rancho Linda Vista Guest Ranch when he saw about six or seven young men pull the girl, VIVA, off a horse. She rode in with a riding whip in her hand. She hit at them with the whip. These young men pulled her off the horse, ripped her clothes all off and she was naked. She was thrown to the ground. One young man jumped on top of the naked VIVA and began to suck her breast. Another young man put his face and head in between her legs. She let them do this to her. They did this for about 10 minutes. After it was over with she got up, put her clothes on and left. He did not see any of the male actors take their clothes off.

The interviews, and the descriptions of the afternoon's activities, kept on coming:

[Source], 18 years of age, living at the Rancho Linda Vista Guest Ranch, advised March 18, 1968, that on Saturday, January 27, 1968, he was with his 15-year-old sister, when he observed the ANDY WARHOL Movie Company take some films of six or seven naked young men. He and his sister were about 30 feet away when they were taking film of the naked boys lying in some sleeping bags in a rocky wash nearby. The naked young men were in pairs in the sleeping bags. They took these films from a short distance and then moved up real close to take some close movies and would not let them watch. The close movie filming went on for about one hour. He gathered the idea that these naked men were doing acts of sexual perversion. They used very foul language. He stated that night they made a film inside one of the cabins for about one hour and would not let them watch. On March 18, 1968, he observed a pair of men's shorts in the rocky wash where the movie was made and stated that the men had been walking around naked and these shorts must have been left by one of them at the time of the filming on January 27, 1968.

With the FBI now snooping around, and the outraged parents of Oracle concerned by the fact that their children were present at the filming of a semihomoerotic porno flick, it was perhaps inevitable that Warhol and his team would find their time in town severely curtailed. And as Warhol himself later stated: " Eventually, the grips, the electricians, and the people who built the sets formed a vigilante committee to run us out of town, just like in a real cowboy movie. We were all standing on the drugstore porch, except for Eric [Emerson], who was doing his ballet exercises at the hitching post, when a group of them came over and said: 'You perverted easterners; go back the hell where you came from.' "

And so they did. However, it was Warhol's decision to drive from Oracle, Arizona, back to his New York home with the offending film footage in tow that led the FBI to believe that there was a very good chance of prosecuting Warhol under legislation governing the "Interstate Transport of Obscene Matter." That would take some time, however, and the FBI determined that the best course of action was to keep a careful and continuous watch on Warhol and his various activities. They did, and things only proceeded to get much worse for Warhol.

In June 1968, the Department of State sent the FBI a telegram that linked Warhol with the one group that bureau boss Hoover despised and hated more than any other: commies. Prepared by the American Embassy in Warsaw, Poland, the telegram outlined the facts:

Graphics Designer Saul Bass (Protect Source), American Member [of] Warsaw Poster Biennale Jury, told EMBOFF [Embassy Official] American Pop Artist Andy Warhol won one of three first prizes this week at insistence [of] Soviet jury member Orest G. Wierejski. Warhol poster had been tentatively picked for a second prize but Wierejski said it was best entry of a major poster trend (pop art) and should so be recognized by jury. His insistence carried the day, Bass said.

Wierejski's action, to say least, does not square with more normal practice of not awarding top prizes to Americans in Bloc cultural competitions. Other two first prizes were won by Pole and Japanese. Two other American entries won honorable mentions.

The fact that Bass had specifically stressed to American officials that "Wierejski's action . . . does not square with more normal practice of not awarding top prizes to Americans in Bloc cultural competitions," inevitably raised suspicions deep within the FBI that Warhol was either a communist sympathizer, or that, at the very least, the Reds had their own obscure reasons for bestowing such an award upon Warhol. So now in addition to the FBI, both the State Department and the American embassy in Warsaw, Poland, were collating data on Warhol.

As the files demonstrate, copies of those documents were also being shared with senior officials at the American embassy in Moscow, Russia. Available documentation does not reflect the outcome of this aspect of the surveillance of Warhol, however. Nevertheless, the surveillance was far from over.

Five months later, and specifically on November 1, 1968, Warhol's *Lonesome Cowboy* movie was finally ready for its debut screening. Two very heavily disguised FBI agents showed up for a cozy "midnight showing" of the production at the San Francisco Film Festival that was being held at the Masonic Auditorium, and an in-depth summary was provided for Hoover. The FBI's finest were most definitely not impressed—neither by the production nor the stars of the movie:

The characters in the film were a woman, played by VIVA; her male nurse, played by TAYLOR MEAD; a sheriff who resided in a small Arizona town—population, three; and a group of about five cowboys with an additional new member called "Boy Julian." All of the males in the cast displayed homosexual tendencies and conducted themselves toward one another in an effeminate manner. Many of the cast portrayed their parts as if in a stupor from marijuana, drugs or alcohol. It appeared that there was no script for the film but rather the actors were given a basic idea for a plot and then instructed to act and speak as they felt.

Worse was to come for the straight-laced FBI agents who had to endure Warhol's surreal piece of work:

The movie opened with the woman and her male nurse on a street in the town. Five or six cowboys then entered the town and there was evidence of hostility between the two groups. One of the cowboys practiced his ballet and a conversation ensued regarding the misuse of mascara by one of the other cowboys. At times it was difficult to understand the words being spoken, due to the poor audio of the film and the pronunciation by the actors. The film also skips from scene to scene without continuity.

And the antics of the ballet-dancing, mascara-wearing cowboys had barely begun:

As the movie progressed, one of the actors ran down a hill. The next scene showed a man wearing only an unbuttoned silk cowboy shirt getting up from the ground. His privates were exposed and another cowboy was lying on the ground in a position with his head facing the genitals of the cowboy who had just stood up. A jealous argument ensued between the cowboy who was observed running down the hill and the one wearing the silk shirt. The man in the silk shirt was then seen urinating; however, his privates were not exposed due to the camera angle. Later in the movie the cowboys went out to the ranch owned by the woman. On their arrival, they took her from her horse, removed her clothes and sexually assaulted her. During this time her private parts were exposed to the audience. She was on her back with her clothes removed and an actor was on his knees near her shoulders with his face in the vicinity of her genitals; but a second actor with his back to the camera blocked the view. The position of the male and female suggested an act of cunnilingus;

however, the act was not portrayed in full view of the camera. At the end of this scene the woman sat up and said, "Now look—you have embarrassed those children." There were no children in the movie.

Certainly the biggest indignity suffered by the FBI agents that had to watch *Lonesome Cowboys* was the portrayal of one of their own, namely a law-enforcement officer, in this case the local sheriff, who was portrayed canoodling in one particular scene with a male nurse. Even worse still in the eyes of the FBI, was the fact that Warhol had committed the heinous and unforgivable crime of portraying the town's sheriff as an outrageous transvestite:

There are other parts in the film in which the private parts of the woman were visible on the screen and there were also scenes in which men were revealed in total nudity. The sheriff in one scene was shown dressing in woman's clothing and later being held on the lap of another cowboy. Also, the male nurse was pictured in the arms of the sheriff. In one scene where VIVA was attempting to persuade one of the cowboys to take off his clothes and join her in her nudity, the discussion was centered around the Catholic Church's liturgical songs. She finally persuaded him to remove all of his clothes and he then fondled her breasts and rolled on top of her naked body. There were movements and gyrations; however, at no time did the camera show penetration or a position for insertion. Another scene depicted a cowboy fondling the nipples of another cowboy. There were suggestive dances done by the male actors with each other. These dances were conducted while they were clothed and suggested lovemaking between two males.

Evidently, the FBI agents relished their role as movie reviewers, since the final entry in the document provides a brief summary of their thoughts and conclusions: "There was no plot to the film and no development of characters throughout. It was rather a remotely connected series of scenes which depicted situations of sexual relationships of homosexual and heterosexual nature. Obscene words, phrases and gestures were used throughout the film."

Despite the fact that the FBI had initially assumed that there were good grounds for believing that a successful prosecution of Warhol could be achieved, it was not to be. In December 1969, officials in Arizona, New York, and Georgia unanimously "declined prosecution." The reason being that despite the presence of the large-headed horse lover, the unnamed actor wildly running around with a woman's panties on his head, the unnamed big sissy who invaded Oracle, and the group of men who insisted on playing with "each other's rear ends," according to the FBI, "at no time did the camera show penetration." And on this unique technicality, Warhol successfully, and very luckily, avoided all prosecution.

Warhol continued to be a prime mover on the New York art scene in the years that followed, and he died on February 22, 1987, as a result of complications from gallbladder surgery. His life was not a long one, but it was one that was, and still is, celebrated by millions, and his contribution to the world of art is, arguably, incalculable.

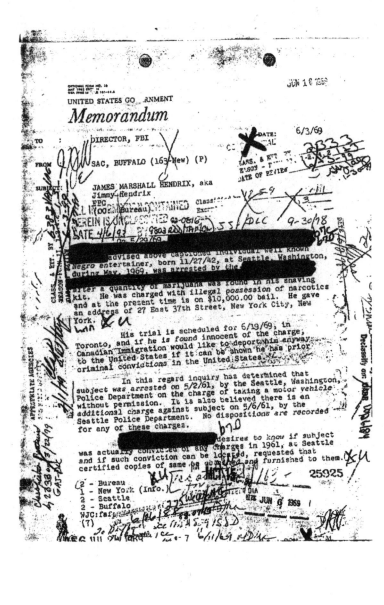

OPTIONAL FORM NO. 10
MAY 1962 EDITION
GSA FPMR (41 CFR) 101-11.6

UNITED STATES GO~~~~RNMENT

Memorandum

TO : DIRECTOR, FBI

DATE: 6/3/69

FROM : SAC, BUFFALO (163-New) (P)

SUBJECT: JAMES MARSHALL HENDRIX, aka
Jimmy Hendrix
EPC
(OO: Bureau)

ALL INFORMATION CONTAINED
HEREIN IS UNCLASSIFIED
DATE 4/6/93 BY 9803 RDD/TAM/DLC

advised above captioned individual well known
Negro entertainer, born 11/27/42, at Seattle, Washington,
during May, 1969, was arrested by the
after a quantity of marijuana was found in his shaving
kit. He was charged with illegal possession of narcotics
and at the present time is on $10,000.00 bail. He gave
an address of 27 East 37th Street, New York City, New
York.

His trial is scheduled for 6/19/69, in
Toronto, and if he is found innocent of the charge,
Canadian Immigration would like to deport him anyway
to the United States if it can be shown he has prior
criminal convictions in the United States.

In this regard inquiry has determined that
subject was arrested on 5/2/61, by the Seattle, Washington,
Police Department on the charge of taking a motor vehicle
without permission. It is also believed there is an
additional charge against subject on 5/6/61, by the
Seattle Police Department. No dispositions are recorded
for any of these charges.

desires to know if subject
was actually convicted of any charges in 1961, at Seattle
and if such conviction can be located, requested that
certified copies of same be submitted and furnished to them.

(2 - Bureau
1 - New York (Info.)
2 - Seattle
2 - Buffalo
WJC:faf
(7)

25925

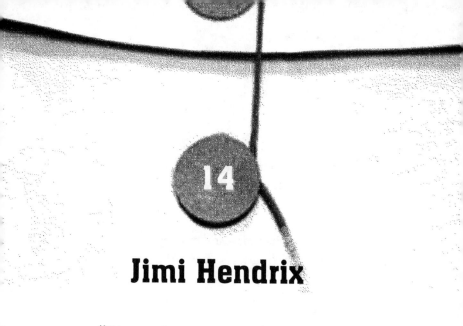

Jimi Hendrix

**"His mind cannot function while
thinking about his guitar."**

Born Johnny Allen Hendrix in Seattle on November 27, 1942,
and renamed James Marshall by his father (his alcoholic mother
having committed suicide when he was a boy), Jimi Hendrix was
undoubtedly one of the most influential and gifted electric guitarists of all time. Tracks such as *Voodoo Chile, Purple Haze, Hey
Joe, The Wind Cries Mary,* and his own, unique version of Bob
Dylan's *All Along the Watchtower* ensured Hendrix a dedicated,
worldwide following that continues to thrive to this day, more than
thirty-five years after the rocker's untimely death. A fan of music
from a young age, Hendrix had been enthralled by Elvis Presley's
performance at Sick's Seattle Stadium on September 1, 1957. And
a decade later, Hendrix had eclipsed the King himself, but not before a brief tour of duty in the military, that began on May 31,
1961, when a file was created on the man known at the time as
Private James Hendrix, United States Army.

Army documentation makes it clear that Hendrix was not exactly what the military was looking for, however. One report generated during Hendrix's short time with the army was particularly critical:

Recommendation is being submitted because: individual is unable to conform to military rules and regulations. Misses bed check; sleeps while supposed to be working; unsatisfactory duty performance. Requires excessive supervision at all times. Was caught masturbating by members of platoon. He appears to be an extreme introvert. This man has the same type problems under two squad leaders. Performance of duty in the barracks and as a supply clerk is unsatisfactory under both supervisors.

Further military documents noted that Hendrix "isn't able to carry on an intelligent conversation, paying little attention to having been spoken to. At one point it was thought perhaps Hendrix was taking dope and was sent to be examined by a medical officer with negative results. He has been undergoing group therapy at Mental Hygiene with negative results."

Evidently, Hendrix's overriding love of the guitar led to his less than enthusiastic approach to his military career. Another document generated by Hendrix's military superiors summed up this point perfectly: "Pvt. Hendrix plays a musical instrument during his off duty hours, or so he says. This is one of his faults, because his mind apparently cannot function while performing duties thinking about his guitar." It is very amusing and ironic that the army described Hendrix's obsession with his guitar as "one of his faults."

The military was also highly critical of Hendrix's apparent financial problems: "Pvt. Hendrix fails to pay just debts. He owes a laundry bill of approximately $80.00 and has made no effort whatsoever to pay it. When Pvt. Hendrix was questioned by the 1st Sergeant and myself concerning this matter, he said he had given the money to a buddy in an infantry unit to pay this debt for him. It was later proven that he had lied about this. To this date the laundry bill is still delinquent."

And once again, Hendrix's sexual habits and his love of the guitar made their way into official files: "This individual requires additional instructions and sometimes requires a supervisor to stay right on the job with him in order to get it done. Approximately 1 month ago, five other men in the billets were on detail in the billets with Pvt. Hendrix. When he was found to be missing, Sp/4 Mattox and Pvt. Stroble began to look for him and later found him in the latrine masturbating.

"Pvt. Hendrix plays a musical instrument in a band and has let this interfere with his military duties in so much as missing bed check and not getting enough sleep. He has no interest whatsoever in the Army. With the counseling and supervision he has had, it is my opinion that Pvt. Hendrix will never come up to the standards required of a soldier."

Having read the above documents, one cannot help but wonder if Hendrix's impressively high laundry bill was in any way connected with his masturbatory habits. On June 1, 1962, things went from bad to worse for Hendrix:

I, Lyndon D. Williams, 2nd Lt, Section Leader of the Supply and Evacuation Section of this unit, make the following statement concerning Pvt. James Hendrix: Since his assignment to my section, Pvt. Hendrix has shown a lack of interest and drive, and apparent inability to concentrate on an assigned task. Even the most simple instructions must be repeated several times before the task is carried out. Constant supervision is necessary to obtain even barely satisfactory results from Pvt. Hendrix. In counseling Pvt. Hendrix, his explanation is that he "has trouble keeping his mind on his work." In addition, Pvt. Hendrix has had disciplinary measures taken repeatedly for failure to repair and for other minor offenses.

Because Pvt. Hendrix has shown little improvement despite concentrated effort on the part of the platoon and company officers and NCO's, because the constant supervision that must be given him deprives other personnel and activities of needed attention, and because of the detrimental effect of his behavior on the morale and efficiency of the men of the section, I believe that Pvt. Hendrix should be eliminated from the service.

Coupled with the fact that on his twenty-sixth parachute jump he had broken his ankle, Hendrix agreed to sign his name to a document of discharge, and after thirteen months of military service, his career with the armed forces was over. But the United States Army would not be the only agency to maintain files on Jimi Hendrix.

At the height of the guitarist's career, an FBI document of June 3, 1969, titled "JAMES MARSHALL HENDRIX aka Jimmy [sic] Hendrix," demonstrates that it, too, was taking an interest in the activities of the legendary guitarist:

On 5/29/69, captioned individual, well known Negro entertainer, born 11/27/42 at Seattle, Washington, during May, 1969, was arrested by the [Canadian Police], after a quantity of marijuana was found in his shaving kit. He was charged with illegal possession of narcotics and at the present time is on $10,000 bail. His trial is scheduled for 6/19/69, in Toronto, and if he is found innocent of the charge, Canadian Immigration would like to deport him anyway to the United States if it can be shown he has prior criminal convictions in the United States. In this regard inquiry has determined that subject was arrested on 5/21/61, by the Seattle, Washington, Police Department on the charge of taking a motor vehicle without permission. It is also believed there is an additional charge against subject on 5/2/61, by the Seattle Police Department. No dispositions are recorded for any of these charges.

Two weeks later, FBI Headquarters recorded that "On June 10, 1969, a certified copy of a conviction for the above-captioned individual was obtained from the Court of Justice of the Peace, William Hoar, State of Washington, County of King, Seattle, Washington, and was forwarded to the Department of Canadian Manpower and Immigration, Toronto, Ontario, Canada."

Ultimately, things did not turn out too badly for Hendrix. Despite the fact that it is very clear the FBI was just as keen as Canadian immigration to see him prosecuted to the full force of the law, bureau documents demonstrate that Hendrix skillfully avoided prosecution and was acquitted of all charges, after it was maintained by his legal team that the offending drugs had, unbeknownst to Hendrix, been placed into his bag by an unnamed fan. Whether or not this was true mattered very little: Hendrix was safe. But still the FBI continued to watch the axe god, and particularly when it became apparent that he was due to perform at the now legendary Woodstock concert of August 1969. An FBI document on September 5, 1969, reveals that the bureau had a mole in the audience at the three-day event.

Today, it might seem strange that the FBI would want to be kept informed of the goings-on at a rock concert, but anything deemed by the FBI to be even remotely subversive—as the rock movement of that time was certainly perceived to be—was ripe for investigation and surveillance. The full report on Woodstock prepared for FBI agents reads:

During the entire festival, no arrests were made at the 600-acre site, but many arrests mainly for drug-related offenses were made on the roads leading to the site. It is also noted that due to a reported instruction from New York's Commissioner of Police, very few New York City officers actually reported for duty in the Peace Service Corps, their places being taken by off-duty officers hastily recruited in other teams in New York and New Jersey.

Entertainers at the festival included the following, Joan Baez, Arlo Guthrie, Tim Hardin, Richie Havens, the Incredible String Band, Ravi Shankar, Sly and the Family Stone, Sweetwater (Friday, August 15), Canned Heat, Credence Clearwater, the Grateful Dead, Janis Joplin, the Jefferson Airplane, Santana, the Who (Saturday, August 16), the Band, Jeff Beck Group, Blood, Sweat and Tears, Joe Cocker, Crosby, Stills and Nash, Jimi Hendrix, the Iron Butterfly, Ten Years After, and Johnny Winter (Sunday, August 17). But these were only the entertainers named in the program; the main entertainment (if that is the correct word) was provided by the bizarre people present, one with another and the unpublicized groups, chief of which was a group known as The Quarry, performing away from the main stage, before an audience of an estimated ten thousand.

The Hog Farm, a commune of hippies, now of New Mexico and formerly of New York's Lower East Side were flown in by the festival organizers, acting as an official "peace-maker between the radicals and the festival management". According to the festival's pre-program publicity, the Hog Farm were supposed to act as a supernumerary, yet official body of the Peace Security Corps, whether they did or not was never established; however they did provide thousands of free meals (boiled rice, lettuce and raisins) and when the LSD (acid) problem became acute they collected many of the worst withdrawal cases, from among the crowd and from the festival's official medical center and cared for them in a quickly constructed tee-pee, where at one time several dozen young people could be found suffering the acute disorders of drug abuse.

The Hog Farm also constructed (they are great builders) a No. 2 stage which became the center for the most uninhibited rock music, most often played by The Quarry from early afternoon until the early hours of the next day; and this music, so-called, unleashed the most unrestrained and lewd behavior. To the repetitious thudding of drums males and females would become involved in strange sexual gyrations.

Had Hendrix's life not been cut tragically short, it seems likely that his FBI file would have continued to grow. Early on the morning of September 18, 1970, Hendrix's body was found in the basement apartment of the Samarkand Hotel, London, England. He had reportedly choked to death on his own vomit after downing nine Vesperax sleeping pills. The all-too-short career of the phenomenal guitarist was over.

In one of life's ironies, however, more than thirty years after his death, the military once again crossed paths with Jimi Hendrix. It was April 2004 and the siege of Fallujah was well under way in Iraq. In an effort to annoy, irritate, and hopefully smoke out enemy snipers, psychological warfare planners at the Pentagon had the bright idea to set up huge and powerful speakers in the streets of Fallujah, where they joyfully pumped out, at ear-splitting volume, songs by Australian rockers AC/DC and none other than the long-departed Jimi Hendrix. This would seem to completely turn on its head the army's earlier comment that, "Hendrix plays a musical instrument in a band and has let this interfere with his military duties."

Perhaps deep within the bowels of the Pentagon, however, someone is still smarting about that unpaid laundry bill.

TO : Mr. Bishop   DATE: 3-9-71

FROM : M. A. Jones

SUBJECT: "ROWAN AND MARTIN'S *"LAUGH-IN"*
LAUGH-IN"
WRC-TV, CHANNEL 4
WASHINGTON, D. C.
MARCH 8, 1971

       During captioned show (beginning 8 p.m. EST) a skit concerning the FBI was performed using various regular members of this show's cast. This portion was introduced by a shorter skit representing a President and First Lady sitting in the White House chatting. Between them was a large vase of flowers. When their conversation turned to the Director, it was made obvious that one of the flowers was actually a bugging device and the President spoke directly to Mr. Hoover by means of this device.

       The longer skit was unified by means of a production-type number consisting of cheerleaders, complete with sweaters emblazoned with "FBI," who sang a "fight song" pertaining to the FBI. This "song," satirical in nature as was the rest of the skit, was interrupted by various minor skits and short gag situations all, of course, bearing on the FBI. A great deal of what purported to be humor related to the Director and his age. For example, a statement was made, "I don't believe that just because the Director of the FBI is named Hoover that there has been a vacuum in that Department for years." A particularly vicious attack was made by means of a "knock-knock" joke in which the answer to "Who is there?" is answered by "Hoover." In reply to the question "Hoover who?" a play on words is made in the statement "Hoover heard of a 76-year-old policeman?" Another sick-type joke pertaining to the Director was an announcement that "J. Edgar Hoover retired one-half hour ago but will be back at his desk first thing in the morning."

       Although, as is common practice in this show, jokes and sight gags were made in rapid fashion, emphasis in terms of subject matter was placed on surveillance-type activities and clandestine-type operations. In one minor skit, two Agents were portrayed meeting and being extremely guarded in their conversation with each other with each trying to elicit information from the other.

REC-6   94-4-2437-1304

1 - Mr. Mohr
1 - Mr. Bishop
1 - M. A. Jones

CONTINUED - OVER   4 MAR 16 1971

paa (5)

57 MAR 17 1971

Tolson
Sullivan
Mohr
Bishop
Brennan, C.D.
Callahan
Casper
Conrad
Dalbey
Felt
Gale
Rosen
Tavel
Walters
Soyars
Tele. Room
Holmes
Gandy

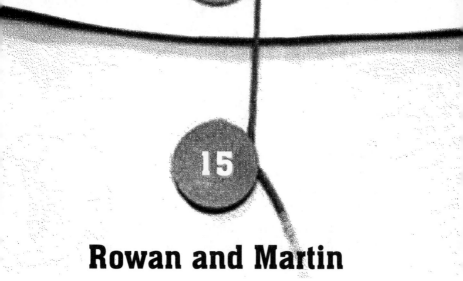

Rowan and Martin

"It's always easy to be a smart aleck."

Laugh-In, the comedy series that debuted on NBC on January 22, 1968, and that ran until May 14, 1973, turned its hosts, Dan Rowan and Dick Martin, into stars across the length and breadth of the entire United States. Although both Rowan and Martin had wide experience as comedy writers, the appeal of *Laugh-In* stemmed largely from the cast's ability to improvise rather than to read from scripts. And it was this fresh, new approach, coupled with vibrant and entertaining characters, unique skits, and memorable catchphrases that attracted a young audience and ensured the show its phenomenally successful five-year run. But not everyone was pleased by Rowan and Martin's *Laugh-In*, and least of all, the CIA and FBI. In fact, what is particularly intriguing about Rowan and Martin is the sheer number of references to the pair that can be found in intelligence files.

Dick 'n' Dan met at a restaurant in late 1951, became friends, and immediately began experimenting as a double act. But it was when Dan Rowan started a double act of a very different kind that the CIA began to take serious notice. Rowan's new double act was a secret affair with Phyllis McGuire, one of the singing McGuire Sisters and the mistress of feared organized-crime mogul, Sam Giancana. The fact that Giancana was already secretly in bed with the CIA at the time, as a result of its plans to assassinate Cuba's Fidel Castro, ensured that any developments that had a bearing on Giancana had a bearing on the CIA, too.

According to CIA files, Giancana met McGuire at one of Morris Dalitz's Las Vegas casinos and "took care of" a $100,000 debt that McGuire owed Dalitz. Needless to say, Giancana's own unique way of taking care of the situation did not involve the transfer of any money to Dalitz. Instead, Giancana told Dalitz that it would definitely be in his best interests to "forget" the debt. Unsurprisingly, Dalitz did exactly what he was told to do.

At some point around the time of the Bay of Pigs debacle (agency files are unclear on the exact date), Giancana began to act on his suspicions that McGuire was secretly seeing Rowan behind his back and was determined to uncover the truth. Both Rowan and McGuire were working in Las Vegas at the time, and as a result Giancana asked one Robert Maheu to handle the bugging of Rowan's hotel room, in an effort to catch Rowan and McGuire in the act. Maheu had joined the FBI in the early 1940s, and during the war had posed as a German sympathizer. After the close of hostilities, he established his own investigative company, and undertook "cut-out" assignments for the CIA, "cut-out" being a term of reference for those jobs deemed too sensitive and controversial for the agency to be officially allied with.

In 1960, CIA bigwigs Richard Bissell and Allen Dulles secretly formulated plans to work with the Mafia in a plot to assassinate Cuba's Castro, and Maheu was seen as the perfect man to coordinate the covert operation, which he then did. Maheu offered the job to mobster Johnny Roselli, who arranged a meeting between Maheu, Giancana, and Santo Trafficante, during which, Maheu revealed the CIA would pay the Mob $150,000 to get Castro taken care of, once and for all. Of course, history has shown that all attempts to assassinate Castro (most of which were ridiculously inept) ended in spectacular failure. But the fact that Giancana had worked alongside Maheu and trusted him to a degree at least led the crime lord to request Maheu's assistance in the Rowan-McGuire caper.

According to the CIA, Maheu declined the job and protested that he really wasn't equipped to handle it at all. A stern Giancana stated in no uncertain terms that he had helped Maheu in the Castro affair, and a favor was now due in return. Perhaps wisely, Maheu decided to modify his position: he agreed to have Dan Rowan's room bugged, but then turned the job over to a Miami-based private investigator named Edward L. DuBois, who duly assigned two men to handle the job: Arthur J. Balletti and J. W. Harrison.

Instead of installing a bug, however, which would have presumably easily recorded the sexual frenzy that Giancana correctly feared was taking place, the pair elected to just tap Rowan's telephone, while Rowan was performing on the Los Vegas stage. Inexplicably and somewhat astonishingly, Balletti, perhaps a fan of Rowan's, exited the room and went to catch the act and carelessly left all of his phone-tapping equipment in full view.

As fate would have it, a maid discovered the equipment while Balletti was watching Rowan's show. The concerned maid called the local sheriff and Balletti was arrested without delay. J. W. Harrison, meanwhile, was long gone. A frantic Balletti then phoned Maheu, who reportedly "fixed" the matter with Las Vegas authorities, thanks to the rapid assistance of mobster Johnny Roselli. However, it was Balletti's call to Maheu that tipped off the FBI to what was secretly going on.

The FBI, in turn, was determined to take action against Maheu under the wiretapping statute. When approached by the FBI, however, Maheu was fast to refer the matter to CIA Director of Security, Sheffield Edwards, who had agreed to handle things if the situation got out of hand. An FBI document outlines its involvement in the events:

Maheu claimed that he ordered coverage of Rowan on behalf of CIA's efforts to obtain intelligence information in Cuba through the hoodlum element, including Sam Giancana, which had interests there. Maheu said he was put in contact with Giancana in connection with these intelligence activities through John Roselli, a Los Angeles hoodlum. Maheu authorized wiring of Rowan's room and discussed this matter with John Roselli.

The technician involved in the assignment was discovered in the process, arrested and taken to the Sheriff's Office for questioning. He called Maheu in the presence of Sheriff's personnel and informed him that he had been detained. Subsequently the Department of Justice announced its intention to prosecute Maheu along with the technician. On February 7, 1962 the Director of Security briefed the then Attorney General Robert Kennedy on the circumstances leading up to Maheu's involvement in the wiretap. At our request, prosecution was dropped.

Of course, Maheu's version of events was not entirely accurate: the whole caper was really just a favor to Giancana, initiated to determine if Dan Rowan was having a secret affair with his girlfriend. According to the story, Roselli was seriously disturbed by the rather farcical events, but Giancana evidently "laughed so hard he nearly swallowed his cigar." That a seething Hoover was forced to back down and drop the planned prosecution of Maheu because it would open up a can of worms linking the CIA and the Mob in secret plans to assassinate Castro, however, was something that apparently amused Giancana no end.

For his part, Dan Rowan breathed a very welcome sigh of relief. Indeed, had he been recorded getting it on with Phyllis in his

Vegas hotel room, it is likely that Rowan would not have been breathing at all. To what extent Rowan had knowledge of the intelligence activities behind the scene as he merrily fornicated with the girlfriend of one of the most influential figures in organized crime is unknown.

But just as Sam Giancana apparently came to view the episode with some humor, Rowan and Martin never missed an opportunity to poke fun at J. Edgar Hoover and the FBI. Declassified FBI files reveal that the bureau received a wealth of complaints from irate viewers of Rowan and Martin's *Laugh-In,* who didn't think the pair's political jibes were in the best interests of the nation. The following letter of September 27, 1968, is a perfect example of the veritable deluge of complaints that the FBI received:

Dear Mr. Hoover,

Mr. Richard Nixon, a Presidential candidate and well-intentioned American appears on a show called "Laugh-In" for his friend Paul Keys. He says "Sock it to me" which has become a catch phrase with the young group. However, it was most controversial, anti-American, anti-establishment.

I never understood how far-reaching and long enduring the conspiracy is. I've learned the first step is to discredit, make fun of, break down, and a so-called innocent show is a very important part of their program.

And Mr. Richard Nixon who is probably the most conscious of all candidates of the great communist conspiracy goes on a show like this just to get more exposure. And prove he's a jolly fellow. What is America coming to?

I'm an American with a proud heritage, and I think there are certain things that a Presidential Candidate should and should not do, and one of them is not to "take jokes." And I know of where I talk.

One month later, on October 24, 1968, Hoover was advised of a development with regard to this letter writer:

On October 21, 1968, the above telephonically contacted the Miami Office and went on to make reference to the Rowan and Martin "Laugh-In" program and in very strong terms stated he considered this program to be seditious in nature and wanted to know what he as a citizen could do. The FBI's jurisdiction was most courteously explained to him; however, he became quite belligerent and then launched into a somewhat disjointed tirade mentioning FDR and pro-German thinking in the United States before World War II.

He indicated it was obvious to him that the FBI was not going to do anything to stop this program on television. At this point he abruptly hung up the phone.

He again called within five minutes and launched into a similar belligerent tirade and again hung up a short time later.

But it was an episode of *Laugh-In* that aired on March 8, 1971, that raised the hackles of the viewing public. Again the FBI was flooded with complaints, and Hoover's agents moved quickly to determine the facts and did so in a document titled "Rowan and Martin's Laugh-In." The bureau was far from pleased:

During captioned show a skit was performed using various regular members of this show's cast. This portion was introduced by a shorter skit representing a President and First Lady sitting in the White House chatting. Between them was a large vase of flowers. When their conversation turned to the Director, it was made obvious that one of the flowers was actually a bugging device and the President spoke directly to Mr. Hoover by means of this device.

The longer skit was unified by means of a production-type number consisting of cheerleaders, complete with sweaters emblazoned with "FBI," who sang a "fight song" pertaining to the FBI. This "song," satirical in nature as was the rest of the skit, was interrupted by various minor skits and shot gag situations all, of course, bearing on the FBI. A great deal of what purported to be humor related to the Director and his age. For example, a statement was made, "I don't believe that just because the Director of the FBI is named Hoover that there has been a vacuum in that Department for years." A particularly vicious attack was made by means of a "knock-knock" joke in which the answer to "Who is there?" is answered by "Hoover." In reply to the question "Hoover who?" a play on words is made in the statement "Hoover heard of a 76-year-old policeman?" Another sick-type joke pertaining to the Director was an announcement that "J. Edgar Hoover retired one half hour ago but will be back at his desk first thing in the morning."

Although, as is common practice in this show, jokes and sight gags were made in rapid fashion, emphasis in terms of subject matter was placed on surveillance-type activities and clandestine-type operations. In one minor skit, two Agents were portrayed meeting and being extremely guarded in their conversation with each other with each trying to illicit information from the other.

All in all, this skit pertaining to the FBI was rather typical of the poor fare which is served on this so-called laugh show, a show which has gained some considerable notoriety by its risqué jokes and irrelevant satirical attacks. Tasteless, sometimes downright vicious jokes and a great deal of forced humor add up to a more telling commentary on this low-grade show itself than on the FBI.

By March 16, the bureau had been inundated with such a mountain of complaints that FBI agents prepared yet another memorandum on the offending episode for Hoover's attention:

Briefly, the skit featured a production-type dance number consisting of cheerleaders wearing sweaters emblazoned with "FBI," who sang a "fight song" pertaining to the FBI. The entire skit was satirical in nature and featured a variety of minor skits, short gag situations and a number of inane captions which were flashed across the television screen.

It is noted that as is typical of this television program, some of the so-called jokes were not only not humorous but did not make any sense, the sight-gags were ridiculously stupid, and the "fight song" featuring the cheerleaders was to a great extent unintelligible.

While supposedly a "laugh show" the portion of the program pertaining to the Bureau, which lasted approximately five minutes, was not at all funny, was typically tasteless, and sometimes downright vicious.

In the final analysis the skit concerning the Bureau added up to a more telling commentary on the low-grade quality of this program itself rather than reflecting adversely on the Bureau. It is noted that "Laugh-In" has been steadily declining in television ratings and it is easy to understand why when you see the type of material they are attempting to foist on the viewing public in the guise of humor.

From that moment on the FBI viewed Rowan and Martin and their attempts to poke fun at the bureau and Hoover with absolute disdain that bordered upon hatred. But as with the Giancana affair in which Dan Rowan was implicated, the FBI was, to its overriding anger and dismay, powerless to act. Curiously, however, the late 1960s and early 1970s saw further links between Dan Rowan and a figure from the covert world of official espionage. In 1967, the comedian had begun a lengthy correspondence with John D. MacDonald, a mystery writer who had established his name in pulp fiction, but who from 1940 to 1946 had worked deep within the Office of Strategic Services (OSS), a forerunner to the CIA.

Those same letters, many of which covered both professional and personal matters, were later published in a book by Rowan titled *A Friendship: The Letters of Dan Rowan and John D. MacDonald, 1967-1974.*

It is unlikely that we will ever know the full story of what really went on beneath the sheets in that Las Vegas hotel room all those years ago, or what remains hidden within the many files pertaining to aspects of the Bay of Pigs affair that are to this day still classified and exempt from disclosure to the public and the media. But, having had sex with the girlfriend of one of the most powerful mobsters in recorded history, having attracted the attention of the highest echelons of the CIA, and having incurred the wrath of Hoover and the FBI, Dan Rowan lived a life that certainly no one can say was run-of-the-mill. You can "bet your bippy" on that, as his partner, Dick Martin, was so fond of saying.

October 28, 1966

ROCK HUDSON *Dr. Roy Dieth*
Summer 11/17/25 Winnetka, Ill
Calif

Rock Hudson has not been the subject of an FBI investigation. During 1965, however, a confidential informant reported that several years ago while he was in New York he had an "affair" with movie star Rock Hudson. The informant stated that from personal knowledge he knew that Rock Hudson was a homosexual. The belief was expressed that by "personal knowledge" the informant meant he had personally indulged in homosexual acts with Hudson or had witnessed or received the information from individuals who had done so. (62-110654-4)

On another occasion, information was received by the Los Angeles Office of the FBI that it was common knowledge in the motion picture industry that Rock Hudson was suspected of having homosexual tendencies.

It is to be noted in May, 1961, a confidential source in New York also stated that Hudson definitely was a homosexual. (105-128834-73)

Our files contain no additional pertinent information identifiable with Mr. Hudson.

The fingerprint files of the Identification Division of the FBI contain no arrest data identifiable with Mr. Hudson based upon background information submitted in connection with this name check request.

NOTE: Per request of Mrs. Mildred Stegall, White House Staff.

MAJ:jer/klg
(8)

Tolson
DeLoach
Mohr
Wick
Casper
Callahan
Conrad
Felt
Gale
Rosen
Sullivan
Tavel
Trotter
T. Room

MAIL ROOM ☐ TELETYPE UNIT ☐ 2 ENCLOSURE 62-5-26386

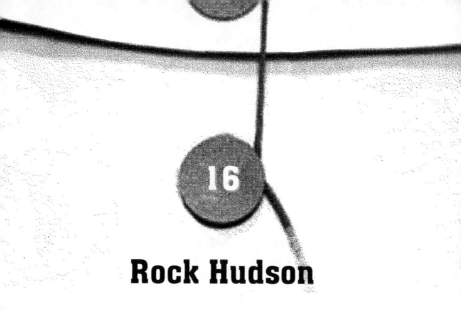

Rock Hudson

**"Prominent individuals have been revealed
as participants in these orgies."**

Born Roy Harold Scherer Jr., in 1925, Rock Hudson became one
of the biggest box-office draws of the 1950s and 1960s, thanks in
part to his role in *Giant,* in which he starred alongside screen
rebel James Dean, as well as a series of highly successful movies
with actress Doris Day. Throughout much of the 1970s, Hudson
costarred with actress Susan Saint James on the long-running
NBC television show *McMillan and Wife,* and he later played in
the TV adaptation of Ray Bradbury's sci-fi series *The Martian
Chronicles,* and the long-running soap series, *Dynasty.* But then,
on July 25, 1985, stark and shocking images of an AIDS-ravaged
Hudson were broadcast around the world, along with the revelation that the Hollywood star had for decades lived a secret, homosexual life. It was quite a surprise to his millions of adoring fans
across the globe.

But it was certainly not a surprise to the FBI. The FBI's dossier
on Hudson demonstrates, perhaps better than anything else, the

overwhelming degree of vicious homophobia that existed within the FBI at the time and that surfaced most graphically in the 1960s, when Hoover learned that the secretly gay actor was planning to portray a bureau special agent in a forthcoming movie.

As far as can be determined, the FBI first delved into Hudson's background in 1959, when two of its agents quietly paid a visit to the Sunset Boulevard offices of "star-maker" Henry Willson, whose career had begun as a talent scout for David O. Selznick, and who was almost single-handedly responsible for both creating and molding the life and the cinematic career of Rock Hudson. When asked by the FBI agents if he, Willson, was a homosexual, Willson said that no he was not, as did his assistant Pat Colby, who, according to writer Robert Hofler, "practically expired on the spot."

The FBI agents then brought up the prime motive for their visit: "We have from good authority that Rock Hudson is a homosexual." Willson vehemently denied the claims, despite the fact that the FBI agents were clearly in possession of incriminating data on Hudson, including information on a variety of his bedmates, orgies in which he had partaken, and motels where he would conduct his secret affairs.

Willson tried to diffuse the situation by pointing out that Hudson had been married to Willson's secretary, Phyllis Gates. However, Willson wisely chose not to confide in the FBI agents that many of Hollywood's elite secretly suspected that the marriage was, in fact, nothing more than a carefully orchestrated sham, designed to deflect attention away from the rumors that behind closed doors Hudson lived a gay life. Unimpressed, FBI agents duly noted that the marriage to Gates had recently ended anyway. The FBI departed, but things were far from over for Hudson.

One year later, in 1960, Hudson's name turned up in an FBI document that, in a section titled "Hollywood Vice," reported on the apparent raid of a Los Angeles establishment that was regularly engaged in arranging wild orgies for high-profile clients. "Files of guests' names were confiscated during the raid and as a result, many prominent individuals have reportedly been revealed as apparently participants in these orgies," said the FBI. Among those "participants" was none other than Rock Hudson.

Heavily redacted FBI memoranda of 1965 reveal that, on June 23 of that year, Hudson was interviewed personally at Paramount Studios by agents of the FBI as a result of its investigation into another, unnamed individual. Although FBI documentation noted that nothing of a truly derogatory nature had been uncovered about Hudson, the Los Angeles office stated in its summary report that, "it is general common knowledge in the motion picture industry that Hudson [is] suspected of having homosexual tendencies." The available documentation on this episode reveals that Hudson discussed with the bureau the whereabouts of his former wife, Phyllis Gates. Precisely why this became a factor in the interview is not made clear, however.

Nor is it made clear why no less than fourteen pages of secret FBI documentation relating to this curious episode remains—to this day—completely classified and exempt from disclosure under clause B1 of the Freedom of Information Act, a clause that specifically governs the protection of data that might seriously harm the national security of the United States of America.

Could one of Hudson's suspected sexual partners have held a position of some influence and authority in government at the time? In view of the FBI's overwhelming desire to keep this specific data firmly under wraps decades later, this possibility cannot be lightly dismissed. And particularly so when it becomes clear that in the following year, 1966, even the White House was apparently asking questions about Hudson. An October 28, 1966, letter from a source at the FBI marked for the attention of Marvin Watson, the special assistant to President Lyndon B. Johnson, included an attachment "memoranda" on Rock Hudson that stated:

Rock Hudson has not been the subject of an FBI investigation. During 1965, however, a confidential informant reported that several years ago while he was in New York he had an "affair" with movie star Rock Hudson. The informant stated that from personal knowledge he knew that Rock Hudson was a homosexual. The belief was expressed that by "personal knowledge" the informant meant that he had personally indulged in homosexual acts with Hudson or had witnessed or received the information from individuals who had done so. On another occasion, information was received by the Los Angeles Office of the FBI that it was common knowledge in the motion picture industry that Rock Hudson was suspected of having homosexual tendencies. It is to be noted in May, 1961, a confidential source in New York also stated that Hudson was definitely a homosexual.

The documentation noted that the original request from the White House had come from one Mildred Stegall, although again for reasons not elaborated upon by the FBI. Whatever the nature of this high-level exchange between the FBI and the White House with regard to the secret sex life of Rock Hudson, it still remains deeply buried within the still classified files and archives of the FBI.

We do know for certain, however, that a small article, which appeared in the September 5, 1967, edition of *Variety*, really raised the collective hackles of the FBI. The article was titled "Rock Hudson and Claudia Cardinale The Quiet Couple" and, in part, read: "Rock Hudson has been signed to co-star in 'The Quiet Couple,' to roll in Italy Nov 15. His role is that of an FBI agent who becomes involved with a jewel thief, essayed by Miss Cardinale. The pair toplined [sic] Universal's 'Blindfold,' incidentally, shot in 1965 in Italy."

Three days later, this brief and seemingly innocuous news story prompted the FBI's special agent in charge at its Los Angeles office to prepare a two-page document for the attention of J. Edgar Hoover that was titled "Portrayal of FBI in Motion Picture 'The Quiet Couple' Research (Crime Records)." It specifically outlined the facts that were then available concerning the movie—evidence that the *Variety* article was of grave concern to the crime-fighting organization.

In early October 1967, the FBI office in Los Angeles provided an update for Hoover on the making of *The Quiet Couple,* after agents began secretly making inquiries in Hollywood about the movie. Days later, the bureau learned from a confidential informant close to Hudson that, contrary to what *Variety* had reported about Hudson portraying one of Hoover's finest, this was actually an "error" and that, "the character Hudson will play is identified as being associated with the U.S. Embassy in Rome, but he is not identified as representing any agency of the U.S. Government. [The informant] believes the final script will follow the story outline in this respect."

Documentation generated on October 30, 1967, makes it quite clear that, thanks to this Hollywood informant, the FBI now knew about all aspects of the planned movie—they were even aware that Hudson was still awaiting his copy of the final script of the movie:

Neither Mr. ROCK HUDSON nor Mr. JOHN FOREMAN (HUDSON's agent) have received scripts of the motion picture "The Quiet Couple." Mr. HUDSON tentatively is scheduled to depart for Italy on 11/6/67 to appear in this film and is concerned that the script has not arrived. [Informant] said Mr. HUDSON will not leave until the script has arrived and he places his stamp of approval on the role. She said she will contact this office as soon as the script is received so that definite information concerning the role will be available.

The special agent in charge ended the memo resolutely: "Los Angeles will closely follow this matter." Ultimately, the movie *was* made. Its title, however, was changed to *A Fine Pair,* and Hudson's role became that of New York City Police Captain Mike Harmon—not that of one of the FBI's finest. One has to speculate, given the very close attention and concern paid to this affair by the FBI, if any official pressure was ever brought to bear on the production company that was making the movie to change the nature of Hudson's character. In an era when homosexuality was still frowned upon by many, the scenario of a gay man portraying an FBI agent was one not easily embraced by Hoover's minions. In view of that fact, the possibility of pressuring the production company may not be too wide of the truth.

In 1969, just two years after this episode, a serious case of déjà vu must have surely overcome a concerned FBI when it learned that the actor—or "sex offender" as he is specifically, and highly controversially, described in the 1969 documentation—was contemplating a role in *another* movie that was set to focus heavily upon the work of the FBI.

An FBI document of July 28, 1969, titled "Proposed Motion Picture Film Entitled 'Chicago 7' Based On Fictional Book Entitled 'The Seven File' Both Written By William P. McGivern," outlined the story:

Euan Lloyd Productions, Ltd, an English motion picture organization, has for some time planned a motion picture on a fictional story concerning a kidnapping case entitled "The Seven File," which was written by William P. McGivern in the mid 1950's. The screenplay has also been written by McGivern and is closely based on the book with the only basic change being the locale of the story being moved from New York to Chicago. We have been following developments with respect to this matter for a number of years.

Briefly the story involves the kidnapping for ransom of an infant daughter of a wealthy couple by two ex-convicts, a confidence man and his girlfriend. The kidnappers' plans are disrupted by the child's nurse whom they are also forced to kidnap. The infant's grandfather calls the FBI into the case despite the kidnappers' admonition not to do so. The FBI's investigation is directed by an Inspector and reflects very favorably and accurately on Bureau operations. The point is made throughout the story that the safe return of the baby and nurse is the FBI's primary interest. At the hideout where the kidnap victim is being held, the brother of one of the kidnappers innocently stumbles on the scene and is held. At the climax of the story, the kidnappers have a falling out, the con man and his girlfriend are killed by the convict, who is in turn killed by his brother. The child and nurse are returned safely.

And again, the FBI was concerned: "Our files indicate that Rock Hudson, a prominent leading man, has been alleged to be a homosexual and/or bisexual. The Los Angeles Office has been instructed to remain alert concerning all developments regarding this motion picture."

The final entry in the FBI's dossier on Rock Hudson dates from May 22, 1972, and focused its attention upon an investigation into Jack Anderson's columns in *The Washington Post*, amid bureau concerns that a source buried deep within the White House or the Secret Service was divulging classified data to the columnist. Perhaps of greater concern to the FBI, however, was the worrying fact that: "Anderson's 5/11/72 column states that 'titillating tidbits' are contained in the FBI's files of Rock Hudson." As a result of this, the bureau noted: "Efforts are continuing to identify Anderson's source for FBI material through analysis of Anderson's columns, to attempt to isolate a single document or item which might pinpoint Anderson's source."

Of course, the FBI was fully aware that its classified file on Hudson did contain "titillating tidbits" of a sexual nature from a national security perspective, and much more. But more important and most significant of all, the Jack Anderson revelations demonstrated to a concerned FBI that the columnist had a legitimate source in government who was leaking classified government secrets.

The outcome of this episode, as it specifically relates to Rock Hudson, remains inconclusive, and the FBI's interest in Hudson trailed off after the 1972 death of J. Edgar Hoover, who was known for his merciless, and unwarranted, treatment and surveillance of homosexuals. With Hoover gone, the folder on Hudson was quietly closed and resigned to the FBI's archives, where it languishes to this day.

Rock Hudson died on October 2, 1985, from AIDS-related cancer of the lymph glands.

Sonny Bono

"In the basement of the Bono residence are two machine guns."

Born in Detroit on February 16, 1935, Salvatore Phillip Bono, better known as half of the 1960s singing duo Sonny and Cher, moved to California with his family as a child and turned to songwriting after high school, supplementing his income by working as a meat-delivery driver. As a songwriter and backup singer, he worked with legendary record producer Phil Spector and the Righteous Brothers, and scored his first hit with "Needles and Pins," co-written with Jack Nitzsche, when it became a Top 20 single for the British group, the Searchers, in 1964. But it was when he teamed up with Cherilyn Sarkisian, the other half of Sonny and Cher, who Bono married that year, that his career reached stratospheric levels, particularly when the pair's worldwide hit "I Got You, Babe" was released in August 1965 and reached Number One on the *Billboard* charts.

In February 1966 Bono received what the FBI described as a "kidnapping threat" from an individual thought to reside in either

FD-36 (Rev. 5-22-64)

F B I

Date: 2/25/66

Transmit the following in _____
                          (Type in plaintext or code)

Via AIRTEL _____ AIRMAIL
                                  (Priority)

b7c

TO: DIRECTOR, FBI   ATTN: FBI LABORATORY

FROM: SAC, LOS ANGELES (7-1000)(P)

SUBJECT: UNSUB;
          SALVATORE BONO, aka
          Sonny Bono - VICTIM

          POSSIBLE KIDNAPPING

          00 - Los Angeles

500649

b7c

          On February 23, 1966, the Los Angeles Office of the
FBI received a letter addressed "Federal Bureau of Investigation,
Los Angeles, California", which contained an anonymous letter
dated 2/12/66.

          Two xerox copies of letter and envelope are being
furnished the Bureau, and one each are being furnished the
Milwaukee and Chicago Office for information, inasmuch as a
suspect may reside in either Chicago or Milwaukee. One copy
of FD-302s containing interview of SALVATORE BONO _____
_____ at Los Angeles, dated 2/24/66, is
being furnished Chicago and Milwaukee.

          Victims are commonly known as "SONNIE _____
and whose rise to national prominence in the rock-n-roll
medium has been rapid and off beat".

b7c

2 - Bureau (4 Encls.)
2 - Chicago (Info)(Encls. 2)
1 - Milwaukee (Info)(Encls. 2)
2 - Los Angeles
JGK/cmr

NEG-75   11343-

MCT-18

54 MAR 2 1966

Approved: _____ Sent _____ M Per _____
          Special Agent in Charge

Chicago or Milwaukee, and who was described as a "possible schizophrenic who is a fan." Even though the affair was definitely a traumatic one for Sonny and Cher, it ultimately died down, the threat being nothing more than the unfortunate product of a seriously deranged mind.

Other hits for the pair, including "The Beat Goes On," "It's the Little Things," "It's a Beautiful Story," and "Laugh at Me," followed, after which the pair turned its attention to television: *The Sonny and Cher Comedy Hour* ran on CBS from 1971 to 1974.

After Sonny and Cher divorced in 1974, their solo television efforts lagged, as did an attempt to revive their partnership with a new TV show in 1976. As a result, Bono all but dropped out of show business, and aside from a few guest appearances on such shows as *Fantasy Island* and *The Love Boat*, he moved into the restaurant business in Palm Springs, California.

The next inkling of FBI interest in Bono came in 1976, when on October 1, papers declassified by the FBI reflect that officials were contacted by "an anonymous caller (male)," who "claiming to be an associate of SONNY BONO (TV's Sonny and Cher), stated that as a result of having a fight with SONNY he wished to advise that in the basement of the BONO residence are two machine guns, an AK 47 and an M 60. Caller hung up before any other information could be obtained." The relevant documentation notes that the Bureau of Alcohol, Tobacco and Firearms was quickly contacted, but that no charges were ever brought against Bono, and the affair was forgotten, after the claims were found to be without foundation.

Of greater interest, however, is the intriguing fact that Bono's name turned up in documentation born out of an early 1980s FBI undercover operation called Star Quest. The operation ultimately resulted in charges being brought against the leadership of New York's Colombo crime family. During the course of its investigations and from June 10 to 12, 1982, the FBI placed two individuals under heavy surveillance who were a key focus of the Star Quest inquiry. Not surprisingly, the FBI has carefully deleted all references to their names from declassified documents generated on June 21, 1982. Enough data can be gleaned from the available material to build up an intriguing picture of the events, however:

[Deleted] was the subject of a three-day surveillance which commenced from the time he arrived at LAX on June 10, 1982, and ended upon his departure from LAX on a late evening flight back to New York on June 12, 1982. Surveillance was terminated at 2300 hours, as there was no further discernible activity. June 11, 1982–0700 hours: surveillance was initiated at the 1330 West Hollywood location. At 1130 hours both subjects left in the MBZ and drove to 9800 Wanda Park Drive, Los Angeles, staying at the residence until 1340 hours. This address, research reflects, is the residence of SALVATORE BONO a.k.a. SONNY BONO. After leaving the BONO residence, subjects proceeded to the shopping district in and around Rodeo Drive, Beverly Hills, stopping in several stores on what appears to have been a shopping excursion. . . .

What were two people who were the subject of intense FBI surveillance relative to the Colombo inquiry doing hanging around with Sonny Bono? The FBI wanted answers, as the document below reflects:

The following investigation was conducted by Special Agent (SA) [Deleted] and Los Angeles County District Attorney's Office Investigator [Deleted], at Los Angeles, California.

On March 8, 1983, Salvatore "Sonny" Bono, 9800 Wanda Park Drive, Los Angeles, California, was contacted at his place of business, Bono's Restaurant, located at Melrose and La Cienga . . . regarding his knowledge of subjects [Deleted] and [Deleted]. Bono was displayed a photograph of [Deleted] and he advised to having no knowledge of [Deleted] by name or likeness. Bono advised that he knows [Deleted] and that he met [Deleted] through his (Bono's) [Deleted] good friend. Bono advised that [Deleted] was in his restaurant for dinner just two weeks ago. [Deleted] is an actor and is currently attending Bono's acting school in Los Angeles. Bono met [Deleted] through [Deleted] approximately two to three years ago. . . . Bono made the statement, "I don't want to know anything more about him," but would not elaborate on that statement. . . . Bono claims no knowledge of any criminal activity on the part of [Deleted] or [Deleted].

The fact that the documentation is highly censored is unfortunate, but it does, at least, indicate that Bono did know one of the individuals of interest to the FBI; the person had stayed at Bono's house for more than two hours. As was the case in 1976, however, when an unnamed source claimed that Bono was packing a couple of high-powered machine guns, the investigation of his activities and associations with "Messrs. Deleted and Deleted" was taken no further.

From 1988 until 1992, Bono served as mayor of Palm Springs. Bono said that his decision to run for mayor was prompted by his sheer frustration at the overwhelming red tape that faced him when he sought to remodel an Italian restaurant in town. Not everyone was happy with Bono's appointment, however, with the outgoing Republican mayor, Frank Bogert, describing him as both a hippie and a squirrel.

In 1994, Bono won the GOP primary in California's 44th District and rode the Republican tide with a 56 percent to 38 percent win over Democrat Steve Clute. At the time, Bogert told reporters: "I don't like to see a darned Democrat go to Congress. But I sure don't want to see Sonny Bono there, making a fool of himself and us." Nevertheless, Bono secured voter approval, won reelection to Congress in 1996, and became the second-most-requested draw at House members' events during the 1996 campaign.

Tragically, Bono's life came to a sudden end on January 5, 1998, when at the age of sixty-two he accidentally skied into a tree at Heavenly Ski Resort, fifty-five miles southwest of Reno, Nevada, and died of severe head and neck injuries. At the time of his death, Bono was married to his fourth wife, Mary.

After Bono's death, his daughter, Chastity Bono, the media spokeswoman for GLAAD, the Gay and Lesbian Alliance Against Defamation, said in a statement to the media: "Of course, I am deeply saddened by the loss of my father and hope the media will respect my family's privacy during this difficult time. Although my father and I differed on some issues, he was very supportive of my personal life and career and was a loving father. I will miss him greatly."

Ironically, the next, and indeed final, example of FBI involvement with Bono came after his death, when the bureau was tasked with coordinating the intense security that surrounded Bono's funeral. A two-page document of January 8, 1998, titled "Funeral of Congressman Sonny Bono" explains the situation:

The Funeral of U.S. Congressman Sonny Bono is scheduled for 11:00 a.m., Friday, 01/09/1998, at St. Theresa's Church, 2800 E Ramon Rd., Palm Springs, California. Approximately 60–75 members of Congress will be transported to Palm Springs by Congressional aircraft to attend the funeral. It is estimated that another 25 Members of Congress may attend the funeral through their own travel arrangements. White House representatives and the Speaker of the House will also be attending.

The Palm Springs Police Department will address traffic for the Members of Congress to and from the Palm Springs Airport and around the church. The California Highway Patrol will handle traffic control surrounding the general area and security for the Governor of California who will be attending. The United States Capitol Police will have approximately 10 officers addressing the personal security of the Members of Congress.

The Congressional Members will be transported by military bus from the Palm Springs Airport, approximately 5 blocks to the church for the funeral. After the funeral the Members of Congress will be transported immediately back to the Congressional aircraft and depart Palm Springs Airport. They will not be attending additional ceremonies at the cemetery.

Notably, the FBI had uncovered rumors that trouble might occur at Bono's funeral:

Unconfirmed intelligence reports have indicated the possibility of an anti-gay and lesbian contingency traveling to Palm Springs to protest at the funeral. Similar reports have indicated the possibility of pro-gay and lesbian groups attending the funeral to counteract the demonstrations. Attempts are being made to obtain additional intelligence, however local gay and lesbian groups have advised the Palm Springs Police Department that they do not intend to attend the funeral.

The FBI's proposed response in this situation will include two agents staffing the command post at the Palm Springs Police Department. . . . Four agents will accompany the Members of Congress seated inside the church during the ceremony. Six additional agents will be present in the general area in the church, before, during and after the funeral. During briefings, it has been explained to other participating agencies that the FBI will be the primary investigating agency in the event of a threat or assault on a Member of Congress. The FBI will liaison with the other agencies concerning any other matters.

Present at Bono's funeral was one Dominic Montemarano, a friend of Bono, and according to writer Ann Louise Bardach, "a reputed Colombo family capo who had done an 11-year stretch in prison for racketeering" and who "pushed back tears." It was, of course, the FBI's Star Quest investigation of 1982 that led to charges being brought against the leadership of New York's Colombo family. And it was within the bureau's investigative files on this particular affair that Bono's name also surfaced. We might speculate that the presence of four FBI agents within the church and six in the "general area" at the time of Bono's funeral was really just due to the heavy congressional presence. If not, this considerable bureau attendance may have been an attempt by its agents to ascertain who in the criminal underworld was paying their last respects to the former singing star, who was speaking to whom at the church, and what other revelations of an underworld nature might conceivably surface if those agents kept their eyes and ears firmly tuned into what was going on. Funerals of high profile individuals may well be an ideal place for FBI agents to do a bit of secret spying.

Also in attendance at the funeral were people from L. Ron Hubbard's Church of Scientology, an organization the FBI had watched very closely from the early 1950s onwards. Commenting on an article written by Ann Louise Bardach and titled "Proud Mary Bono" that had appeared in the late John F. Kennedy's magazine, *George*, in August 1999, MSNBC reported on August 5 that: "Sonny Bono had so much trouble trying to break away from the Church of Scientology, says a source, that he asked the FBI to intervene."

That Sonny Bono had flirted with Scientology since the 1970s is not in doubt. After church founder L. Ron Hubbard's death in 1986, Bono wrote the following tribute that appeared in the church's literature: "My only sorrow is that L. Ron Hubbard left before I could thank him for my new life." Ann Louise Bardach noted Mary Bono's words: " 'Sonny did try to break away at one point, and they made it very difficult for him. . . . I was resentful of that. I did not like the fact that he said, 'Hey, I'm done with it. I'm not a Scientologist.' And they were saying, 'Hey, you can't do that.' He was amazed, and I was upset.' "

Also, the church "had asked if the president of the Church of Scientology, the Reverend Heber Jentzsch, could conduct the service, which would have afforded them an unprecedented showcase. But they lost out to the Catholic Church." When contacted for comment, the church faxed a statement from Mike Rinder of Scientology's board of directors. According to the July 15, 1999, issue of the *New York Post*, Rinder said: "I'm very offended by the statements. . . . I had both a personal and professional relationship with Sonny. He was constantly talking to me, seeking advice and assistance on matters. I had no indication he wasn't a Scientologist. He never said anything discouraging to me. I don't know what Mary Bono's agenda is, but it isn't Sonny's." Despite this, the Reverend Jentzsch did attend Bono's funeral, as did Karen Hollander, who was then president of the church's Celebrity Center International.

Taking into consideration the presence at Sonny Bono's funeral of underworld figures, congressmen, Church of Scientology representatives, and a multitude of FBI agents, it would not be at all surprising if further intriguing revelations and secrets concerning Palm Springs' most famous mayor are one day made public.

Airtel

4/10/72

To: SAC, New York (100-175319) (Enclosures - 2)

From: Director, FBI (100-469910)

JOHN WINSTON LENNON
SM - NEW LEFT

1 - Mr. Horner
1 - Mr. Preusse
1 - Mr. Shackelford
1 - Mr. Pence

ReNYtel 3/16/72.

Enclosed for information of New York are two copies of
Alexandria airtel dated 3/31/72 captioned "White Panther Party,
IS - WPP; CALREP; MIDEM," which contains information from Alexandria
source relating to current activities of subject.

It appears from referenced New York teletype that subject
and wife might be preparing for lengthy delaying tactics to avert
their deportation in the near future. In the interim, very real
possibility exists that subject, as indicated in enclosed airtel,
might engage in activities in U.S. leading toward disruption of
Republican National Convention (RNC), San Diego, 8/72. For this
reason New York promptly initiate discreet efforts to locate subject
and remain aware of his activities and movements. Handle inquiries
only through established sources and discreet pretext inquiries.
Careful attention should be given to reports that subject is heavy
narcotics user and any information developed in this regard should be
furnished to narcotics authorities and immediately furnished to
Bureau in form suitable for dissemination.

1 - Alexandria
1 - San Diego

RLP:mcm (9)

CLASS. & EXT. BY
REASON-FCIM II, 1-2, 4.2
DATE OF REVIEW

EX-105   REC-33

100-469910-4

MAILED 21
APR 7 - 1972

SEE NOTE PAGE TWO   APR 10 1972

ALL INFORMATION CONTAINED
HEREIN IS UNCLASSIFIED
DATE 13/9/81 BY

ALL INFORMATION CONTAINED
HEREIN IS UNCLASSIFIED EXCEPT
WHERE SHOWN OTHERWISE.

Tolson
Felt
Campbell
Rosen
Mohr
Bishop
Miller, E.S.
Callahan
Casper
Conrad
Dalbey
Cleveland
Ponder
Bates
Walters
Soyars
Tele. Room
Holmes
Gandy

51 APR 12 1972

TELETYPE UNIT

10

John Lennon and the Beatles

"I'm going to throw a hand grenade instead of jelly babies."

When the Liverpool, England-based group, the Beatles, toured the United States in 1964, it led to a rock revolution that truly changed the face of music forever. It also caused the FBI to sit up and take notice. A bureau document of August 20, 1964, reveals the events of August 9 of that year, when the Beatles played the Cow Palace at Daly City, California: "Approximately 17,000 persons, predominantly juveniles, jammed Cow Palace to see performance. Crowd, which was generally orderly, became extremely noisy and excited on appearance of Beatles. Numerous spectators treated for fainting, exhaustion and minor injuries. San Mateo County Sheriff's Office and Daly City Police Department handled minor local violations and issued two juvenile citations for drunk [*sic*] and switchblade knife."

And while it just wouldn't be a rock concert without the obligatory fainting and drunkenness, the FBI's real concern with regard to the Beatles' tour ran much deeper than that: "The San Francisco and Los Angeles Divisions were on August 18, 1964, alerted to the fact that thousands of teenagers gathering for the appearances of the Beatles in Los Angeles and San Francisco could be a perfect vehicle for riots if racial elements or organization, subversive or otherwise, would decide to capitalize on this vehicle."

History has shown that the concerts ran smoothly. But one month later, on September 18, the FBI was still voicing its secret concerns regarding "a few apparently baseless and unverifiable rumors . . . suggesting that one or two Muslims or ex-Muslims, unidentified, had been overheard to say 'some trouble might occur' at the stadium in connection with the appearance of the Beatles. . . ."

Despite the fact that the FBI was told on several occasions that the rumors were utterly without foundation, J. Edgar Hoover's all-seeing eyes continued to watch the Fab Four, particularly when an anonymous letter that made a worrying prediction was brought to the FBI's attention while the Beatles were in the middle of their American tour:

On 8–18–64 Denver, Colorado, Police Department, advised that on this date he had received a threatening letter in the mail. . . . This letter contained another letter which was addressed to the Beatles, Denver, a.m., and marked urgent and important. The envelope was postmarked 8–17–64, Greeley, Colorado, a.m., and the letter was comprised of cut out letters from a magazine pasted on plain white paper, which read as follows: "If you know what's good for you cancel Denver engagement. I'll be in the audience and I'm going to throw a hand grenade instead of jelly babies. Beatle Hater."

The FBI evidently took this threat very seriously, since a follow-up memorandum added that, "On 8–19–64 [Source] made available the above described letter and advised that the Denver Police Department will have approximately 200 police officers assigned to handle the crowd when the Beatles perform and that they are all being advised of the receipt of this letter." Despite the fact that a twenty-five-page investigation file was opened on this threat, the source of the letter was never identified. That the concert went ahead without a hitch, however, suggests that the letter was nothing more than the product of a deranged mind. Five years later, the Beatles had disbanded and the four members, George Harrison, John Lennon, Ringo Starr, and Paul McCartney had moved on to solo careers. And it was during this period that official surveillance of the most controversial of the four Beatles, namely John Lennon, began in earnest.

On January 31, 1969, United States Congressman Ancher Nelsen received a letter from a correspondent with whom he was on first-name terms, and who expressed major concerns about John Lennon's activities, specifically the infamous cover of the 1968 album he recorded with Yoko Ono, *Two Virgins: Unfinished Music No. 1* that depicted a naked Lennon and Ono. Nelsen had hoped that some sort of statute had been violated by Lennon. But much to his dismay, the FBI (which certainly had no love for the former Beatle) was forced to grudgingly advise him that "A representative of the Department of Justice has advised that he is familiar with the photograph contained on the cover of an album by John Lennon. He stated that no violation with regard to obscenity exists concerning this photograph as it does not meet the criteria of obscenity from a legal standpoint."

As a new decade dawned, however, the FBI's interest in John Lennon increased dramatically and raised some extremely provocative questions. Was Lennon, the former Beatle and hero to millions, a major threat to the national security of the United States and Britain in the late 1960s and the early-to-mid 1970s? Was his every move secretly monitored by shadowy sources from worldwide espionage agencies? And, certainly most controversial of all, was John Lennon, at one point in the 1970s, covertly donating funds to Irish Republican Army (IRA) terrorists?

Only weeks after Lennon was shot and killed outside of his New York home in December 1980 by Mark Chapman, a professor of history at the University of California named Jon Wiener began probing the links that existed between Lennon and American authorities: "It began out of simple curiosity, a desire to check out a few rumors that [FBI boss, J. Edgar] Hoover was not Lennon's greatest fan. It then started snowballing into a crusade when I realized how many obstacles were being thrown in my path," stated Professor Wiener.

Twenty years on, and as a direct result of his research and investigations, Wiener found himself embroiled in one of the most talked-about court cases of all time. On February 18, 2000, in Court 23 at the Federal Court Building in Los Angeles, Judge Brian Q. Robbins ordered the FBI to release two letters from a batch of ten documents it was withholding concerning its intense surveillance activities of Lennon. The FBI flatly refused to comply with the order, citing overwhelming national security considerations. Although the FBI had already released a substantial amount of documentation from its files on Lennon by the time the case came to court, what set this final, elusive batch of papers apart from the already-declassified files, is that they almost certainly originated with none other than Britain's ultrasecret, domestic security service: MI5.

That MI5 has information on file pertaining to the activities of John Lennon is not in dispute at all. MI5 whistleblower David Shayler has stated unequivocally that he saw the files in 1993 while serving with the security services, and that they dealt with MI5's surveillance of Lennon during the late 1960s. According to the documentation, Lennon donated £45,000 to the Trotskyist Workers' Revolutionary Party (WRP) and gave support to *Red Mole*, a Marxist magazine edited by student protest leader, Tariq Ali.

At the time MI5's F Branch, the so-called "anti-subversion division," was already monitoring closely the activities of the WRP and even had its very own "mole" buried deep within the organization. It is strongly suspected by those who have followed this entire controversy that MI5's mole, whose identity remains a secret to this day, may very well have been Lennon's contact within the group, too, hence the reason MI5 and the FBI were so keen to keep this information under wraps several decades later.

It is also believed that the MI5 source within the WRP had intercepted at least one letter from Lennon that was destined for the party. The British *Mail On Sunday* newspaper took things a step further, referring to an "insider" who had asserted to their staff that not only would Lennon's correspondence have been closely monitored by MI5, but his telephone would have been tapped, and listening devices would almost certainly have been placed in his home, which at the time in question was a Georgian mansion at Tittenshurst Park, near Ascot.

And, as an FBI source stated, "[The British] don't want these pages released because they show Lennon was being monitored in ways that might now prove to be embarrassing." However, Professor Jon Wiener said, *The Sunday Times*, a British newspaper that had also reported on the controversy, "somehow failed to consider the possibility that the MI5 files Shayler described contained erroneous information. Lennon never had anything to do with the WRP, widely regarded as the looniest group on the left. In the late sixties Lennon was friendly with the International Marxist Group, who published the underground *Red Mole*, edited by Tariq Ali and Robin Blackburn, which had a completely different political orientation from the WRP. A former member of the WRP executive committee, Roger Smith, told *The Observer* (UK) the MI5 information was wrong: 'There was absolutely no link between Lennon and us.'"

The Workers Revolutionary Party aside, what of the more controversial rumors suggesting that John Lennon may have donated funds to the IRA? In 1971, when internment without trial was introduced in Northern Ireland, Lennon held a sign at a rally in London that read: "Victory for the IRA against British imperialism." And Lennon himself stated at the time, "If it's a choice between the IRA and the British Army, I'm with the IRA." For its part, the political wing of the IRA, Sinn Fein, has stated with regard to these allegations that Lennon donated funds: "It is not unbelievable." Similarly, Hunter Davies, a biographer of the Beatles, says, "I wouldn't be at all surprised if he gave money to the IRA. John liked stirring it up."

Not everyone is in agreement, however. Lennon's widow, Yoko Ono, denied such controversial claims when they were made public, and Lennon's friend, Beatle chronicler Ray Connolly, said that "daft though he sometimes may have been, naive though he certainly was, and absolutely the softest of touches for all kinds of causes, [John Lennon] was hardly a bogeyman—and absolutely not a supporter of terrorism." With regard to Lennon's I'm-with-the-IRA statement, Connolly concluded that, "Knowing him, it was, I'm certain, an emotional, unconsidered retort, about an organization about which he and virtually his entire generation knew hardly anything."

The surveillance of Lennon by MI5 aside, how did the man come to be targeted by the FBI? To answer that question we need to take a look at those FBI files that have already been released into the public domain via the terms of the Freedom of Information Act. It is clear that the bulk of the FBI's concerns surrounding John Lennon and his politically related activities began when he moved to live in the United States in the early 1970s and was trying to secure permanent residency in the country. Of particular concern to the American government, was the fact that Lennon was vehemently, and very vocally, against the Vietnam War. At the time President Richard Nixon instructed the FBI to look for any damaging information that would allow American authorities to get Lennon summarily thrown out of the country and back to Britain on a permanent basis. The last thing Nixon and the FBI wanted was a famous and influential rock star, with millions of fans, no less, getting his teeth firmly into the scalding hot potato that was Vietnam.

That is when the FBI approached MI5 in an attempt to obtain any information on Lennon that would be useful to it. MI5 was reluctant to do so, not because it was against lending assistance to its American counterpart, but because MI5 feared, and history may one day prove its fears to be entirely justified, that if it shared too much of its data with the FBI, its classified files would eventually surface into the public domain via the U.S. Freedom of Information Act. A middle ground was reached, however, and MI5 prepared a summary of its surveillance of Lennon that was forwarded on to the FBI. Thus began the FBI's spying operations on John Lennon.

But what do the hundreds of previously classified files on Lennon's activities in the United States tell us? The Vietnam War aside, much of the documentation centers upon Lennon's financial donations to a host of left-wing organizations in the United States, which were perceived by the FBI to be nothing but undesirables, troublemakers, and subversives. One particular document, a January 1972 FBI Teletype, confirms the fact that Lennon's activities were of interest to the CIA, as well as to the FBI:

Classified Secret—No Foreign Dissemination/No Dissemination Abroad" since information being furnished in CACTUS channel and CIA has asked that all such information be so classified. CIA has requested details of information we furnished in daily summary teletype captioned, "Protest Activities and Civil Disturbances", dates 1/24/72, reporting that John Lennon contributed large sum of money to [the Election Year Strategy Information Center (EYSIC)].

An additional document on this aspect of the surveillance was routed to the FBI's Liaison Desk in London and may well have found its way into the files of MI5:

The Election Year Strategy Information Center has been formed to direct movement activities during coming election year to culminate with demonstrations at Republican National Convention, August next. Sources advise John Lennon, former member of The Beatles singing group, has contributed seventy-five thousand dollars to assist in formation of EYSIC.

The same file made it very clear that the FBI intended that this information be quickly made available to senior officials within both the State Department and the Immigration and Naturalization Service (INS):

EYSIC, apparently dedicated to creating disruptions during Republican National Convention, obviously being heavily influenced by John Lennon, British citizen who is currently in US attempting to obtain US citizenship. Inasmuch as he is attempting to stay permanently in US, it is anticipated pertinent information concerning him will be disseminated to State and INS.

There can be absolutely no doubt at all that this was a direct attempt to prevent Lennon from obtaining American citizenship. And lo and behold, on March 16, 1972, the Communications Section of the FBI dispatched the following Teletype to FBI director, J. Edgar Hoover:

On March 16th Mr. Vincent Schiano, Chief Trial Attorney, Immigration and Naturalization Service, New York City advised that John Lennon and his wife Yoko Ono appeared at INS, NYC, this date for deportation proceedings. Both individuals thru their attorney won delays on hearings. Lennon requested delay while he attempted to fight a narcotics conviction in England. Yoko Ono requested delay on basis of child custody case in which she is involved. Mr. Schiano advised that new hearings would be held on April 18 next. If Lennon wins overthrow of British narcotic conviction, INS will reconsider their attempts to deport Lennon and wife.

Another FBI document from this time, generated by the FBI's Domestic Intelligence Division, states: "We are closely following these proceedings. . . ." Only days later the special agent in charge in New York informed bureau headquarters of a new development in the controversy surrounding John Lennon's political activities:

[Lennon] and his wife might be preparing for lengthy delaying tactics to avert their deportation in the near future. . . . Careful attention should be given to reports that [Lennon] is heavy narcotics user and any information developed in this regard should be furnished to narcotics authorities and immediately furnished to Bureau.

Meanwhile, the attempts to get Lennon slung out of the United States continued. An April 18, 1972, FBI Teletype refers to Lennon's comments made to the media, "in which he inferred INS was attempting to deport him due to his political ideas and present policy of the U.S. government as to aliens who speak out against the administration." Interestingly, a memo prepared several days afterward refers to the fact that following a drug bust in London in 1968, the FBI felt there were very good reasons why Lennon should never have been allowed into the United States in the first place. Curiously, however, the document states that the decision to allow him entry "was due to unexplained intervention by State Department with INS." In other words, the very people who were now doing their utmost to deport Lennon back to Britain were the same ones who had originally granted him open access to the United States in the first place.

For the most part, the files continue in a similar vein and concentrate on two primary issues: (a) the attempts of American authorities to get Lennon out of America; and (b) his links with organizations and individuals that, from a political perspective, the FBI perceived as being troublesome, such as the Election Year Strategy Information Center (EYSIC). In 1974, Lennon won his battle to stay in the States and remained there until his life was cut short in December 1980 by the bullets of Mark Chapman. So, in the final analysis, was John Lennon really a major national security risk who donated funds to the IRA and others? Or, was he simply, as his friend Ray Connolly puts it "daft," "naïve," and "the softest of touches for all kinds of causes?"

We may one day have a conclusive answer to those questions. If those questions are ultimately answered, however, then it is very likely that we will also be exposed to never-before-seen papers that reveal the ways in which Britain's security services conduct their own top secret surveillance of celebrity figures. How ironic it would be if some of MI5's deepest secrets on famous stars surfaced not as a result of a long-term Russian mole, but via the provisions of the U.S. government's Freedom of Information Act, and as a direct result of the FBI's decades-old investigations of a dead rock star.

It is perhaps apposite to close with the words of Professor Jon Wiener, who states that the official surveillance of Lennon amounted to nothing less than "an abuse of power by the government, engaged in illegitimate surveillance of dissidents engaged in lawful political activities."

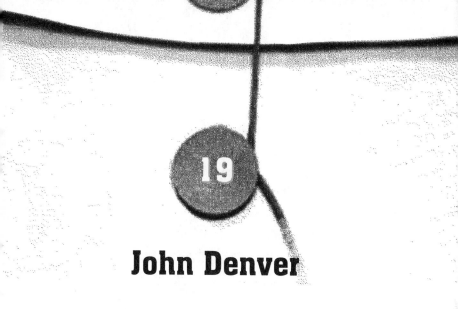

John Denver

"Denver was pretty well strung out on cocaine."

Born into an air force family in the town of Roswell, New Mexico, in 1943, Henry John Deutschendorf Jr. gained worldwide fame as singer-guitarist John Denver, who is perhaps best known for his hits "Take Me Home, Country Roads;" "Rocky Mountain High;" "Thank God, I'm a Country Boy;" and "Leaving on a Jet Plane," the latter having been recorded by Peter, Paul and Mary and reached number one on the charts. But as Denver's popularity grew in the 1970s, so did his passion for politics and pressing social and humanitarian issues. It was this passion that led officials to take note of the man's activities, as a May 22, 1975, FBI document generated as a result of interagency interest in Denver makes abundantly clear.

According to the document, a "Dump the War Rally" had taken place at the Metropolitan Sports Center, Bloomington, Minnesota, on May 23, 1971, and among those listed as speakers was folk singer John Denver, along with Congressman Paul Mc-Closkey Jr., former U.S. congressman Allard Lowenstein, former

Memorandum

Eece AV Adm. _____
Eece AD Inv. _____
Eece AD LES _____
Asst. Dir.: _____
Adm. Servs. _____
Crim. Inv. _____
Ident. _____
Insp. _____
Intell. _____
Lab. _____
Legal Coun. _____
Off. Cong. &
Public Affs. _____
Rec. Mgnt. _____
Tech. Servs. _____
Training _____
Telephone Rm. _____
Director's Sec'y _____

To   :   Mr. Christensen   Date .   2/12/90

From   :   W. M. Baker

SSP

CLASS
SRC'D   Subject :   JOHN DENVER   *none check*

SIR
REC

PURPOSE: To advise the results of an Organized Crime Information
System (OCIS) name search in connection with captioned subject.

RECOMMENDATIONS: That the Executive Agencies Unit (EAU) contact
Las Vegas and St. Louis field offices in order to further
investigate the results concerning captioned subject.

APPROVED: Adm. Serv. ___   Intell. ___   Off. of Liaison
            Crim. Inv. ___   Laboratory ___   & Int. Affs. ___
Deputy ___   Ident. ___   Inspection ___   Public Affs. ___
Asst. Dir.: ___   Legal Coun. ___
Asst. Dir.: ___   Legal Court. ___

DETAILS: Subsequent to a request of the EAU, Records Management
Division, the name John Denver was searched in OCIS with regard
to captioned matter.

The results of this search indicate the possibility of
the following hit concerning a John Denver. Denver is listed
as an entertainer and a narcotics user. John Denver is also
listed as the owner of ████ Auto Sales. ████ Auto Sales
b7C is listed as having an address of ████
████ ████ This information is sourced to Las Vegas
file ████ and St. Louis file ████

It is recommended that the EAU contact Las Vegas and
St. Louis in order to determine what additional information may
be available.

1 - Mr. Christensen
     (Attn: Ms. ████ Room ████
b7C 1 - Mr. Baker
     (Attn: Mr. ████ Room ████
1 - Executive Searches File
████ (4)

62-5-69835

b7C

/ ENCLOSURE

b7C

U.S. senator Eugene J. McCarthy, U.S. congressman Donald Reigel, and former navy lieutenant (and, later, presidential candidate) John Kerry.

The FBI further noted that an article had appeared in the May 3, 1971, issue of the *Minneapolis Star* newspaper, quoting the rally sponsors denying that "the antiwar rally is part of a 'dump Nixon movement.' " Nevertheless, the FBI recorded, "Wheelock Whitney, a Republican leader, would not endorse this rally because he considers it a 'dump Nixon effort.' " The FBI had further noted that a spokesman for the Bipartisan Caucus to End the War had said, "We're not waiting for November 1972," and that the same spokesman had informed the *Minneapolis Star* that it wanted to "persuade the political animal who holds the presidency to change his course of action before the election."

The document concluded, "The above is being furnished to the Bureau for information. Since this affair is clearly political in nature, no coverage through established informants contemplated unless positive evidence received of disruptive or destructive activity being involved therewith." In this case, the FBI took no action beyond filing the data for potential future reference, and the "Denver File" seems to have remained largely inactive until December 1979 when, the FBI reported, threats were made to kill the singer:

Approximately seventeen threatening phone calls directed at singer John Denver have been received in Los Angeles since December 1, 1979. A female, speaking German and English has called daily from Germany demanding first to speak to Denver and then stating that her mother's boyfriend is coming to Los Angeles to kill Denver. John Denver, who is presently at his home in Aspen, Colorado, is aware of the threats. Legat Bonn is requested to ascertain through local authorities if captioned individuals pose any threat to John Denver.

This affair ultimately fizzled out, and the FBI determined that Denver was never in any real danger. But surveillance of the country boy was not going to go away anytime soon. In fact, it was only destined to increase. Official records reflect that a great deal of interest, not to mention a distinct raising of eyebrows, was shown within the FBI when, in 1985, Denver was invited by the Soviet Union of Composers to perform in the USSR at an event that would inspire the antiarms-race song "Let Us Begin (What Are We Making Weapons For?)," which subsequently appeared on Denver's *One World* album.

Aside from politics and humanitarian issues, Denver's other big passion was outer space; he even took, and notably passed, NASA's physical and mental examination to determine if he was fit enough to cope with the extreme rigors of a journey into space. Plans were made for Denver to travel on the *Challenger* Space Shuttle. But a twist of fate prevented him from joining the ill-fated January 1986 mission that ended in utter disaster when *Challenger* exploded shortly after takeoff, killing the crew. (This event led to an FBI investigation of the accident that ran to 170 pages.)

Five years after his trip to Russia, John Denver was still being watched, as declassified FBI files of February 1990 demonstrate:

Purpose: To advise the results of an Organized Crime Information System (OCIS) name search in connection with captioned subject.

Recommendations: That the Executive Agencies Unit (EAU) contact Las Vegas and St. Louis field offices in order to further investigate the results concerning captioned subject.

Subsequent to a request of the EAU, Records Management Division, the name John Denver was searched in OCIS with regard to captioned matter.

The results of this search indicate the possibility of the following hit concerning a John Denver. Denver is listed as an entertainer and a narcotics user. John Denver is also listed as the owner of [Deleted] Auto Sales.

It is recommended that the EAU contact Las Vegas and St. Louis in order to determine what additional information may be available.

During the course of a Racketeer Influenced Corrupt Organizations; La Cosa Nostra-Narcotics investigation being conducted [Deleted] information was received [concerning] a recent benefit concert [in] Colorado, with entertainer John Denver. It was alleged Denver was pretty well strung out on cocaine.

No further data has surfaced from the FBI on this aspect of John Denver's activities. And if all he did was to try and make the world a better place, while snorting a few lines of coke in the process, then he could hardly have been considered public enemy number one. But there is one genuinely weird saga in the life and career of John Denver that touches upon official secrecy and that deserves to be mentioned. One of those aboard the tragic Space Shuttle *Challenger* flight that Denver was due to travel on was astronaut Ellison Onizuka. He had told his close friend Chris Coffey that, while serving in the air force at McClelland Air Force Base in 1973, he had viewed a piece of black-and-white film footage that showed "alien bodies on a slab," alien bodies not unlike those supposedly recovered from a crashed UFO by the military in 1947 at Roswell, New Mexico. Roswell just happens to be John Denver's hometown.

John Denver died on October 12, 1997, when his private plane plunged into the ocean near Pacific Grove, California.

the involvement of CIA employees in fabricating these fraudulent documents." Upon information and belief, the OIG was prevented from fully investigating the allegations by the CIA's Office of General Counsel, despite the fact that current or former CIA personnel may have been involved in an illegal scheme to defraud Al Fayed.

Unanswered Questions

68. As with many controversial high-profile events, oftentimes there exists more unanswered questions than those that appear to have been answered. This lawsuit seeks the release of information to answer at least some of those questions including, but not limited to:

- Do agencies of the United States government possess any information regarding the deaths of Princess Diana, Dodi Al Fayed and Henri Paul?

- With all of its forensic and criminal expertise, was the United States government ever requested to lend assistance to the French investigation into the August 31, 1997, tragedy?

- Does the United States possess any satellite imagery of the City of Paris from the night of August 31, 1997, that could be used to determine the movement of vehicles in the area of the tragedy?

- Does the United States possess information, as alleged by Gerald Posner, that Henri Paul was employed by MI6 as reported by Richard Tomlinson to the judge, or any other foreign intelligence service?

- Was Henri Paul meeting his French intelligence handler in the three hours before he returned to the Ritz as claimed by Gerald Posner?

- To what extent did the NSA intercept telephonic communications between Princess Diana and others, the existence of which has been confirmed by Gerald Posner?

- What documents did Defense Secretary William Cohen's Chief of Staff, Robert Tyrer, review relating to the tragedy, and were the searches conducted to locate these records intentionally narrow?

- What is or has been the CIA's relationship with Oswald LeWinter, Pat McMillan and the other individuals involved with the plot to defraud Al Fayed of $20 million dollars?

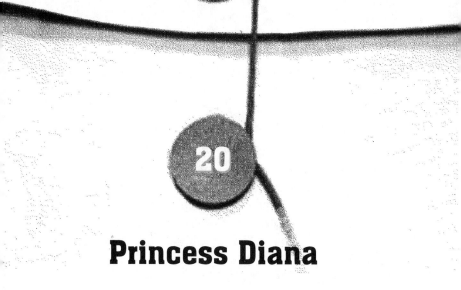

Princess Diana

"Their disclosure could cause exceptionally grave damage to the national security."

Agencies such as the FBI, the CIA, and the State Department have declassified a wealth of documents on numerous celebrity figures. There can be no doubt, however, that those same agencies, and many more, continue to withhold materials on other famous individuals, most notably on the late Diana, Princess of Wales. Along with her lover Dodi Fayed and driver Henri Paul, Diana was killed in a horrific car crash in Paris, France, on August 31, 1997. And while it is certainly true that secret files on Diana are known to exist within the archives of various departments and official bodies, the exact circumstances surrounding her untimely death are massively confused by other files, namely, unofficially released files that many view firmly as nothing more than hoaxed material but that some believe may be real.

In December 1998, the United States' supersecret National Security Agency admitted that it was holding more than a thousand pages of classified documents on the princess. The fact that many view Diana's death as highly suspicious has roused major concern and interest on a worldwide basis, no less, about what those documents actually contain. And the fact that the NSA has flatly refused to declassify its files on Diana has made the story even more intriguing in the eyes of both the press and the public.

British tabloids reported extensively and sometimes sensationally on the revelations at the time they first surfaced: "America's spy chiefs admitted last night they snooped on Princess Diana for years—and learned some of her most intimate love secrets" the *Daily Mirror* loudly proclaimed, while the *Daily Record* stated that the NSA's surveillance had continued, "right until she died in the Paris car crash with Dodi Fayed." *The Washington Post* took the view that "the truth" was likely to be less "lurid," however, and cited the comments of a "U.S. intelligence official" who asserted that the references contained within the files to Diana were merely "incidental." The *Post* added, "In denying the request, the NSA disclosed existence of a 1,056-page Diana file and reported that Fort Meade, where the agency is located, had produced 39 'NSA-originated and NSA-controlled documents,' totaling 124 pages."

These documents, the NSA explained, were being withheld "because their disclosure could reasonably be expected to cause exceptionally grave damage to the national security" and if released, would potentially disclose "sources and methods" utilized by the U.S. intelligence-gathering network. But, as the *Post* also reported: "The giant spy agency, Maryland's largest employer, has been the subject of intense controversy in Britain and across Europe since a report released in January by the European Parliament concluded that 'within Europe, all email, telephone and fax communications are routinely intercepted by the United States National Security Agency.' "

The NSA is not the only agency known to be holding files on the dead royal. According to an NSA freedom of information officer, the CIA also has at least two classified documents on file that relate to the princess. And the Defense Intelligence Agency has admitted that it possessed both "information" and "product" on Diana. When asked why the DIA would have a classified document mentioning Diana, a spokesman for the DIA admitted that he had "no idea why. All of our stuff is on military. Obviously she wasn't in the military." Diana *was*, however, a major player in the long and drawn-out battle to have land mines outlawed, which *would* have been of prime concern to the military, as well as to the defense contractors of numerous nations.

Interestingly, in 1999 Britain's *Guardian* newspaper learned that at least *some* of the material held by the NSA originated with the British intelligence services, MI5 and MI6, portions of which were officially classified top secret. "The documents on the dead princess seem to have arisen because of the company she kept rather than through any attempt to target her," said the *Guardian*, "and the agency goes out of its way to say that it did not compile any of the spy reports itself."

The *Guardian* also noted that the NSA had stressed that its policy did not involve targeting "British subjects" as a part of its "foreign intelligence mission." However, it was also reported that the NSA did admit that "other countries could communicate about these subjects; therefore, this agency could acquire intelligence concerning British subjects."

And there can be little doubt that at least some of that classified documentation surely must relate to the data that was collected by Mohamed Al-Fayed, the father of Diana's lover Dodi Fayed, and the subsequent lawsuit filed by Al-Fayed in 2000 in the U.S. District Court for the District of Columbia. The lawsuit in question, which was bravely designed to force numerous agencies to relinquish their files on Diana, but that has unfortunately failed thus far, began as follows:

This is an action under the Freedom of Information Act . . . for the expedited processing and disclosure of agency records pertaining to the deaths of Princess Diana and Dodi Fayed, and events and individuals associated with the tragedy, that were improperly withheld from plaintiffs Mohammed Al Fayed and Punch Limited by defendants Central Intelligence Agency, the National Security Agency, the Defense Intelligence Agency, the United States Departments of Defense, Justice and State, the Federal Bureau of Investigation, the Executive Office of United States Attorneys, the Immigration and Naturalization Service and the United States Secret Service.

In a section, titled "Background," an outline was provided of the fatal crash that killed Diana and Dodi:

On August 31, 1997, at approximately 12:25 A.M. local time, an automobile carrying Diana Francis Spencer, Princess of Wales, and Dodi Al Fayed crashed into the thirteenth pillar in the tunnel under the Place d'Alma in Paris, France. Princess Diana and Dodi Al Fayed were killed along with the automobile's driver, Henri Paul, a French security officer at the Ritz Hotel. Bodyguard Trevor Rees-Jones was the sole survivor. Shortly after the tragedy, Premier Juge d'instruction Hervé Stephan, a French investigating magistrate, instituted an investigation. On or about January 29, 1999, it was announced that the investigation had ended and concluded that the tragedy was caused by drunk driving by Henri Paul, excessive speed and a dangerous stretch of road. Nine photographers and a press motorcyclist were placed under formal investigation—a step immediately before being formally charged—for manslaughter and failing to render aid to accident victims. On or about September 3, 1999, Judge Stephan dismissed all charges against the photographers and motorcyclist.

The decision to formally end the investigation is presently under appeal by Al Fayed, and judicial proceedings are scheduled for September 2001.

The document then focused its attention upon the revelations of a British government agent, Richard Tomlinson:

Richard Tomlinson, 37, is a former MI6 (British foreign intelligence service) officer who served from September 1991 through April 1995. On or about August 28, 1998, Tomlinson informed investigating magistrate Hervé Stephan that Henri Paul, the chauffeur killed in the tragedy, had been on the MI6 payroll for at least three years. He also revealed that the death crash resembled a MI6 plot to kill Yugoslavian President Slobodan Milosevic in Geneva. A copy of the affidavit Tomlinson provided to Judge Stephan is available at www .alfayed.com/dianaanddodi/tomlinson.html.

In or around September 1998, Tomlinson traveled to the United States on board a Swiss Air Flight in order to appear on a NBC television program to discuss his recent revelations. Upon arrival at John F. Kennedy International Airport in New York, Tomlinson was escorted off the plane by United States government officials and detained for several hours. He was never permitted to enter the United States, and instead was placed back on a plane to Europe.

Upon information and belief, the United States government prevented Tomlinson from entering the United States at the request of MI6 or other British government officials.

Oswald LeWinter ("LeWinter"), 70, has claimed to be a former United States intelligence operative for more than two decades. He has been linked to several high profile controversies here in the United States and Europe, all of which involved allegations of intelligence connections and specifically the CIA. These controversies have included LeWinter providing what apparently turned out to be disinformation regarding "October Surprise", which involved allegations that individuals associated with Ronald Reagan's presidential campaign delayed the release of American hostages in Iran in order to defeat President Jimmy Carter; claims by LeWinter that the CIA was involved in the 1986 assassination of former Swedish Prime Minister Olof Palme; his appearance in a 1994 documentary on the bombing of Pan Am Flight 103 entitled The Maltese Double Cross in which LeWinter claimed that the CIA knew that Libya was not responsible for the terrorist attack; and a 1998 attempt, more fully described below, to sell fraudulent CIA documents concerning the deaths of Princess Diana and Dodi Al Fayed.

In his book October Surprise (1991), Professor Gary Sick describes LeWinter as an "intelligence operative", who was a "graduate of University of California at Berkeley and had a master's degree in English literature from San Francisco State." "He spoke German and English, but he had also acquired a working knowledge of Hebrew, Persian, and French, and some Urdu." Sick stated LeWinter "had served with U.S. forces in Vietnam and also claimed long experience with various U.S. and Israeli intelligence agencies."

Upon information and belief, LeWinter previously formally maintained a relationship with the CIA, at least to the extent he provided information to the Agency during the 1970s. The CIA presently maintains in its possession records that confirm a relationship, as well as information pertaining to the fraud attempt described below.

In a lengthy section of the court document titled "The Effort To Defraud Mohamed Al Fayed," the strange story is told of a series of controversial documents that surfaced not long after the death of the Princess of Wales, documents that were purported to be official leaked United States government documents about the secret surveillance of Diana. According to a lawsuit filed by Mohamed Al Fayed in the United States District Court for the District of Columbia, it was alleged that:

In late 1997 or early 1998, George Williamson ("Williamson"), an independent journalist, Pat Macmillan ("Macmillan") [*sic*] and LeWinter—the latter two are both alleged former CIA agents—participated in an enterprise to sell forged documents purportedly stolen from the CIA that indicated MI6—the British foreign intelligence agency—had plotted to murder Princess Diana and Dodi Al Fayed. Other individuals who are alleged to have played a role in the scheme include [Keith Fleer ("Fleer"), a prominent California attorney,] Linda Tumulty, who is tied to the late film producer Alan Francovich, and another former CIA operative named Thompson.

LeWinter, Macmillan, and other associates apparently forged the documents and planned to misrepresent them as genuine to induce potential buyers to purchase the documents. Along with Williamson, who was also aware that the documents to be sold were not authentic, LeWinter, Macmillan, and their colleagues agreed that a sale of the forged documents to a tabloid newspaper should be arranged. The participants in the scheme anticipated a sale price of over $1 million.

Upon information and belief, at the suggestion of Gaby Leon (phonetic), an individual who allegedly formerly worked for the Argentine Secret Service, Williamson was advised to contact Fleer, an entertainment attorney in Los Angeles, for advice on the sale of the documents and to serve as a broker for their sale.

In their course of discussions, Fleer [reportedly] noted that Al Fayed had offered a reward of up to $20 million for information concerning the deaths of his son and Princess Diana and he suggested that they should approach Al Fayed in lieu of a tabloid and offer him the information for $20 million. Fleer stated that he knew one of Al Fayed's attorneys in Washington, D.C. and would make the necessary approaches to him. Upon information and belief, Fleer was to receive 5% of any monies obtained through the sale of the alleged CIA documents.

On or about March 24, 1998, Fleer contacted Douglas Marvin ("Marvin"), Al Fayed's legal representative in Washington. Marvin, in turn, put Fleer in contact with John MacNamara ("MacNamara"), Al Fayed's chief of security. In a series of telephone conversations over the first two weeks of April 1998, between Fleer and MacNamara, Fleer [allegedly] stated that he had been approached by reliable individuals with credible information that the deaths of Dodi Al Fayed and Princess Diana were not accidental but in fact were the product of a carefully planned assassination carried out at the behest of British intelligence with the knowledge and acquiescence of Buckingham Palace. Fleer indicated that his immediate contact was Williamson, an investigative reporter, and that several "principals" were also involved.

[Court papers allege that] according to Fleer, Williamson had connections with CIA sources who had been reliable in the past. Those CIA employees, Fleer stated, would be prepared to disclose their information concerning the deaths of Dodi Al Fayed and the Princess, provided that Al Fayed would provide them with the financial security and assistance to "take measures to protect themselves"—a price of $20 million. While it was unlikely that the CIA employees would agree to testify in any manner, they could provide authentic and sufficiently detailed CIA documentary evidence to prove the involvement of British intelligence agencies in the assassination plot. [It was alleged] that the CIA sources knew that a CIA operative in Europe had been contacted by someone within the British intelligence agency MI6. The British agent indicated that an assassination team was being compiled and asked for assistance. The CIA employee subsequently cabled for instructions and received in return a telex indicating that the CIA was not to become involved directly but that the agent could give British intelligence the name of a contact with a Mossad-affiliated "K team" operating out of Switzerland.

In addition to the telexes from and to the CIA operative, Fleer [allegedly] indicated that the CIA sources could and would supply Al Fayed with a relevant intelligence collection report and a medical document indicating that the Princess was pregnant at the time of her death. Fleer also [reportedly] indicated that there was a report of the results of an internal CIA investigation into the agency's involvement with the assassination of Dodi Al Fayed and Princess Diana, but that this document could only be obtained through a "seven figure" cash payment.

On or about April 8, 1998, Fleer [allegedly] requested that MacNamara arrange for the wire transfer of $25,000 "expense money" so that Al Fayed's representatives and the "principals" could meet in a foreign country to arrange for the inspection of the CIA documents and their subsequent sale to Al Fayed.

Given that alleged classified information was being offered for sale, on or about April 13, 1998, Al Fayed's representatives contacted and began cooperating with officials from the FBI and the CIA. From here on, all actions taken by Al Fayed's representatives were done so with the approval and supervision of law enforcement and intelligence officials of the United States government.

On or about April 13, 1998, Fleer [reportedly] requested that MacNamara send the $25,000 via wire transfer to the account of Garland and Loman, Inc., a New Mexico company with an affiliate in Juarez, Mexico, at the Western Bank, 201 North Church Street, Las Cruces, New Mexico 88001. Fleer [allegedly] explained in a subsequent call to MacNamara that the Western Bank would contact Williamson when the funds were received. The FBI directed Al Fayed's representatives to wire the money from a bank in the District of Columbia so that criminal jurisdiction would lie with the United States Attorney's Office for the District of Columbia. MacNamara was told that at the very least the transmittal and receipt of the funds would constitute wire fraud, even if nothing else came of the intended transaction to sell the documents.

On or about April 14, 1998, with the approval of U.S. law enforcement authorities, Marvin ordered the wire transfer of $25,000 from a NationsBank branch in Washington, D.C. to the Garland & Loman account. FBI, CIA and EOUSA officials were all aware of the ongoing events.

Upon information and belief, Williamson traveled to the Garland and Loman premises in New Mexico to withdraw the $25,000 wire transfer with the intent to use those funds to finance and further the sale of the forged documents to Al Fayed. Williamson subsequently traveled to London, England and disbursed some or all of the $25,000 to his co-conspirators; including, but not limited to, LeWinter.

On or about April 14, 1998, following confirmation from Williamson that the $25,000 wire transfer had been received, Fleer [reportedly] informed MacNamara that the meeting to exchange the documents for payment was to take place in Vienna, Austria. Fleer [allegedly] stated that in Austria, Al Fayed's representatives would meet with four "principals," who would offer for sale two CIA telexes and a doctor's certificate that Princess Diana was pregnant at the time of her death. Fleer [reportedly] emphasized that the internal CIA investigative report on the circumstances of the crash would not, however, be provided at the Vienna meeting because "they" had yet to procure it.

The court filing further alleges that:

With the intent to render the proceeds of the sale difficult or impossible to trace, and in an effort to conceal their source, Fleer [allegedly] instructed MacNamara during their conversation on or about April 14, 2000, that he should arrange to have the $15 million negotiated purchase price (having been reduced from $20 million) for the documents deposited at the Austrian bank Kredit Anstalt in a Sparbuch, an anonymous, bearer passbook account. Fleer [reportedly] stated that the passbook was to be handed over to the "principals" at the Vienna meeting as payment for the documents.

On or about April 20, 1998, MacNamara received a telephone call in Austria from Williamson, who stated that he was at the Hilton Hotel, New York City. Williamson confirmed that he dealt regularly with the "principals" supplying the documents and that he served as their go-between. He also stated that the "principals" would be present in Vienna and that at least one of them, whose identity remains unknown, had traveled from the United States to meet with Al Fayed's representatives. At an initial meeting, Al Fayed's representatives would be shown at least one of the CIA telexes dealing with the assassination of Dodi Fayed and Princess Diana, and that a serving member of the CIA would be on hand to authenticate the document. Additionally, Williamson also stated that the $25,000 wired by MacNamara had been spent and that "nobody's cheating on you."

Following additional negotiations concerning the time, place, and format of the Vienna meeting, MacNamara received two telephone calls from an unknown individual on his mobile phone discussing the mechanics of the document exchange and setting a meeting for April 22, 1998, 2:00 p.m. at the Hotel Ambassador, 1010 Vienna, Neuer Markt 5. Mac-Namara was to sit on the Kartner Strasse side, where he would be approached by one of the "principals." With the approval of United States and Austrian law enforcement authorities, MacNamara followed the instructions that had been given to him regarding the planned rendezvous.

At approximately 2:30 p.m. local time, a man (later identified as LeWinter) approached MacNamara and identified himself as an ex-CIA agent who was in Vienna with six CIA and

Mossad agents to deal with "the business." LeWinter spoke to MacNamara for approximately one half hour, briefing him on the provenance of the CIA documents, and indicated that there had been a meeting in London between an MI6 operative named Spelding and a CIA agent named Harrison, who was attached to the United States Embassy in London. At that meeting, Spelding asked Harrison for the CIA's assistance in assassinating Dodi Al Fayed, who had formed a close relationship with Princess Diana. Harrison allegedly cabled CIA headquarters in Langley, Virginia for instructions and was informed via telex that the CIA would not become involved but could refer the British to the Mossad "K team" in Geneva. LeWinter indicated to MacNamara that these two telexes were for sale, and he also gave a brief description of the CIA investigative report that could be obtained, including a reference in that report to Princess Diana's pregnancy.

At the conclusion of their meeting at the Hotel Ambassador, LeWinter provided a telephone number and requested MacNamara to call him there under the name George Mearah at 5:00 p.m. Law enforcement personnel working with MacNamara traced the telephone number to the Hotel Stadt Bamberg, where they confirmed that the hotel had as a guest an American named Oswald LeWinter who matched Mearah's description.

By arrangement, and with the approval of United States and Austrian authorities, MacNamara met with LeWinter later that afternoon at the Ambassador Hotel. Following further discussions with MacNamara, LeWinter was taken into custody at the Ambassador Hotel by Austrian law enforcement officials. On information and belief, two associates (one of which has apparently been identified as Thompson) of LeWinter who were nearby evaded capture. In fact, it turns out that one of the individuals who assisted LeWinter during his time in Vienna was Karl Koecher, a Czechoslovakian intelligence operative who had infiltrated the CIA as a "sleeper" agent during the 1970s. After more than a decade of spying on the United States, Koecher was arrested and ultimately exchanged in a spy trade for Soviet dissident Anatoly Shcharansky on February 11, 1986. Upon information and belief, Koecher and LeWinter became acquainted while serving in prison together in New York State.

http://www.dcd.uscourts.gov/00-2092.pdf

As part of a settlement to a lawsuit brought by Al Fayed against Fleer, Williamson, Pat Macmillan, and LeWinter, Fleer agreed to make a donation to a charitable organization in Dodi Al Fayed's honor. Fleer issued a prepared statement apologizing to Al Fayed for supporting the mistaken belief that his son was murdered. "My role in the offer to sell Mr. Al Fayed information supporting this belief and which involved, as I later learned, the creation of forged documents in order to give greater credibility to the information being sold, is one I bitterly regret."

There can be little doubt that even if the documents were faked, a great deal of thought had certainly gone into their content, as can be seen from the text of one of the documents contained within the collection that was circulated to the British media. Indeed, the lead-in to one of the documents, dated June 17, 1997, looked very impressive. It was headed "DOMESTIC COLLECTION DIVISION Foreign Intelligence Information Report Directorate of Intelligence WARNING NOTICE—INTELLIGENCE SOURCES AND METHODS INVOLVED REPORT CLASS: TOP SECRET" and read:

1. Relationship initiated between Diana POW and Dodi aF according to reliable intel sources in November 1996. Intimacy begins shortly after they meet. (Report filed).
2. Reliable source reports Palace seriously disturbed by liaison. PM considers any al Fayed relationship politically disastrous. [The Duke of] Edinburgh sees serious threat to

dynasty should relationship endure. Quote reported: "Such an affair is racially and morally repugnant and no son of a Bedouin camel trader is fit for the mother of a future king," Edinburgh. (Report filed).

3. Request from highest circles to DEA attaché UK for 6 on Dodi re: Cocaine. See File forwarded to UK embassy DC. (Copy filed).

4. US liaison to MI6 requested by David Spedding for assistance in providing permanent solution to Dodi problem. Blessing of Palace secured.

5. WHuse [White House] denies Spedding request. Harrison authorized only to arrange meeting for MI6 representative with K-Team Geneva.

6. Meeting in Geneva reportedly successful (Report filed).

7. al Fayed Mercedes Limo stolen and returned with electronics missing. Reliable intel source confirms K-team involved. Source reports car rebuilt to respond to external radio controls. (Report filed).

8. COBGeneva reports that on May 28, 1997 heavily weighted Fiat Turbo.

And there the document ends. In an intriguing twist, a July 23, 1999, article titled "Fayed, the spies and the $20m plot to show Palace was behind Diana's death," written by journalists Stuart Millar and Duncan Campbell, reported that "Le Winter has since claimed, during two meetings with the Harrods head of security, that although the papers shown to Mr. Fayed were forgeries, they were copies of real documents held by the CIA." No wonder then that the death of Diana, Princess of Wales, continues to provoke intense controversy nearly a decade after her untimely demise.

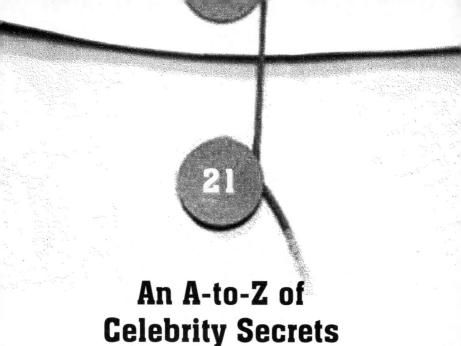

An A-to-Z of Celebrity Secrets

Government agencies have compiled documentation on a whole host of other famous individuals, some of which is either very brief in nature, or is of great length but contains only snippets and fragments of truly eye-opening data, as the following items reveal. Interestingly, the subjects of concern to the FBI vary little. Those celebrities not plagued by extortion claims were generally seen by the FBI as either Communists or dope smokers.

Gracie Allen and George Burns

FBI files from 1931 show that comedians George Burns and Jack Benny, along with their wives, Gracie Allen and Mary Livingston, were investigated and subsequently fined by New York City authorities for having the unmitigated gall to bring jewelry and clothing into the United States from Europe without paying duty tax. Amusingly, contained within the George 'n' Gracie file is a reference to an FBI informant, who advised bureau officials that he had been told by "an individual, presently in the Federal

July 23, 1969

MICKEY MANTLE

Mickey Mantle, former well-known baseball player of the New York Yankees, has not been the subject of an investigation by the FBI. However, our files reveal that information received in June, 1956, indicated that Mickey Mantle was "blackmailed" for $15,000 after being found in a compromising situation with a married woman. Mr. Mantle subsequently denied ever having been caught in a compromising situation. Mr. Mantle readily admitted that he had "shacked up" with many girls in New York City, but stated that he has never been caught. (139-243

A confidential source, who has furnished reliable information in the past, advised in June, 1957, that a very prominent Washington, D. C., area gambler and bookmaker arranged dates for members of the New York Yankees baseball club at a Washington, D. C., house of prostitution. Allegedly, Mr. Mantle was one of the members of the team who was entertained at this house of prostitution. (62-9-53-31, p. 34)

In February, 1962, it was alleged that an individual, described as a Dallas, Texas, playboy, night club operator and former boy friend of a notorious Dallas stripper, was purchasing the University Club, Dallas, Texas, from a former Dallas gambler. It was further noted that the University Club was a private night club, and that Mickey Mantle of the New York Yankees was one of the individuals financially backing this purchase. (62-9-12-294

In January, 1963, a confidential source, of unknown reliability, advised that a well-known Dallas, Texas, gambler, who frequently made "heavy bets" on professional football games and other athletic contests, would make a number of telephone calls

NOTE: Per request of John D. Ehrlichman, Counsel to the President.

JCF:clw
(8)

MAIL ROOM ☐   TELETYPE UNIT ☐

House of Detention from Alcatraz," that "both Burns and Allen use narcotics and that this is the reason Gracie wears long sleeves all the time. The individual claims he has sold narcotics to George and Gracie."

Elizabeth Arden

Two years later, an FBI investigative file was opened on Elizabeth Arden, the famed operator of the cosmetic firm of the same name, upon receipt of a letter in 1941 alleging that she was opening branches of her firm to be used specifically as clearing houses for Nazi activities. The investigation led nowhere.

Louis Armstrong

Claims of Communist affiliations had been made about Louis Armstrong for years by, and to, the FBI. Although, what incensed the FBI more than anything about Armstrong was the less-than-overwhelming fact that he liked to "smoke" now and again, as a partially withheld FBI report makes clear: "Louis Armstrong and his orchestra were playing at the Flamingo Hotel and Armstrong was dissatisfied with the situation. [Source] said he would take care of Armstrong by calling him on the phone and by sending him 'a bottle of scotch or a couple of reefers.' "

Gene Autry

Renowned on-screen cowboy Gene Autry became the subject of an FBI "Extortion Main File" in the 1940s, after a man made a threatening telephone call to one of Autry's radio stations and attempted to extract a sizeable amount of money. However, an investigation undertaken by the bureau's Richmond field office determined that the "individual" had made the threats "while intoxicated" and, as a result, "the U.S. Attorney declined prosecution because the incident did not violate the Extortion Statute nor the Federal Statute dealing with Interstate Obscene or Harassing Telephone Calls."

Lucille Ball

Particularly notable is the FBI's file on the *I Love Lucy* star, Lucille Ball. According to a 1950s FBI report, Ball had been moving in highly controversial circles:

Rena M. Vale, a Hollywood writer and an admitted former Communist Party member in Los Angeles, California, furnished a sworn deposition to the Assembly Fact Finding Committee on Un-American Activities in California in 1943. She stated that in 1937 she attended a Communist Party new members' class at the home of actress Lucille Ball. Vale added that Ball was not present at the meeting but that the person in charge specifically said that Lucille Ball knew the character of the meeting and approved of its taking place in her home.

Could it be true? Was the beloved Lucy secretly a dirty, no-good Red? Well, the jury is still out on that possibility. But it has to be said that on December 16, 1953, the FBI recorded some remarkably illuminating data on the legendary star that suggests there was some truth to the rumors:

[Lucille Ball] furnished an executive statement to William A. Wheeler, West Coast Representative, House Committee on Un-American Activities, on September 4, 1953, at Hollywood, California. Ball stated that in 1936 she registered to vote as a Communist or intended to vote the Communist Party ticket because her grandfather, Fred Hunt had been a Socialist all his life and she had registered as a Communist to make him happy and to do him a favor. She stated she at no time intended to vote as a Communist.

Ball stated she has never been a member of the Communist Party to "her knowledge"; had never been asked to become a Communist Party member; did not ever attend any meetings which she later discovered were Communist Party meetings; did not know whether or not any meetings were ever held at her home at 1344 North Ogden Drive; stated she did not know Emil Freed and if he had appointed her as a delegate to the State Central Committee of the Communist Party in 1936 it was done without her knowledge or consent; did not recall signing the document sponsoring Emil Freed for the Communist Party nomination to the office of member of the assembly of the 57th District; and has never heard of the California Conference for Repeal of the Criminal Syndicalism Act, the Southern California Council for Constitutional Rights, or the Committee for the 1st Amendment. [Note: Emil Freed was a Communist activist in California at the time.]

Even though Ball had openly admitted that "she registered to vote as a Communist or intended to vote the Communist Party ticket because her grandfather, Fred Hunt, had been a Socialist all his life and she had registered as a Communist to make him happy and to do him a favor," the FBI was apparently satisfied that by the 1950s Ball had put all alleged Communist affiliations behind her: "A review of the subject's file reflects no activity that would warrant her inclusion on the Security Index. The subject's file is being maintained in a closed status."

However, the fact that Rena M. Vale had specifically sworn that, in 1937, she had attended a Communist Party new members' class at the home of Lucille Ball, and that, furthermore, Ball "knew the character of the meeting and approved of its taking place in her home," suggests that there may still be more notable secret tidbits to this story that have failed yet to surface.

Tallulah Bankhead

The actress Tallulah Bankhead, along with other cast members, was accused of the devilishly heinous crime of smoking weed during the 1948 stage production of Noel Coward's *Private Lives*.

This outrageous depravity, as the FBI somewhat amusingly perceived it, did not prevent Bankhead from having a very cordial and regular correspondence with J. Edgar Hoover, however. Nor did it prevent her from being granted a tour of FBI HQ, along with her husband, John Emory.

Maurice Chevalier

The internationally acclaimed actor and singer Maurice Chevalier was born on September 12, 1888, in Paris, France, and in both 1951 and 1954 was refused a visa to the United States by the Department of State as a direct result of his "association with Communists and Communist causes." And although Chevalier was never the direct subject of an FBI investigation per se, his name does appear in several bureau reports, where he was described as "a card-carrying member of the French Communist Party."

Nat King Cole

Contained within an FBI file of 1951 titled "Nat King Cole—Security Matter," is the following: "From information furnished the office in 1945 . . . it appears that Cole and [Deleted] were members of the Communist Party and the Communist Political Association during that period, probably attached to the cultural groups in Hollywood. A confidential informant of known reliability advised in August 1949 that 'King' Cole was a member of the Music Division of the Southern California Chapter of the Arts, Sciences, and Professions Council. (AS&PC)." According to the bureau, the AS&PC had been "cited as a Communist front."

Gary Cooper

John Wayne, Audie Murphy, and Gene Autry were not the only Hollywood cowboys who were of interest to the FBI. Born Frank James Cooper, on May 7, 1901, in Helena, Montana, Gary Cooper caught the attention of J. Edgar Hoover in 1947 when a Rio de Janeiro, Brazil-based newspaper reported that the actor had made a speech in which he "praised the American Communist Party." However, according to the FBI, this was seemingly not true:

The Daily Worker, an East Coast Communist newspaper published an article which stated: "Press Agent Hoax in Brazil Makes hero of Wrong Actor." The article said that this was a cheap trick to get the people to see his films—to take their money under false pretenses. The November 1951 issue of the bulletin 'Counterattack' contained an article that stated for years Gary Cooper was prominent in the motion picture alliance for the preservation of American ideals which had led the fight against Communist infiltration in Hollywood. Mr. Cooper's house was burglarized on several occasions and incurred a loss of several thousand dollars each time. He also was the target of numerous extortion attempts.

Sammy Davis Jr.

Rat-Packer Sammy Davis Jr. caught the FBI's attention on numerous occasions. And although the bureau's "Sammy File" is a lengthy one, it is not particularly enlightening or titillating. However, there *is* the following report of December 27, 1963:

This is to advise that the Chicago Courier, a Chicago, Illinois newspaper, on 12–21–63 carried an article alleging that Sammy Davis, Jr., the well-known entertainer and associate of Frank Sinatra, Sr., was kidnapped in Las Vegas several years ago by a pair of tough Chicago gangsters. According to this article, Davis was released when told by his kidnappers to "forget about any plans you have to wed movie actress Kim Novak." The article went on to state that this incident was just disclosed a few days ago following the kidnapping of Frank Sinatra, Jr.

The article states that this incident was known by a few of Sammy Davis, Jr.'s close associates but that Davis did not discuss it at the time. The article alleges that Broadway columnist Frank Farrell leaked this item a few days ago and that it was not known what action Federal authorities might take in regard to this matter. It is reported that this kidnapping was arranged by certain people in show business as a "friendly kidnapping" to convince Davis not to marry Kim Novak. The article concluded by alleging that a "death note" was left in Davis' dressing room at a benefit show in Santa Monica, California, within the past week.

No information was located in Bureau files concerning the above-mentioned kidnapping or the recent "death note." This story may well be an attempt by Davis to obtain publicity similar to that afforded the Sinatras in the recent kidnapping of Frank Sinatra, Jr.

But the FBI could not apparently summon up the energy to get even remotely enthused about this affair, as Alan Belmont, widely acknowledged as the "Number Three Man" in the bureau at the time, noted in an internal document generated as a result of the allegations concerning the kidnapping of Sammy Davis Jr.:

I do not think we should interview Sammy Davis, Jr., based on information in the Chicago Courier, alleging Davis was kidnapped "several years ago," nor concerning the alleged death note left in his dressing room last week. If there is any substance to either of these allegations, Davis had a responsibility to notify the FBI or other appropriate authorities.

Marlene Dietrich

Marlene Dietrich was born on December 27, 1901, as Marie Magdalene (or Maria Magdalena) Dietrich, in Berlin-Schöneberg, Germany. In 1932, she made a movie in the United States under contract to Paramount Pictures, and subsequently took the oath of United States citizenship in Los Angeles. Never known for her financial wizardry, Dietrich received notice from that most feared of all organizations, the Internal Revenue Service in 1942, that she owed them a substantial amount of money and needed to make arrangements to pay them, or they would be forced to take action against her. Dietrich paid up. And according to the FBI:

During June and July of 1943, Dietrich toured the Midwest in connection with the Treasury Department's War Bond sales. She was married to a German citizen, and had a daughter by him. They accompanied her to New York where the husband stayed most of the time, while Dietrich lived in Los Angeles. Ms. Dietrich was the victim of an extortion attempt in 1940, and was also threatened with kidnapping along with another actress from the same film studio.

Douglas Fairbanks Jr.

According to an FBI report of February 27, 1953, titled "Douglas Fairbanks, Jr.," the renowned actor had a few secrets that were of distinct interest to the United States government:

The "New York Times" issue dated October 10, 1941, carried a full-page advertisement for Russian War Relief, Inc. Under the caption "These Eminent Americans Ask For Your Help on Behalf of the Russian People" appeared the name of Douglas Fairbanks, Jr.

The name of Douglas Fairbanks, Jr., appeared as a sponsor on a program of a dinner which was held at Ciro's Restaurant, Hollywood, California, under the joint auspices of the American Committee to Save Refugees, Exiled Writers Committee, and the United American Spanish Aid Committee on November 10, 1941.

The American Committee to Save Refugees was cited as a Communist front by the Special Committee on Un-American Activities.

The Exiled Writers Committee was cited by the California Committee on Un-American Activities as follows: "Established by the Communist League of American Writers to Save refugees. The Exiled Writers Committee worked with other Communist fronts in the Spanish Communist refugee agitation."

The United American Spanish Aid Committee was cited as a Communist organization by the Attorney General.

The "Worker," east coast Communist newspaper, issue dated November 9, 1947, carried an article captioned "Hollywood Fights Back." According to this article, the Committee for the First Amendment had sponsored a radio program protesting the action of the House Committee on Un-American Activities. It was reported that Douglas Fairbanks, Jr., had participated in this program.

The Committee for the First Amendment was cited as a Communist front by the California Committee on Un-American activities.

The "Daily Variety," a trade publication of the motion picture industry issue dated December 29, 1947, identified Douglas Fairbanks, Jr., as a member of the "anti-Communist group of motion picture people who were members of both the major political parties in the United States, who felt there was a great danger of confusion over the difference between liberalism and Communism." The article further reported that the "anti-Communist" group would not have as a member any person who had appeared as a witness before the House Committee on Un-American Activities.

The "New York Sun" issue dated January 22, 1948, carried an article captioned "Secret Plans Laid for Drive to Attack Thomas Committee." This article reported, among other things, that the Committee of One Thousand was making plans for a stage show, and that Douglas Fairbanks, Jr., would be among those to participate.

The Committee of One Thousand was cited as a "Communist created and controlled front organization" by the California Committee on Un-American Activities.

The "Daily Peoples World," west coast Communist newspaper, issue dated December 27, 1948, in a column captioned "Political Arena," attacked as to veracity a booklet entitled "Red Stars in Hollywood." The article pointed out that the booklet had been prepared by Miron C. Fagan. According to this article, Douglas Fairbanks, Jr., appeared in the booklet as one of the "red stars in Hollywood."

There was more to come. An FBI document of August 29, 1972, practically implicated Fairbanks in the now notorious Profumo spy scandal of 1963 that rocked the British government to its very core. John Dennis Profumo, the British government's Secretary of State for War, was married to movie star Valerie Hobson, and moved effortlessly within the highest echelons of English society. It was his affair with hooker Christine Keeler that proved to be his downfall, however. Keeler had left home at sixteen and gravitated to London where she found work at Murray's cabaret club and became close friends with Marilyn "Mandy" Rice-Davies, another figure on the capital's cabaret circuit. It wasn't long before both girls drifted into the sex-fueled circle of Stephen Ward, a West End osteopath and socialite who had numerous high-profile friends and influential contacts within the British government. Thanks to Ward's contacts, Keeler and Rice-Davies began climbing the social ladder, a ladder that, for Keeler, led right to War Secretary Profumo.

When details of their secret affair reached the British press, however, the clandestine relationship became the talk of the nation. And in a situation that in some ways eerily mirrored the

Clinton-Lewinsky affair of more than three decades later, in March 1963 Profumo assured the Government that there was "no impropriety whatever" in his relationship with Keeler. Only two and a half months later, however, he appeared before Members of the British Parliament to admit "with deep remorse" that he had misled the House, and would resign. He *did* have sexual relations with that woman, after all.

But what really destroyed Profumo was not so much the deceit over his affair with Keeler, but the startling, and potentially very serious, revelation that Keeler had also been having a sexual relationship with one Eugene Ivanov, who was none other than the naval attaché at the Soviet embassy in London. It was that highly significant detail that led the FBI to compile a detailed report on the whole sorry saga that was code-named "Operation Bowtie."

Profumo resigned and Stephen Ward was prosecuted for living on immoral earnings. In her 2001 autobiography, *The Truth At Last*, Keeler claimed that Sir Roger Hollis, chief of MI5, the British equivalent of the FBI, was a Soviet spy, and that Stephen Ward, who, on the last day of his trial, committed suicide with an overdose of sleeping tablets, ran a spy ring that included Hollis and Sir Anthony Blunt, whose title was Surveyor of the Queen's Pictures.

And from the FBI's "Operation Bowtie" file comes the following background data on Douglas Fairbanks Jr.'s links to the controversy:

[Douglas Fairbanks, Jr.] who you advised resides at Chateau Marmont, 8221 Sunset Boulevard, Los Angeles, California, was the subject of an applicant-type investigation conducted by the FBI in 1951 in connection with his appointment as a consultant with the Voice of America Program.

The investigation revealed that during the 1940's, Mr. Fairbanks' name was associated with several organizations cited as communist front groups, but acquaintances, associates, and other sources all described him as anticommunist and loyal American citizen.

Fairbanks' name was also mentioned in connection with the trial of Stephen Ward on morals charges in England during 1963. The case received worldwide publicity and was highlighted by the testimony of two admitted prostitutes, Christine Keeler and Marilyn Rice-Davies, who, according to press reports, named Fairbanks as among those whom the girls described as their "boyfriends."

Fairbanks reportedly received osteopathic treatments from Ward, and through Ward, became acquainted with Keeler and Rice-Davies, but denied that he had ever been associated with the two women.

Clark Gable

Throughout his career, movie legend Clark Gable was dogged by threats of extortion, all of which he was quick to share with the FBI. Indeed, as the bureau noted: "On February 21, 1938, Gable received an extortion letter from Fonda, Iowa, demanding that he send $1,000. The investigation revealed that the letter had been written by an Iowa farmhand, not the woman whose name was signed to the note. The farmhand had sent the note after the woman spurned him. On August 18, 1936, a Philadelphia, Pennsylvania, man sent Gable an extortion letter demanding $5,000 from Gable and MGM Studio. He advised that if he didn't receive all $10,000, he would do bodily harm to Gable."

A strange letter that Gable had received on May 12, 1939, via the Hollywood offices of Metro-Golden-Mayer (MGM) was also turned over to the FBI for scrutiny. The letter was postmarked Columbus, Ohio, and read: "Just who do you think you are that you can hook me and keep my human respect and marry another woman. Prophesy or no—anyone that is small enough to live with another wife when he is hooked, I don't wish to ever see. I demand my freedom and I'll get it or I'll know the reason why."

Needless to say, Gable was not engaged in bigamy as the letter suggested, and the bureau reported that: "Efforts to locate the person who wrote the letter were not successful."

And, as the FBI also recorded: "On July 6, 1940, an attorney at the MGM Studios opened a letter addressed to Clark Gable requesting that he deposit a generous amount of money in the American Trust, Jefferson Street Branch in San Francisco. On December 3, 1940, Clark Gable and his wife, Carole Lombard, received a letter wherein they were threatened with kidnapping to be held for ransom."

Marvin Gaye

The late singer Marvin Gaye (shot and killed by his father in 1984) will forever be remembered for the massive contribution that he made to the world of soul music. However, he is less likely to be remembered for the brief time that he spent in the United States Air Force in 1957. Declassified files on Basic Airman Marvin Gay Jr., (he added the "e" to his last name as his musical career took off) prepared by Major William B. Mayes of the 802nd Supply Squadron at Schilling Air Force Base, Kansas, suggest that Gaye would not have done well at all on the battlefield:

Airman Gay is uncooperative, lacks even a minor degree of initiative, shows very little interest in his assigned duties, and does nothing to improve his job knowledge. He has been a constant problem to his supervisor and to the First Sergeant ever since he has been assigned to this Squadron. He evidences a dislike for the service and indicated nothing that can show that he can meet Air Force standards. I am convinced that further retention in the service would be a waste of time, effort and money. Request that he be discharged from the service with the least possible delay.

Rita Hayworth

Hollywood legend Rita Hayworth did not fare much better. On September 13, 1953, Hayworth and her fiancé, Dick Haymes received a letter at the Sands Hotel in Las Vegas where they were staying at the time, telling them that if they got married, Princess Yasmin Khan, Hayworth's three-year-old daughter by Aly Khan, would be killed. Again, the FBI dug deep into the affair but it remained unresolved, and no harm came to Hayworth's daughter.

Aldous Huxley

Renowned author Aldous Huxley also became a target for FBI interest when it was revealed that his classic book *Brave New World* was creating waves of trouble in Michigan. It was March 14, 1962, when a special agent from the bureau's head office in Michigan informed Hoover, under cover of a document titled "Activities in Educational Institutions," of the fuss that Huxley's book was causing:

On March 9, 1962 [Deleted of] Michigan, advised she has children attending Forest Hills High school, 5091 Hall SE, Ada, Michigan, near Grand Rapids. She said she and other parents of children at the above school are concerned about the conduct of certain of the teachers there, and particularly the use of a book, "Brave New World", by Huxley, which is a subject of study at the school. [Deleted] said she had heard through sources that a history teacher at Forest Hills, had displayed a Russian flag in his classroom during the visit of Soviet Premier Khrushchev to the United States, explaining that he did so in honor of a visiting head of state. She said she heard he had not displayed flags of other nations when their heads of state visited the United States.

[Deleted] said [a] recent graduate of Dartmouth College, who is an English teacher at Forest Hills, is using the novel "Brave New World" by Huxley, as a text for classroom study.

She said she heard [Deleted] had a picture of a Russian flag on the blackboard or bulletin board in his classroom.

[Deleted] advised he had received several reports regarding the controversy at Forest Hills High School, which appeared to center around classroom use of the book, "Brave New World" by Aldous Huxley. The Forest Hills School Board had apparently ordered this book banned from use at the school, but a review of this decision was ordered when faculty members showed that only three of the seven members of the School Board had read the book. [Deleted] said he had no indication that any subversive activity was involved in the above controversy.

John F. Kennedy Jr.

Although John F. Kennedy Jr. was not the subject of an FBI investigation per se, a substantial file on him *was* opened when the FBI learned of various "alleged plots" to kidnap the son of the late president John F. Kennedy in 1985 and 1995. Interestingly, the FBI has also stated that their "files also contain a reference to laboratory examinations in 1994 to determine the true writer of a threatening letter received by a United States Senator. The letter was written by an unknown person and signed, 'John F. Kennedy, Jr.' "

Jack London

Acclaimed author Jack London was never the focus of an FBI investigation. However, the FBI has stated that "London was mentioned in FBI files as co-founder of the Inter-Collegiate Socialist Society. The FBI was interested in the society because of its views on socialism." This interest can be demonstrated by the following FBI report of October 15, 1941:

Jack London, Upton Sinclair and Clarence Darrow founded in 1905 the Inter-Collegiate Socialist Society for the Purpose of creating students of Socialism. After the World war the organization was known as the League for Industrial Democracy (L.I.D.). In 1931 the Communist students in the L.I.D. became dissatisfied with the Socialist leadership and split off forming the New York Student League, which became the National Student Union. In December, 1935, the Student League for Industrial Democracy and the National Student Union amalgamated into the American Student Union. (The Socialists and the Communists united for a common front.) Membership of this amalgamation amounted to 20,000 representatives, 175 in college chapters and 100 in high school chapters.

Peter Lorre

Born on June 26, 1904, in Austria-Hungary, now Slovakia, Peter Lorre became a well-known Hollywood motion picture actor in the 1940s. In answer to questions, the FBI has stated, "Mr. Lorre was not a subject of an FBI investigation, but his name was found in the FBI files of other persons. Lorre associated with Otto Katz, Bertolt Brecht and Hanns Eisler; just a few of the better-known communist sympathizers."

Mickey Mantle

The glitterati of Hollywood aside, the elite of the sporting world also caught the attention of J. Edgar Hoover, including none other than celebrated baseball star Mickey Mantle. An FBI document of July 23, 1969, reveals that Hoover had penetrated Mantle's secret world of sex, hookers, and gambling:

Mickey Mantle, former well-known baseball player of the New York Yankees, has not been the subject of an investigation by the FBI. However, our files reveal that information received in June, 1956, indicated that Mickey Mantle was "blackmailed" for $15,000 after being found in a compromising situation with a married woman. Mr. Mantle subsequently denied ever having been caught in a compromising situation.

Mr. Mantle readily admitted that he had "shacked up" with many girls in New York City, but stated that he has never been caught.

A confidential source, who has furnished reliable information in the past, advised in June, 1957, that a very prominent Washington, D.C., area gambler and bookmaker arranged dates for members of the New York Yankees baseball club at a Washington, D.C., house of prostitution. Allegedly, Mr. Mantle was one of the members of the team who was entertained at this house of prostitution.

In February, 1962, it was alleged that an individual, described as a Dallas, Texas, playboy, nightclub operator and former boyfriend of a notorious Dallas stripper, was purchasing the University Club, Dallas, Texas, from a former Dallas gambler. It was further noted that the University Club was a private nightclub, and that Mickey Mantle of the New York Yankees was one of the individuals financially backing this purchase.

In January, 1963, a confidential source, of unknown reliability, advised that a well-known Dallas, Texas, gambler, who frequently made "heavy bets" on professional football games and other athletic contests, would make a number of telephone calls to various professional athletes to obtain information concerning certain games. Some of the professional athletes contacted by this individual allegedly included Mickey Mantle of the New York Yankees.

Dean Martin

Dean Martin's FBI file is of an impressive length. However, much of its content is related to a variety of attempts to extort huge sums of money from the ultimate lounge lizard, none of which succeeded, and all of which were similar and overwhelmingly inept in nature. As a result, and somewhat surprisingly when one considers that he regularly hung out with buddy-to-the-Mob Frank

Sinatra, the file offers us few real insights into the secret world of the hard-drinking rat-packer. However, a bureau document of August 21, 1972, titled "Dean Martin Summary," does at least hint at the secrets of the inner, private world of Martin:

Captioned individual was born Dino Crocetti on June 17, 1917, at Steubenville, Ohio. . . . He has reportedly been associated with several known hoodlums and is well known to the gambling interests in Las Vegas, Nevada. In 1961 he reportedly owned one per cent in the Sands Hotel, Inc., at Las Vegas, and had an interest in the Cal-Neva Lodge at Lake Tahoe. Martin was also reported to be associated with prostitutes and officials of the Teamsters Union.

A confidential source who has supplied reliable information in the past advised in May, 1956, that Dean Martin had made an extremely obscene phonograph record while cutting a record advertising one of their motion pictures. The source explained the obscene portion was supposed to have been destroyed but the master disc was saved and additional records were made and circulated. Martin also was alleged to have been involved in the negotiations for an obscene film to be distributed outside the United States.

Another confidential source of reliable information reported Frank Sinatra and Dean Martin flew to Miami, Florida, to attend [Deleted], Samuel M. Giancana, a well-known Chicago hoodlum.

In May 1950, a representative of [Deleted] advised that the names of [Deleted] and Dean Martin were contained in a book of alleged prospective customers which was found in a Chicago, Illinois, house of prostitution which allegedly catered to Hollywood male clientele.

In November 1955, unsubstantiated information was received from an admitted homosexual identifying numerous stage and screen personalities as homosexuals. This individual also stated that a number of other personalities in the entertainment business were known among homosexuals as "gay." He stated he heard Dean Martin and [Deleted] were classified as "gay."

Of course, much of the above was merely hearsay and unfounded gossip of the type that proliferates throughout the FBI's dossiers on the rich and the famous. And the fact that the FBI would apparently waste its time bothering to investigate Dean's "obscene phonograph" record, which had simply been recorded in a drunken moment for the amusement of his drinking pals and largely no one else, demonstrates the sheer absurdity of some of the bureau's absolute money-wasting investigations.

Roddy McDowall

Roddy McDowall, the London, England-born movie star and acknowledged soul of discretion when it came to Hollywood gossip, who achieved everlasting fame as a talking primate in both the *Planet of the Apes* movie franchise and the television spin-off series, might have seemed the least likely person to be the subject of FBI interest. But not even Cornelius the Chimpanzee could escape the wrath of the feared crime-fighting organization. Considering that, in late 1974, the FBI was astonished to learn that McDowall possessed a huge collection of illegal pirated movies with a "conservative" value in excess of five million dollars, perhaps the reason for that interest becomes somewhat understandable, to say the very least.

Although McDowall was ultimately not prosecuted by officials, the fear of God was certainly put in him by the FBI. Not only did a quivering McDowall spill his guts on the full story of how his collection of cinematic masterpieces grew and grew, he also fingered a variety of other famous figures in Hollywood who possessed similar collections, including Rock Hudson, Dick Martin, and Mel Torme. Doubtless, given the fact that they were *al-*

ready the subjects of highly disapproving FBI files, Rock Hudson and Dick Martin, in particular, would hardly have been enamored by McDowall's actions. But for the bureau, it was just another day in the challenge to both create and update its secret celebrity files.

MC5

On February 25, 1969, the Detroit, Michigan, office of the FBI reported to J. Edgar Hoover on the activities of a rising rock band named the MC5 that was creating controversy on a large scale within the city of Detroit. Little did the bureau know it at the time, but the MC5 would ultimately go on to become one of the most legendary and inspirational groups within the annals of rock and roll, with their all-time classic album *Kick out the Jams,* heralded by practically anyone and everyone who has been moved by the raging distortions of an electric guitar and the unbridled emotion of enraged youth. But to the FBI, which was overwhelmingly unimpressed by the cultural revolution of the 1960s, there were other, far more serious reasons for taking note of the activities of Detroit's finest. J. Edgar Hoover was advised by Neil J. Welch, the special agent in charge at the bureau's Detroit office, that the January 3, 1969, edition of *Time* magazine had carried an article titled "The Revolutionary Hype" that described the MC5's music as "the most violent expression of revolutionary rock so far."

Time elaborated further and reported that the group's manager, 26-year-old John Sinclair, who ran their "hippie-style communal household in Ann Arbor," had proclaimed the MC5 to be "a free, high-energy source that will drive us wild into the streets of America, yelling and screaming and tearing down everything that would keep people slaves."

And Hoover undoubtedly sat up and took notice when *Time* added that, "the MC5 are self-styled 'musical guerillas,' who flaunt their membership in a minuscule left-wing organization called the White Panther Party." If that alone was not enough to enrage the powerful FBI boss, the fact that *Time* had learned that members of the MC5 had a "string of arrests," on charges including possession of pot, and were on occasion given to "burning the United States flag," certainly was.

The White Panthers was very much a proactive political body that had been founded in 1968 by MC5 manager John Sinclair, his wife Magdalene "Leni" Arndt, and Lawrence Plamondon, and its origins can be traced back to an interview in which Huey P. Newton, cofounder of the Black Panther Party, was asked: 'What can white people do to support the Black Panthers?' Newton replied that, quite naturally, they could form a White Panther Party, and thus was born the WPP.

Hoover's concerns about the activities of Sinclair and the FBI were largely born out of the WPP's manifesto that, in part, stated that the party supported: "Total assault on the culture by any means necessary, including rock and roll, dope and fucking in the streets; free exchange of energy and materials—we demand the end of money; free food, clothes, housing, dope, music, bodies, medical care—everything, free for everybody;" and "free access to information media—free the technology from the greed creeps."

As John Sinclair noted: "Our program is cultural revolution through a total assault on the culture, which makes use of every tool, every energy and every media we can get our collective hands on. We take our program with us everywhere we go and use any means necessary to expose people to it."

Today, forty years on, the White Panther Party is long gone. The same cannot be said for the MC5, however. Although vocalist Rob Tyner died in 1991, followed by the band's guitarist, Fred "Sonic" Smith in 1994, in 2003 the surviving members, guitarist Wayne Kramer, bassist Michael Davis, and drummer Dennis Thompson, teamed up with a number of guest singers, including Dave Vanian from the Damned, Ian Astbury from the Cult, and Motorhead's Lemmy, and flew the flag of the MC5 proudly. In the following year, 2004, the group toured again, as DKT/MC5. They continue to piss off parents and officials everywhere.

George Raft

Famed actor of the 1930s, 40s, and 50s, George Raft grew up in New York's Hell's Kitchen and received his first starring role in the 1932 version of *Scarface*. He had numerous Mob ties, and was a lifelong friend of notorious underworld character Bugsy Siegel, who actually lived at Raft's Hollywood home for a while as he sought to make inroads into Hollywood on behalf of the world of organized crime. Raft's tough guy image earned him numerous hard-hitting roles. Perhaps his most memorable gangster-style portrayal was, ironically, a parody—in Billy Wilder's *Some Like It Hot*, in which he appeared alongside Marilyn Monroe, Tony Curtis, and Jack Lemmon. As FBI files demonstrate, however, Hoover's special agents were surprised to find that Raft's on-screen image did not seem to gel at all with that of the actor's private life. The FBI's files note that Raft had been investigated in 1949 under the White Slave Traffic Act as a result of his associations with a prostitute at New York's Sherry-Netherland Hotel. In 1952 and 1953, FBI files reflect, Raft was interviewed by personnel from the Los Angeles bureau office with regard to what was described as "another investigation." The FBI's substantially blacked-out files on Raft tell an interesting story:

In an attempt to locate Raft at his residence in Beverly Hills, it was determined that his house was occupied by a young woman who Raft later advised was his girl friend. He stated he allowed the girl to live in his house with her parents while he was absent from California, and upon returning found that her parents were ill and he could not move them from the house so he took an apartment in Beverly Hills where he was interviewed.

Doubtless, Raft would have been mortified (as, certainly, would all of his underworld buddies) if he had known that the interviewing FBI agents had added in their report to Hoover that,

"Raft is small in stature, has a very limp hand shake and gives the personal impression quite contrary to that which he portrays in motion pictures and television shows."

Sex Pistols

There is good evidence to suggest that John Lennon was not the only rebel rocker being closely watched by Britain's security services. According to MI5 whistleblower David Shayler: "I saw something from the seventies called *Subversion in Contemporary Music*. It was cuttings about bands like the Sex Pistols. . . . You can imagine some Colonel Blimp [a British caricature of an out-of-touch military man] character compiling this file, whereas anybody with half a brain knew the Sex Pistols talked a good talk—wrote a lot of songs about it, but when it came to political activism did absolutely nothing."

Interestingly, when the Sex Pistols embarked upon their January 1978 tour of the United States, it was widely rumored at the time that Warner Brothers had hired former "CIA goons" to roadie the band. Similarly, in the 2002 documentary *The Filth and the Fury*, Sex Pistols guitarist Steve Jones confirmed that, while on tour in the United States, the band had indeed been followed by elements of both the CIA and the FBI.

Official files also shed some light on one of the most mysterious aspects of the Sex Pistols' short career: the October 12, 1978, death of Nancy Spungen, girlfriend of Pistols bass player, Sid Vicious, at the Chelsea Hotel, New York. A declassified "Voluntary Disclosure Sheet Supplement," that was prepared at an official level after Vicious's arrest by the New York Police Department for the murder of Spungen, reveals some intriguing data concerning the death of the drug-addicted Nancy:

To the detectives [Vicious] said in substance that:
He and the deceased had taken tuinal that night and he went to sleep about 1 AM. Nancy was in the bed with him

when he went to sleep. Nancy was sitting on the edge of the bed flicking a knife. They had an argument.

He claimed when he woke up in the morning the bed was wet with blood. He thought he had "pee'd" himself. He found the deceased in the bathroom sitting on the floor (same position as found by police). She was breathing. She had a stab wound in her stomach.

He left her. He went out to get her methadone—at Lafayette Street. When he returned she was full of blood. He washed off the knife and he attempted to wash her off. When he could not wash the blood off her he called for help. He did not know what happened to her. He had slept the entire night through. At various times he said, "my baby is dead" or words to that effect. He denied stabbing her (various times).

Notably, the record reveals that, at one point, Vicious had made a confession of sorts with respect to Spungen's bloody death:

The defendant also said that he did not remember what their argument was about and that she hit him and he hit her on top of the head and knocked her onto the bed—but he did not knock her unconscious. He said, "I stabbed her but I didn't mean to kill her. I loved her, but she treated me like shit."

However, Vicious later denied saying this, as police noted: "At other times the defendant said the deceased must have fallen on the knife and that she must have dragged herself into the bathroom. When asked why he left the deceased in the bathroom, wounded, and went out to get his methadone he said, 'Oh! I am a dog,' or similar words." The murder was never solved; twenty-one-year-old Sid Vicious died of a heroin overdose on February 2, 1979, while out on bail.

Paul Simonon, former bass guitarist with fellow British punks the Clash, echoed the fact that prominent punk rock figures in late 1970s Britain were watched by elements of the government. Responding to questions as to whether or not an official file might have existed on the Clash, too, Simonon stated: "There probably is, yes, alongside the file on the Sex Pistols. It's hard to fully appreciate now, but we certainly stood out back then, we really made a noise. It wasn't just us, it was every punk—anyone, in fact, who wasn't wearing flares was making a big political noise that terrified the Government."

MI5 man David Shayler also stated that similar files had been compiled on the British band UB40, who, mostly in the early 1980s, were very well known for their politically oriented songs and their scathing, and wholly justified, attacks on the utterly fascist regime of then British prime minister Margaret Thatcher.

Lana Turner

Data contained on the FBI's official website states: "The FBI files indicate that in 1945 Lana Turner was the victim of an extortion attempt. On April 4, 1958, Lana Turner had a fight in her bedroom with her boyfriend, Johnny Stompanato, an underworld mob figure. Lana's fourteen-year-old daughter, Cheryl Crane, feared that Stompanato was going to disfigure her mother and stabbed him with an eight-inch carving knife. The coroner's jury found the stabbing to be justifiable homicide. Santa Monica, California's juvenile court ordered Cheryl to a school for wayward girls."

Mae West

According to another summary that can also be located at the FBI's website, 1930s actress Mae West had asked for the bureau's help:

The FBI files indicate that in 1935, Mae West, a Hollywood film star, received an extortion letter threatening to disfigure her with acid. In 1943, Mae West, Betty Grable, and other

Hollywood notables, received additional extortion letters. An eighteen-year-old boy was apprehended trying to mail another letter in which he demanded $85,000. The extortionist was from Omaha, NE and received a five-year sentence for the crime.

Conclusions

Having examined an absolute wealth of previously classified documentation on numerous personalities from the world of show business, what can we conclude about the true nature of official surveillance of, and interest in the rich and the famous? Certainly, the files reveal as much about Hoover, the FBI, and the mood of the country at the time as they do about the celebrities themselves. After all, they are human, just like the rest of us.

As far as the army, navy, and air force's files on Jack Kerouac, Marvin Gaye, and Jimi Hendrix are concerned, it seems safe to conclude that free-spirited artists—whether they are singers, rock guitarists, or writers—do not adapt at all well to the rigid conformity of life in the military, hence the reason why they shine like stars in public, but fare far less well when being told what to do by others. And, paradoxically, the exact opposite seems to be true, too: even those Hollywood players who *did* have notable military careers, such as war hero Audie Murphy in particular, never seemed happy; Murphy's highly successful movie career was forever dogged by the horrors of post-traumatic stress disorder. The same goes for Frank Sinatra; although he was conveniently able to avoid wartime military service, his emotional condition was the last thing the army wanted to deal with, anyway. In other words, Hollywood stars should stay as far away from the battlefield as possible—for everyone's sake.

As for the fact that Abbott and Costello, Mickey Mantle, Frank Sinatra, Andy Warhol, Marilyn Monroe, and Errol Flynn, among many others, enjoyed wild and varied sex lives, or had a particular penchant for pornography, well, so what? That hardly made them criminal outlaws. In fact, surveillance of the Hollywood glitterati purely on the basis of their bed partners, was mainly the result of the outdated and antiquated prejudices of the agency—which, as we have seen with respect to such issues, was almost unanimously the FBI. And, on this track: was it really that important to government agents that Rock Hudson, a man born gay who just wanted to enjoy his life and his privacy, might have been contemplating a movie role as an FBI agent?

The fact that J. Edgar Hoover was vehemently antigay, as various files cited within this book amply demonstrate, has led some commentators to conclude that his tirade against famous homosexuals was because he, too, was gay but was never able to come to terms with the fact. Interestingly, FBI files occasionally focused their attention upon rumors to the effect that Hoover himself was a secret homosexual. One such file, dated June 30, 1942, reported on stories in circulation that "the Director was a homosexual and kept a large group of young boys around him." Similarly writer Marilyn Bardsley states: "The single factor that gave rise to the strongest rumors was Hoover's lifelong intimacy with Clyde Tolson," who was Hoover's number-two man in the bureau.

Or, perhaps, "right-hand man" would have been a better description. An Internet article titled "J. Edgar Hoover 1895-1972," notes: "It is widely believed that Hoover and Clyde Tolson, the FBI's Associate Director, were lovers. The two were inseparable for over forty years. They regularly had lunch and dinner five times a week over this same period. The two vacationed together, and Hoover's scrapbooks (found after his death) were almost entirely of Tolson." It is unlikely, however, that we will ever know the real story of Hoover's sexuality, or to what extent that may have had a bearing upon his unwarranted treatment of homosexuals and particularly those in the entertainment industry.

Sex lives aside, what about those numerous claims of communism and espionage that proliferate in celebrity files? The records on Errol Flynn and Rudolf Nureyev, in particular, definitely suggest that some of those investigations had some merit to them. But, with so much information of an undetermined value provided to the FBI, or where the data had been made available by a source that was of unknown reliability, we are also faced with a scenario in which the FBI chased down every rumor, tale, innuendo, and fact and viewed them all as being of equal value— which, of course, was not true—and, as a direct result of those conclusions, made sweeping judgments about the celebrity under investigation.

The files on John Lennon tell us much about the FBI's methods and motives. The former Beatle was simply trying to exercise his right to freedom of speech, yet the FBI's response was to try and find ways to get him deported and sent back to England— hardly the reaction one would hope to receive from an agency that supposedly wanted to protect the right of the individual to free speech.

The FBI's relationship to John Wayne was very different and somewhat unique, in the sense that he was arguably the one and only celebrity who never incurred Hoover's dreaded wrath. Of course, Wayne's hatred of communism was an overriding factor in this, and is an indicator of the "with-us-or-against-us" attitude that was prevalent within the FBI of the Cold War era.

Remember also, that of the many files on the famous that have been declassified, a substantial amount have whole passages of data deleted from them—and occasionally for reasons allegedly affecting the national security of the United States of America. It must be said that if those redacted portions were made available to us, our impressions of some of the stars of the silver screen might be radically altered, and perhaps not necessarily for the better.

But, having reviewed sixty years of files, of one thing we can be truly certain: the FBI's documents on the world of the celebrity were, and still are, as varied, as unusual, and as outrageous as the famous figures that they were watching.

References

Other than the actual official government, military, and intelligence documents cited within the pages of this book, the following additional sources were consulted.

Chapter 1: Abbott and Costello
The Official Abbott and Costello Website: www.abbottandcostello.net.
"Russell Dodd's Abbott and Costello, Forever!": www.louandbud.com.

Chapter 2: Jack Kerouac
Big Sur, Jack Kerouac, Foreword by Adam Saroyan. Penguin Books 1992.
On the Road, Jack Kerouac. Viking Compass, 1959.
www.thesmokinggun.com.
www.archives.gov/publications/prologue/2006/spring/vips-military.html.

Chapter 3: Errol Flynn
Errol Flynn: The Untold Story, Charles Higham. Granada Publishing Ltd.,
    1980.
The Life and Crimes of Errol Flynn, Lionel Godfrey. Robert Hale Ltd., 1977.
Errol Flynn, Michael Freedland. Arthur Barker Ltd., 1978.
The Young Errol, John Hammond Moore. Angus & Robertson, 1955.
Errol and Me, Nora Eddington. Signet Books, 1960.
"British Documents Prove Errol Flynn Spied for Allies, Not the Nazis,"
    David Bamber and Chris Hastings. *Daily Telegraph*, December 31, 2000.
"The Back Half—The Missing Errol Flynn File," Charles Higham. *New
    Statesman*, April 17, 2000. www.newstatesman.com.

Chapter 4: Ernest Hemingway

"Ernest Hemingway, Introduction," Caroline Hulse: www.ernestheming
way.com.

"Timeless Hemingway," Josh Silverstein: www.timelesshemingway.com.

Ernest Hemingway Chronology: www.ehfop.org.

"Ernest Hemingway, Biography": nobelprize.org/literature/laureates/1954/
hemingway-bio.html.

Chapter 5: Billie Holiday

"Sad Am I," Julia Blackburn, *Guardian*, March 26, 2005. books.guardian
.co.uk/review/story/0,12084,1445169,00.html.

With Billie, Julia Blackburn. Pantheon, 2005.

The Unofficial Billie Holiday Website: www.ladyday.net.

The Official Site of Billie Holiday: www.cmgww.com/music/holiday.

"Farah Griffin, Author of *In Search of Billie Holiday: If You Can't Be Free,
Be a Mystery*": www.jerryjazzmusician.com/linernotes/billie_holiday.html.

Chapter 6: John Wayne

"Book Tells How John Wayne Survived Soviet Assassination," Nick Paton
Walsh. *Guardian*, August 1, 2003. www.guardian.co.uk/russia/article/
0,2763,1010266,00.html.

"The John Birch Society," Barbara Aho: watch.pair.com/jbs-cnp.html.

Conquerer Film Location Site: ludb.clui.org/ex/i/UT3174/.

John Wayne: The Man Behind the Myth, Michael Munn. NAL Trade, 2005.

"Conspiracy of Silence," M. D. Schwartz, A. Kalet: bmj.bmjjournals.com/
cgi/content/full/309/6948/207.

Chapter 7: Audie Murphy

Post Traumatic Stress Disorder: The Invisible Injury, David Kinchin. Success Unlimited, 2001.

Audie L. Murphy Memorial Website: www.audiemurphy.com.

"Audie Leon Murphy": www.jrotc.org/audie_murphy.htm.

Chapter 8: Frank Sinatra

"Frank Sinatra Biography": www.hotshotdigital.com/OldRock/FrankSinatra
Bio.html.

"Biography": www.spiritofsinatra.com/pages/bio.html.

Chapter 9: The Kingsmen

"Chronological History of the Kingsmen": www.louielouie.org.

"Louie, Louie": www.snopes.com/music/songs/louie.htm.

www.thesmokinggun.com.

Chapter 10: Elvis Presley

"All About Elvis, Biography": www.elvis.com.

The Original Unofficial Elvis Home Page: www.ibiblio.org/elvis/elvis-hom
.html.

The Fifties Web, Candace Rich: www.fiftiesweb.com/elvis.htm.

Elvis Presley News, Always First with Elvis News Worldwide: www.elvis
presleynews.com.

Chapter 11: Marilyn Monroe

Goddess: The Secret Lives of Marilyn Monroe, Anthony Summers. Macmillan Publishing Company, 1985

"The Death of Marilyn," Rachael Bell: www.crimelibrary.com/notorious
_murders/celebrity/marilyn_monroe/.

"The 'Assassination' of Marilyn Monroe," Mel Ayton: crimemagazine.com/
05/marilynmonroe,0724-5.htm.

"John F. Kennedy & Marilyn Monroe Papers—Inside Information on the Controversy and Litigation Concerning the Files of JFK's Secret Advisor, Attorney Lawrence X.Cusack, Sr.," Carl E. Person: www.lawmall.com/
jfk.mm.

"Kennedy-Monroe Forger Lawrence 'Lex' Cusack Gets 10 Years," David Hewett: www.maineantiquedigest.com/articles/cusa0100.htm.

"Official Washington Chortles over Legendary Reporter Seymour Hersh's Troubles with Camelot. But Hersh May Have the Last Laugh," Eric Alterman. Media Circus: www.salon.com/media/1997/10/13hersh.html.

The Marilyn Conspiracy, Milo Speriglio with Steven Chain. Corgi, 1986.

UFO, Vol. 10, No.2, 1995.

Crypt 33: The Saga of Marilyn Monroe—The Final Word, Adela Gregory and Milo Speriglio. Carol Publishing Corporation, 1993.

Marilyn Monroe: Murder Cover-Up, Milo Speriglio. Lawman, 1982.

The Assassination of Marilyn Monroe, Donald H. Wolfe. Firebird Distributing, 1999.

Chapter 12: Rudolf Nureyev

"Rudolf Nureyev Biography": www.nureyev.org.

"Rudolf Nureyev Biography," Ballet Theater Foundation, Inc.: www.abt.org/
education/archive/choreographers/nureyev_r.html.

"FBI Watched Nureyev's Every Step," Michael Dobbs, *Moscow Times*:
www.themoscowtimes.ru/stories/1999/07/20/035.html.

Chapter 13: Andy Warhol

"Lonesome Cowboys (1968)," Gary Comenas: www.warholstars.org/filmch/
lone.html.

The Warhol Collections: www.warhol.org
"Viva is Born": www.warholstars.org/chron/192862.html#viv42.
"Viva Meets Andy": www.warholstars.org/chron/1967.html#v67.
"Viva Threatens Andy": www.warholstars.org/chron/1969.html#v69.
"Andy Warhol (1928–1987)": www.artchive.com/artchive/W/warhol.html.
www.thesmokinggun.com.
www.warholstars.org/warhol/warhol1/andy/warhol/can/lone15.html.

Chapter 14: Jimi Hendrix
"News and Events": www.jimi-hendrix.com.
www.thesmokinggun.com.
www.archives.gov/publications/prologue/2006/spring/vips-military.html.

Chapter 15: Rowan and Martin
"Fidel Castro FBI-CIA Files": www.paperlessarchives.com/castro.html.
"The Revolt of the Bureaucrats," Edward J. Epstein: www.edwardjay
    epstein.com/agency/chap31.html.
Agency of Fear: Opiates and Political Power in America, Edward J. Epstein.
    G.P. Putnam & Sons, 1977.
"JFK Revisited: A Noted Historian and Kennedy Insider Refutes the Revi-
    sionist Version of JFK's Legacy," Arthur Schlesinger, Jr.: www.cigar
    aficionado.com/Cigar/CA_Profiles/People_Profile/0,2540,17,00.html.
"Document: CIA Plot to Kill Castro": www.parascope.com/mx/articles/
    castroreport.htm.
"Foreign Relations of the United States, 1961 to 1963, Department of
    State": www.jfklancer.com/cuba/wiretap4-26-62.html.
"NORM: Interesting Tale in 'JFK and Sam,'" Norm Clarke: www.review
    journal.com/lvrj_home/2005/Dec-18-Sun-2005/news/4859332.html.
*A Friendship: The Letters of Dan Rowan and John D. MacDonald, 1967–
    1974*, Dan Rowan. Random House, 1986.

Chapter 16: Rock Hudson
"Remembering Rock Hudson": www.imdb.com/name/nm0001369.
The Official Website of Rock Hudson: www.cmgworldwide.com/stars/hudson.
*The Man Who Invented Rock Hudson: The Pretty Boys and Dirty Deals of
    Henry Willson*, Robert Hofler. Carroll & Graf, 2005.

Chapter 17: Sonny Bono
New York Post, July 15, 1999.
"Proud Mary Bono," Ann Louise Bardach. *George* magazine, August 1999.
"Sonny Bono—From TV to D.C.": www.cnn.com.

Sony and Cher: www.classicbands.com/sonnycher.html.
www.thesmokinggun.com.

Chapter 18: John Lennon and The Beatles

Defending the Realm: MI5 and the Shayler Affair, Mark Hollingsworth and
  Nick Fielding. Andre Deutsch Books, 1999.
Mail On Sunday, August 24, 1997.
Sunday Times, October 5, 1997.
Sunday Express, February 20, 2000.
Sunday Times, February 20, 2000.
Observer, February 20, 2000.
Mail On Sunday, February 20, 2000.
Daily Mail, February 21, 2000.
"Shaylergate" Explained, BBC News, August 20, 2000: news.bbc.co.uk/
  1/hi/uk/885588.stm.

Chapter 19: John Denver

"Biography": www.johndenver.com.
"John Denver": www.hotshotdigital.com/WellAlwaysRemember.4/John
  Denver.html.
"John Denver Killed in Plane Crash," CNN Interactive: www.cnn.com/US/
  9710/13/denver.nc.
UFO Crash/Retrievals, Leonard Stringfield, published privately, 1989.

Chapter 20: Princess Diana

"Fayed, the Spies and the $20m Plot to Show Palace Was Behind Diana's
  Death," Stuart Millar and Duncan Campbell. *Guardian,* July 23, 1999:
  www.guardian.co.uk/uk_news/story/0,3604,282806,00.html.
"NSA Admits to Spying on Princess Diana," Vernon Loeb, *Washington
  Post.* December 12, 1998: www.washingtonpost.com/wp-srv/national/
  daily/dec98/diana12/htm.
"Diana Feared Being Watched and Diana *Was* Being Watched," Jackie Jura:
  www.orwelltoday.com/princessfeared.shtml.
"Were the Deaths of Princess Diana and Dodi Al Fayed Part of a Conspir-
  acy?" CNN: transcripts.cnn.com/TRANSCRIPTS/0008/30/tl.00.html.
"My Beliefs: In Memory of Dodi and Diana," Mohamed Al Fayed, Sep-
  tember 29, 2000: www.alfayed.com/details.asp?aid=55.

Chapter 21: An A-to-Z of Celebrity Secrets

"1963: The Profumo Scandal," Derek Brown. *Guardian,* April 10, 2001.
"The Profumo Affair," Nostalgia Central: www.nostalgiacentral.com/pop/
  profumoaffair.htm.

"A Tribute to Roddy McDowall": http://www.xmoppet.org.

Defending the Realm: MI5 and the Shayler Affair, Mark Hollingsworth and Nick Fielding. Andre Deutsch Books, 1999.

"The Clash: We Were Spied On," Breaking News, October 6, 2004: www.breakingnews.ie/2004/10/06/story169796.html.

" 'Shaylergate' Explained," BBC News, August 20, 2000: news.bbc.co.uk/1/hi/uk/885588.stm.

www.MC5.org.

www.dkt-mc5.com.

www.thesmokinggun.com.

Conclusions

"Gangsters and Outlaws, Cops and Other Characters, Homosexual?" Marilyn Bardsley: www.crimelibrary.com/gangsters_outlaws/cops_others/hoover/6.html.

"J. Edgar Hoover 1895–1972": members.aol.com/matrixwerx/glbthistory/hoover.htm.

Acknowledgments

I would like to thank the following, without whom this book would not have appeared: the Federal Bureau of Investigation; the Central Intelligence Agency; the Departments of State, Army, Navy, and Air Force; and everyone at Paraview Pocket Books, but particularly Patrick Huyghe, Josh Martino, Marco Palmieri, Stephen Llano, and Sandra Martin. I must also offer sincere thanks to my wife, Dana, for her unswerving understanding, love, and support when I was busy burning the midnight oil.